Out Behind the Desk

Out Behind the Desk: Workplace Issues for LGBTQ Librarians is number one in the Series on Gender and Sexuality in Librarianship, edited by Emily Drabinski.

Forthcoming in the series:

Documenting Feminist Activism, edited by Lyz Bly and Kelly Wooten

Gender, Sexuality, Information: A Reader, edited by Rebecca Dean and Patrick Keilty

Ephemeral Material: Queering the Archive, by Alana Kumbier

Out Behind the Desk

Workplace Issues for LGBTQ Librarians

Edited by Tracy Marie Nectoux

Library Juice Press
Duluth, Minnesota

Published by Library Juice Press, 2011
PO Box 3320
Duluth, MN 55803
http://libraryjuicepress.com/

This book is printed on acid-free paper meeting all present ANSI standards for archival preservation.

Cover designed by Alana Kumbier.

Layout designed by Martin Wallace.

Library of Congress Cataloging-in-Publication Data
Out behind the desk : workplace issues for LGBTQ librarians / edited by Tracy Marie Nectoux.
    p. cm.—(Litwin Books/Library Juice Press series on gender and sexuality in librarianship ; no. 1)
    Includes bibliographical references and index.
    Summary: "An anthology of personal accounts by librarians and library workers relating experiences of being gay, lesbian, bisexual, transgendered, or queer at work. A broad spectrum of orientations and gender identities are represented, highlighting a range of experiences of being and/or coming out at work"—Provided by publisher.
    ISBN 978-1-936117-03-1 (acid-free paper)
    1. Gay librarians—Employment—United States. 2. Bisexual librarians—Employment—United States. 3. Transgender librarians—Employment—United States. I. Nectoux, Tracy.
    Z682.4.G39O98 2011
    020.86'6—dc22
                                    2011001445

Acknowledgments

I wish to thank Rory Litwin of Library Juice Press, the University of Illinois at Urbana-Champaign Library, the Social Responsibilities Round Table and the Gay, Lesbian, Bisexual, and Transgendered Round Table of the American Library Association for the enormous good that they do.

I thank Emily Drabinski, my brilliant series editor, for trusting me, giving me this chance, and supporting me through this, my first time at editing a book. I couldn't have done it without her. More specifically, I literally *wouldn't* have done it without her. Thank you, Emily.

Ellen Greenblatt's generous agreement to write the Foreword to this book is an enormous compliment. My sincere thanks to her.

Much, much thanks to my partner in everything, Stuart Albert, for his infinite support, patience, and love.

Finally, tremendous gratitude to the articulate, generous, intelligent, and brave contributors to this book. What they've done here is fiercely important. My thanks to all of them.

Dedication

The editor dedicates this book to its contributors.

The contributors dedicate this book to the following:

Char Booth; Dr. James V. Carmichael, Jr.; Betty Garity; Barbara Gittings; Joseph Gregg; George Hoemann; William Inge; Libba Kelly; Prof. Laroi Lawton; Leather Archives & Museum; Constance Merritt; National Gay and Lesbian Task Force; "My parents"; "Our brothers and sisters who came before us and blazed the trail that we can follow"; Mark Paquette; Pat Parker/Vito Russo Center Library; "People who have shown me their love and their support and have accepted me for who I am"; Michelle Pesavento; Albert Lloyd Smith; Kathleen Smith; "Those trying to be their entire self who are role models for the rest of us, and our straight friends and supporters who help make it so"; "Those who bravely opened the doors for so many of us"; Janet Thrush; Libby Vaugh; Michael Wachter; and Karen Whittlesey.

Contents

Acknowledgments	v
Dedication	vi
Foreword by Ellen Greenblatt	xi
Introduction	1
Part One: Trajectories	9
A Small Town Start ~Ryan Donovan	11
Sexuality, Students, and Disclosure ~Johnnie Gray	17
Girl meets girl. Girl works with girl. Girl falls in love with girl... ~Brenda Linares and Emily Vardell	23
It's Okay to *BE* Gay... A Librarian's Journey to Acceptance and Activism ~Jason D. Phillips	33
Out of the Frying Pan: Coming Out As a Culinary School Librarian ~Rachel Wexelbaum	49
Part Two: Sex and the Institution	61
Gay Librarians on the Tenure Track: Following the Yellow Brick Road? ~Paul Blobaum	63
Out All Over: Giving Voice to LGBTs on Campus ~Donna Braquet and Roger Weaver	69

Managing Outside the Closet: On Being an Openly Gay Library
Administrator
~Matthew P. Ciszek   83

Homophobia in San Antonio
~David Allen White   91

Part Three: The Rest of the Rainbow   97

Leather Librarian
~John P. Bradford   99

Gender Changer
~Jim Van Buskirk   107

The Secret Life of Bis: On Not Quite Being Out and Not Quite Fitting In
~BWS Johnson   113

Passing Tips and Pronoun Police: A Guide to Transitioning at Your Local
Library
~K.R. Roberto   121

Part Four: Coming Out in Time   129

Out Lines: An LGBT Career in Perspective
~Robert Ridinger   131

Outness and Social Networks: From Closet to Container Store
~Lia Friedman   141

The Challenges of Coming and Being Out in Historical Perspective
~Richard P. Hulser   147

Curating William Inge
~Marcel LaFlamme   155

Part Five: Coming Out in Place   165

Activism in Colorado: How Life and Librarianship Bloomed in the Desert
West
~Chris Hartman   167

In and Out Behind the Desk—In and Out of the Country
~Kimberli Morris   175

Table of Contents

"Do They Know?" A Gay Librarian at a Catholic University
~Martin Garnar 187

All About My Job Hunt: The Diary of a Wannabe Librarian
~Andy Foskey 197

Part Six: Coming Out in the Field 203

Pride and Paranoia @ Your Library
~Maria T. Accardi 205

When is the Personal not Professional? An Exploration
~Kellian Clink 219

Out in the Classroom
~Ann L. O'Neill 233

Taking the Homosexual Highroad
~Nicola Price 237

Patricia's Child, Patrick's Penis & the Sex of Reference: A Lesbian Librarian's Log of Perverse Patronage
~Shawn(ta) D. Smith 241

On Being *As If*,
Imagination and Gay Librarianship
~William Thompson 255

Contributors 267

Index 273

Foreword by Ellen Greenblatt

On May 18, 1970, Michael McConnell and Jack Baker applied for a marriage license in Minneapolis, Minnesota – allegedly the first same-sex couple in the United States to do so. Why, you may ask, do I feel obliged to mention this in a book about library workplace issues? Well, McConnell had recently been hired by the University of Minnesota as head of cataloging. All his paperwork had been processed, and he was awaiting approval from the Board of Regents – in most cases, a rubber stamp situation. However, due to the publicity generated from McConnell's and Baker's attempt to marry, the Regents of the University of Minnesota refused to approve his appointment, stating that his conduct was "not in the best interests of the University" (Bjornson 17). The fledgling Taskforce on Gay Liberation[1] of the American Library Association (ALA), the first professional gay caucus in the nation, took on McConnell's case, trying, unsuccessfully, for three years to get ALA to champion McConnell's cause.

Fast forward forty years. We all know how much progress has been made on the same-sex marriage front – but how have we fared in the library workplace? This book, *Out Behind the Desk: Workplace Issues for LGBTQ Librarians,* introduces you to library workers who candidly share their disparate experiences. Some are humorous, some wistful, others poignant – most a combination of peaks and valleys. All are compelling.

Let me add my own library coming out story to the mix here. I was working in the cataloging department at Princeton University Library in the early 1980s, barely a decade after the McConnell incident. While I was pretty much out in college – I ran for student senate on a gay platform with two gay buddies and later on a multicultural platform with a coalition of gay, chican@, and black students (activities that somehow didn't make it

---

1. The name of this organization, which was founded in 1971, has since morphed to the Gay, Lesbian, Bisexual, and Transgendered Round Table (GLBTRT).

onto my resume) – being out at work was different. However, overall, the library seemed pretty gay-friendly – definitely much more so than the veterans' hospital where I worked previously. And there were out librarians, even in my department. So, I screwed up my courage and decided that I would ease myself out of the closet at work. Since this was pre-Internet, I called the local lesbian and gay helpline to seek support and find out about resources in the area. Uncomfortable mentioning the actual small academic town in which I lived, I asked about resources for a town about an hour away. The voice on the other end sounded familiar, but I thought I was just being paranoid. Then all of a sudden I heard, "Ellen, is that you?" And I realized that, yes indeed, the voice on the other end of the line belonged to my supervisor. After an initial moment of panic on my part, a wondrous conversation ensued. And thereafter, my supervisor became my mentor, introducing me to other lesbians in the area, as well as helping me locate affirmative resources and activities.[2] Luckily, I was in the right place at the right time. And more than a quarter century of work in LGBTIQ[3] librarianship derives from that extraordinary moment.

While my coming out at work was a fairly benign process, other friends who came out around the same time have vastly different experiences to relate, many negative. However, I thought (hoped!) things had improved over time, and so I was surprised by the accounts of some recent graduates that appear in this book. For example, I was astonished that a job coach questioned one of the contributors about including his involvement in the ALA GLBT Round Table on his resume. I just don't want to believe that a professional advisor would *still* make such a recommendation!

Flash back to the mid-1990s – When my partner was just about to graduate from library school, we attended an ALA conference. She had signed up for a resume/vitae clinic where she was promised "expert advice." Although I had been a librarian for almost fifteen years and worked in three different libraries, I tagged along, figuring I'd see what they had to say about my vitae as well. I was floored when I was told to "take out all this gay stuff." That "gay stuff" consisted of a book, several articles, national and regional presentations, and lots of professional service activities – in brief, the bulk of my vitae. I was aghast that this so-called "expert" was telling me that years of scholarship and service should be

---

2. Ironically, years later, my former supervisor made national headlines when she and her intended sued a religious organization for refusing to let them rent their beachfront facility for the couple's civil union service.
3. I use the acronym LGBTIQ to stand for Lesbian, Gay, Bisexual, Transgender, Intersex, and Queer/Questioning.

removed from my vitae, simply because *she* didn't approve of the subject content. Obviously, as a successful mid-career librarian, I wasn't about to take her advice, but I was worried that she, and other advisors like her, would intimidate newly-minted librarians into closeting themselves. I emphatically suggested to the organizers of this clinic that in the future they should be more discerning in their choice of advisors.

Far from being a liability, my work in LGBTIQ librarianship has enriched my career. It is undeniably my passion and has afforded me opportunities to participate in so many extraordinarily rewarding adventures, including teaching library school courses, serving on advisory committees, creating thesauri, editing books, and so much more. The best part has been the many people I've met through this work. Unlike many of my coworkers who meet mostly academic librarians in their own narrow discipline or functional area through professional organizations such as ALA, I have been fortunate to meet colleagues from across the country and around the globe, folks from every conceivable type of library, working in a variety of fields and functions. Sexual orientation and gender identity cut across all these boundaries and make these connections possible.

But enough about me and back to the book. The depth and breadth of perspectives within its pages are remarkable. From those reminiscing about decades-long careers to those anticipating their journeys, these essays view librarianship in a variety of contexts, including those you expect to read about – public, school, and academic libraries – and others which you may find surprising – cooking school, legislative, and leather libraries. Some address professional organizations, while others speak to library education. Venues vary, with tales emanating from both rural and urban settings. Positions run the gamut from line librarians to administrators, cross the borders between public and technical services, and pass beyond library walls themselves.

As its title suggests, the theme of the book revolves around how our identities intersect with our professional roles. Some narratives focus more on the professional aspects, others on the personal, some on the tension between personal validation and professional obligation. I found this last group of essays, those relating to professional ethics, particularly provocative.

Another salient feature of this book is its historical significance. As the first out generation of librarians is poised on the verge of retirement, collections like the current volume and earlier works, *Liberating Minds* (Kester, 1997) and *Daring to Speak Our Names* (Carmichael, 1998), ensure that representative voices of that first wave have been recorded. And it does so in tandem with capturing the aspirations of the generation to follow.

While I know many of the people in this book personally, in various roles as colleague, teacher, mentor, and friend, it's inspiring to read about their lives, to learn about their struggles and victories, about how their identities and professional lives coincide, co-exist, collide. The contributors to this book generously share their reflections and observations, vulnerabilities and successes with us. I was touched by their openness and their candor. I hope you'll find the stories of the individuals who inhabit these pages equally compelling.

References

Bjornson, L. "Librarians abandon McConnell: Three year limbo ends." *The Advocate* 16 Jan. 1974: 17. Print.

Carmichael, J. V., ed. *Daring to Find Our Names: The Search for Lesbigay Library History.* Westport, Conn: Greenwood Press, 1998. Print.

Kester, N. G., ed. *Liberating Minds: The Stories and Professional Lives of Gay, Lesbian, and Bisexual Librarians and Their Advocates.* Jefferson, N.C: McFarland, 1997. Print.

Introduction

Jesus said, "If you bring forth what is within you, what you bring forth will save you. If you do not bring forth what is within you, what you do not bring forth will destroy you."

~Saying 70[1]

Come out, come out, wherever you are!

~Harvey Milk

Out Behind the Desk is not the first book that focuses solely on the experiences of lesbian, gay, bisexual, transgender, and queer/questioning librarians, and it won't be the last. But it is one of only a few. I cannot speak highly enough of Norman Kester's *Liberating Minds* and James Carmichael's *Daring to Find Our Names.* Carmichael's historical perspective on "lesbigay" librarianship is especially informative and insightful scholarship, and I highly recommend it. But it has been over a decade since these groundbreaking anthologies were published. It's time to check out the landscape and assess our progress.

I find it necessary to come out as bisexual at least once every few months. Granted, I'm married to a man and I have a big mouth. Eliminate at least one of those things, and I'd not have all of these "necessary" coming out moments. But, alas, my mouth and my determination to not let my "opposite marriage" misrepresent me are stronger than my sense of decorum.

I remember a day when I was working in the University of Illinois at Urbana-Champaign (UIUC) Library's cataloging department. I'd recently

---

1. Pagels, Elaine. *The Gnostic Gospels.* New York: Vintage, 1989. 124.

graduated from library school (I received my MLIS in 2006), and they'd kindly kept me on as an academic hourly employee until I could find something permanent. We (present and former) graduate students worked closely together in a kind of cubicle cluster, and one of them asked me if I was attending the upcoming graduation ceremony.

> **Me**: No, but I'm attending the Lavender Graduation.
> **She**: *Lavender* Graduation?! But you're not gay.
> **Me**: I most certainly am.
> **She**: But you're married.
> **Me**: Madame, I am bisexual.
> **She**: Oh! I have lots of bisexual friends!
> **Me**: And now you have another one.
> **She**: Score!

Since coming out completely in 2001, I have engaged in many variants of this conversation. They never offend me; they never hurt me; and they never tire me. I know that, no matter my activism, no matter my research, no matter my stated ideologies, most straight people – because I've partnered with a man – will assume that I'm straight. And it makes complete sense that they would.

What's also true is that very few gay people assume that I'm straight. And that also makes sense.

So when I come out to people, I do it in a fun, joking manner, and – out of respect for my spouse – I try not to divulge too much about my personal sex life. And surprisingly enough, coming out at work has been just as easy, though with fewer jokes, and *no* sex talk. Absolutely none (for the most part).

My first library job was a part-time shelver/processor position at Urbana Free Library.[2] At that time I was a volunteer distributor for Illinois' downstate free LGBT newspaper, the *Prairie Flame,* and when I applied for the job, I included this in my resume under "Service and Other Activities." It didn't stop me from getting the job. (In fact, Urbana Free was one of my drop spots for the newspaper.)

When I later began library school at UIUC, while applying for graduate assistantships, I again listed my volunteer work for the *Prairie Flame* – this time as an interviewer and columnist writing about bisexuality. The original purpose of my column (absurdly titled "Living Bi with a Straight Guy") was to write about my experiences as a bisexual woman. I had fully

---

2. I adored this job, and it was what led to my eventual decision to go to library school.

come out the previous year and I was ready to talk, rant, talk, consider my navel, talk, contemplate the gloriousness of my own existence, and talk some more. I was desperately fascinated with myself.[3] And I did write about myself for awhile (and – to his abject horror – occasionally about Straight Guy). But within six months I was sick of myself, and moved on to more interesting topics of culture, politics, and homophobia.

But I digress. Back to the job hunt! Just as with my city's public library, the university from which I needed a job did not bat an eye at anything on my vitae. I was granted an assistantship, and after graduating, I was eventually hired full-time.

Since beginning library school, my activism and involvement in social justice and gay rights issues have only increased. Even before I graduated, I'd already joined both the Social Responsibilities Round Table and the Gay, Lesbian, Bisexual, and Transgendered Round Table of the American Library Association. It was enormously meaningful to me to find both of these organizations within ALA, and I didn't hesitate to include my memberships in them on my vitae. I didn't hesitate because back in 2001 when I came out, I decided that I'd not work for anyone who had issue with what I am. I am out and determined to fight for full civil rights for all, and I simply will not work for an organization that might be offended by this. It's who I am, and to try to hide it would not only be impossible, but would be detrimental to me. Yes, this has limited my choices, but there is simply no other option for me. I would rather work two, lower-paying part-time labor jobs and be out, than one, high-paying full-time cushy job and be closeted. At the same time, I absolutely understand that my decision is my own, and I neither expect, nor do I suggest that others agree with or emulate either me or my choices.

~~*~~

Unlike most librarians I know (gay or straight), libraries did not play a large role in my development or life. I enjoyed reading and I attended good schools, and my father was even a teacher, but I was not encouraged to visit or use libraries (not that I can remember, at least). We moved every few years, and – with one brief exception – we didn't live in areas where libraries were easily accessible. From kindergarten on I didn't enjoy school, and today I couldn't even tell you if any of my elementary schools had libraries. My high school had a library, but by then school was such

---

3. I cringe when I think of those articles now. I was so idle-on-angry back then, and mean to my parents.

a low priority in my life, vampire slayers could have used it as their intelligence headquarters and I'd not have noticed.

So why am I, today, a librarian who holds libraries in highest esteem? The answer is easy, and it's one that many librarians give: I love books. I don't just love reading; I love *books*. It is why I loved my shelving and processing job; it is why I eventually decided to go to library school; and it is why I love cataloging today. And it was in library school that I learned that the mission of libraries is to protect the information *in* those books (journals, newspapers, CDs, etc.) – no matter what it is – and to make it accessible to everyone. Libraries ensure that intellectual freedom reigns within their walls. Librarians fight censorship; librarians fight ignorance. I was told this in library school, and I believed it. And because I was told that libraries don't censor information, I credulously believed that libraries don't censor *people*. And my personal experiences seemed to prove me right: I've never, in the six years I've worked at the UIUC Library, experienced negativity or censorship due to my research, my activism, or my sexuality. From my first day working in a library, and especially at UIUC, I've known I was lucky to be a librarian, and I've always appreciated the respect I received from my various supervisors and coworkers. But I admit that I didn't deem my situation all that unique in librarianship. When I reflected on my good fortune, it was in the sense that I was now working in a library, and wouldn't have to worry about prejudice or backlash. Because libraries embrace everyone, regardless of their sexuality, right?

It wasn't until reading the contributions to this book that I have come to understand that I am much more fortunate than I knew.

In his introduction to *Daring to Find Our Names,* James Carmichael explains that – as a rule – the particularly unique connection of lesbian, bisexual, and gay librarians with libraries didn't begin in library school. It began when libraries helped us "first find confirmation" of our identities and reassured us that we "are not alone" (1). We found ourselves there, on the shelves. We learned that we'd existed since the beginning; the Greek classics said so! It was only later that professional librarianship dawned on many of us as an option. LGBTQ librarians have all heard the rumor – often true – that libraries are "safe havens" for queer people. We've all probably said this ourselves; indeed, many authors in this very book say this. Perhaps we say it so often because they actually were for us. Perhaps we say it because we were told they are in library school. Or perhaps we say it because we want so badly for it to be true. And sometimes it *is* true.

But it has not always been true, and sometimes *it still is not,* and when it's not, we are at risk of "ostracism, threats of violence, and overt and

Introduction

covert discrimination," even as professionals (Kester 2). Perhaps it won't surprise you – as it did me – that every one of these threats and inequities listed by Kester are mentioned in this book. And they came from professional colleagues, patrons, students, and administrators. It seems that homophobia respects no hierarchy.

~~*~~

The authors in *Out Behind the Desk* bring over three decades of historical perspective on being out at work. Their stories are powerful and vital for anyone in librarianship, whether they be library school students, brand-new graduates, or skilled veterans. And their experiences are relevant to librarians in all settings – public, academic, and private. Here you will find a current crop of librarians who have bravely held a mirror up to the present landscape and aren't afraid to critique it honestly. Their stories are told in narratives, anecdotes, essays, memoirs, and, in one delightful instance, a journal. And though many of the chapters are personal accounts rather than focused on library science, they are no less eloquent, informative, self-reflective, and important for that.

You will read about librarians who transitioned genders on the job, successfully changed their library school's curriculum to include courses in LGBTQ library issues, and who fearlessly stood up to closed-minded colleagues, administrators, and even patrons. Topics range from the ways our experiences shape our scholarship to the decisions we make while preparing for that first job interview (a challenge Andy Foskey wrestles with), from coming out, as Jason Phillips did when library school finally gave him the space to feel safe, to being outed, as happened when David Allen White was working at San Antonio Public Library. There are stories about awkward conversations with students and patrons, to even more awkward conversations with coworkers and supervisors: BWS Johnson's particular exchange with a Library Friend is probably the most infuriating within these pages, but it is not unique in its aspect. Librarians write about combating discrimination to finding allies where least expected, even in the rural wilds of Colorado, as Chris Hartman describes. Also included are accounts of academic projects, administrative challenges, and theoretical inquiry, as well as blunt discussions of particular issues in librarianship that tend to get ignored, even by LGBTQ librarians. These librarians are reshaping the landscape of our profession so that it can better appreciate and take advantage of our unique and necessary perspective. Drawing on their personal stories, they offer valuable advice and insight for librarians who are coping with similar issues.

In a political climate and society where simply being out *is* oftentimes its own form of activism, many of the reflections and experiences described here present the subtle difference between being out in the workplace and being an out *activist* in the workplace. Fair or not, those of us who are out at work must often balance our desire to affect change with the ethical and practical requirements of our professional lives. Maria Accardi demonstrates this balancing act when she describes the misery she felt while watching patrons peruse her Gay Pride Month display, nervously anticipating the inevitable negative reaction. And yet, fear didn't prevent Maria from engaging in a "teaching moment" when a patron unabashedly expressed his bigoted beliefs to her. These are choices that LGBTQ librarians continually face, not just once and for all, but every day they walk through their libraries' door. Every librarian in *Out Behind the Desk* has faced an option between self-expression and self-censorship, self-integrity and self-preservation, and they have generously shared the decisions they made here.

~~*~~

In *Liberating Minds,* Norman Kester implored librarians to "be catalysts for social change in our profession and society." He encouraged gay librarians to declare, "We exist!" because it is crucial for all of us to "express our voices in the continuing struggle for our own liberation" (2-6). I don't know if Mr. Kester will ever read *Out Behind the Desk,* but if he does, he'll see that – a decade later – many LGBTQ librarians are *doing just that.* We're out in "safe" libraries; we're out in not-so-safe libraries; we come out in red states, blue states, and purple states; we come out to our coworkers, our supervisors, our students, and our patrons. And as can be seen in the diverse essays in this book, we come out for an enormous variety of reasons.

We come out when *we can.* Sometimes ... we cannot. Most of the authors in this book are out, but as of this writing a few are (or were) not. And those few who trusted me enough to contribute to this book are saying, "We exist!" too.

It has become a byword that libraries are safe havens for LGBTQ patrons; the accounts in *Out Behind the Desk* challenge and complicate that sweeping generalization. And though it is clear that some situations have improved, there is still much work to be done. As this book was entering the production phase, we watched and read in helpless horror as six gay teens committed suicide in a span of just four weeks. These suicides remind us that it is still a brave and radical act to be who we are. The response from some librarians has been swift; ALA's GLBT Round Table has reached out to our young patrons, hoping to show them what many of us discovered for ourselves: LGBT people will find themselves in their libraries.[4] And they will have the help and privacy they need while doing so. If libraries ever do become that "safe haven" that we want so badly to make them, it will be, in large part, because of the librarians represented herein.

Works Cited

Carmichael, Jr., James V., ed. *Daring to Find Our Names: The Search for Lesbigay Library History.* Introduction. Westport, Conn.: Greenwood Press, 1998. Print.

Kester, Norman G., ed. *Liberating Minds: The Stories and Professional Lives of Gay, Lesbian, and Bisexual Librarians and Their Advocates.* Introduction. Jefferson, N.C.: McFarland, 1997. Print.

---

4. *Speaking OUT Against Bullying.* American Library Association. http://www.ala.org/

Part One: Trajectories

A Small Town Start

Ryan Donovan

For me, being gay and working in a library has always gone hand-in-hand. I got a job working as a page at my local library at the same time that I started the process of coming out in high school. I am from an urban, but somewhat conservative, area in the great state of New Hampshire. I didn't know very many gay people growing up. When I turned 18 in 2001, I learned that there was one local gay bar in town, but it only stayed in business for about three months. This was a time when gay people were still heavily underrepresented in the media. I also did not know anyone who was gay in real life. There simply were not any gay role models for me to look up to. Most of the things I had heard my parents or my friends say about gay and lesbian people led me to believe that they wouldn't necessarily be tolerant if I did start being honest about who I was with them. To be perfectly honest, I was not even that tolerant of myself. I think this had a lot to do with me not acknowledging my own gay feelings before then. I was still just a teenager. I wanted people to like me. I had no idea whom I was going to be.

A lot of my sheltered lifestyle came from the fact that my parents decided to yank me from public school and stick me in a small New Hampshire private school that promised a brighter future. At the time, I was fifteen years old, and I could not see much else other than the fact that I was having to essentially start my life over. A new school meant new friends, a new understanding of how everything worked, and essentially a new identity. Previously, I had been accepted by my peers. But now, while it seemed that everyone my age was taking a few steps forward, getting that much closer to growing up, I was thrown into a completely different environment with an entirely different social order. My parents had sacrificed to send me to private school, and several of the children who attended my new school were wealthier beyond what I had previously encountered. We try to pretend that there is little difference between the haves and the have-nots, but I experienced firsthand the fact that it really does matter who we are and how much money our parents make. It was a good life lesson in dealing with people that I would need in the future.

Private school was really where my innocence ended. So, when I turned 18, and my parents couldn't tell me where to go to school anymore, I got the hell out of there. I couldn't stand the class issues and the smug incestuousness anymore, and I don't think anyone shed too many tears at my departure in the end ... except maybe Mrs. Thompson. The only place I ever found refuge was with Mrs. Thompson, the librarian. She made the library a place where everyone could go, no matter how popular or rich you were.

Now firmly rooted back in the public school system, I had to start myself over a third time. I decided the best thing to do was to become an amalgam of the two people I had been: take my experiences from private school and tack them on to the person I was before I left. Become the best of both worlds. I threw myself into the experience, eager to reinvent myself better than before. The first thing I had to think about was, "What do I want to be when I grow up?" When I took one of those career tests my junior year, the results came back blank; I had a special note that said my interests were "too varied" for them to narrow down one particular career for me. I hadn't decided yet where I wanted to go to college or what I was going to do. Basically, I was grown up already, having just turned eighteen. I still wasn't really thinking that hard about my future.

It was one of my friends, a boy named Adam, who changed everything. This boy Adam, who in a twist of fate, brought me along with him when he had a burning desire to watch fishing videos for free at the library ... this is what led to my first job and future career field. I thought back to Mrs. Thompson. She made the library a great place to be. I always felt safe and strong there. To me, this was an important feeling to remember when I began looking for work.

My first library job actually helped me create an identity for myself. I began feeling more comfortable in my own skin. Never before had I felt such a surge in confidence. People would come to me, ask for help, and I was able to help them! I knew where everything in the library was and all the services that the library offered. I had never really stepped up or taken charge of anything before this. I loved it. There was a distinct change in my personality that began taking place. No longer was I content to sit shyly in the background. On the contrary, I willingly stood up and spoke my mind. I was a lot more comfortable with the person I was starting to become. This would help me immensely with not only my work, but ultimately in identifying as a gay man.

For me, coming out at work was simply about not hiding this amazing person I was becoming. I didn't have a problem being *me* when I was in the library. Honestly, it was usually the times that I wasn't in the library that I felt uncomfortable and out of place. The library was where I was truly in my element. I felt – surrounded by all those books, videos, and other materials – that I was in my own little world. That's really what the library is: a world where everything has its specific place and its own order. When I was behind the information desk, people needed me. They couldn't navigate the system, the world, like I could. They asked me questions that I could answer. Up until that point, my life had been completely the opposite. I felt like I never had the answers, especially the answers that pertained to my own feelings. I had spent over eighteen years not really dealing with who or what I was. But when I had a level of control over myself as I did in the library, as fleeting as it was, it still made me feel like I was worthwhile. I think that's something every LGBTQ kid needs. It was the library that made me feel worthwhile. I will always be grateful for that. I want that for every gay boy, lesbian girl, or trans kid everywhere.

I never really formally came out at work. Most people, after talking to me for five minutes or less, usually "get" it. I'm gay. It's not like I'm coming to work in a rainbow tie every day, but once I start talking and moving it's something most people usually just *get* about me. That bothered me at first, but after awhile ... what can you really do? I embraced it. I was glad that people weren't whispering about it behind my back. Some of the staff members my age would come right out and ask me sometimes. I didn't deny it. Still, I didn't think there was a reason to sit my supervisor down and have a discussion explaining to him that I like other guys. People that I was close with at work that needed to know *did* know. It was as simple as that.

After being at my job for several years, I started to learn about library school and the fabled MLS that every librarian has to get to be taken seriously. I decided that that's what I was going to do. It seemed perfect. I had started school in the area, but really had no idea what I was going to do with myself afterward. Really, I was content to work as a page forever where I had discovered myself so completely. I was happy there. But there's always trouble looming in paradise.

Shortly before I left for Boston to begin library school at Simmons College, a woman was hired at my library who taught me a valuable lesson. The woman, an extremely conservative religious fundamentalist, wasn't shy about expressing her own values and morals at work. This included a very deep fear and hatred of any and all homosexuals. This was not something that she expressed in so many words, but a passive aggressive comment here, an eye roll there ... this woman was very good at expressing exactly how she felt without actually speaking her bigotry outright. One evening when I was working alone with her, she made me overtly uncomfortable. She told me that she and her husband attended a "pro-marriage" rally over the weekend in Massachusetts. When I asked her exactly what a "pro-marriage" rally was, she said it was to protect marriage against people who would ruin it. Then she narrowed her eyes at me.

I had never had a conversation with this woman about being gay. As with all the people with whom I worked, it was understood. I wasn't doing anything "gay" at work. I wasn't wearing a rainbow jumpsuit or making out with my boyfriend during my 15-minute break. There was nothing that I was doing to which this woman could actually object. But she didn't like me. I knew it. Everyone I worked with knew it. And we all knew why. My boss was a great guy, but he wasn't able to do anything about this woman unless she did or said anything directly to me. For all her faults, she was actually pretty good at her job; she got everything done; the public liked her; and she got along great with all the other staff members. If she didn't bring up her religious beliefs and her political views at work every single day, I probably would have even liked her. But she couldn't let certain things go, especially that one big gay elephant in the room: me.

I frequently had to work with this woman by myself. She was often in charge of our department for the evening, and I had to defer to her if there were any problems. It goes without saying that I wasn't comfortable doing that. This was the beginning of a tumultuous work relationship that lasted for nearly three years. I *had* to find a way to make it work, and I did. Again, it was really as simple as that. As horrible as this woman was, she taught me that I wasn't always going to be in control of my work environment – that the library could sometimes *not* be the safe place that I thought it was. It was a healthy dose of reality, the result of which made me truly commit to becoming a librarian. I wanted to make sure that, in the future, people like this woman would be held accountable for expressing themselves inappropriately at work. I hoped that perhaps one day, I could be the supervisor of someone like the young college age me who had to deal with the venomous verbal diarrhea coming out of that horrible woman's mouth. They would know that they could come to me, and I would understand and solve the problem. I would make her stop. She taught me that it's not the library itself that's safe, but rather the librarians who work there that make

A Small Town Start

it that way. Ultimately, I wanted to be one of those librarians. That's what I wanted to do with my life.

I graduated from Simmons last winter. I moved to New York City, and initially got a job working in one of the smaller branches of the New York Public Library. I primarily worked with young adults, running programs and specific library services to teenagers. One of the first roles I took on at my library was leadership of the weekly Teen Advisory Group. There I encountered several colorful high school students who were not unlike myself at that age. It took a few weeks, but some of them started to warm up and confide in me. Several of our teen patrons came out to me after I had been here for a few months. Often I was the only person that these kids would talk to when they came in to the library. While I encouraged the teens to build relationships with other staff members as well, I did get a secret thrill that sometimes, I'm their favorite. I tried to be the type of guy that I would have liked talking to if I was coming into the library every day after school. The teens were receptive to that, and I was thankful.

I have now moved on to the Mid-Manhattan Library on 5th Avenue. I work on the first floor, usually serving as an ambassador to the library's many first-time visitors. I have a whole new set of job responsibilities. I'm excited for the challenge that this new position will bring. Ultimately, my career and relationship with libraries has been a worthwhile and rewarding experience. I've learned a lot and I'm happy with the way things turned out. Sure, things haven't always been perfect. But sometimes, that's the best education. My experiences were what helped me find my way. Most importantly, work is the place where I truly get to be who I am: a gay librarian.

Sexuality, Students, and Disclosure

Johnnie Gray

Sexuality and openness in the workplace is undoubtedly a complicated and personal decision. Add to this the disclosure of your sexuality to students and younger patrons, and things become more complicated and new issues arise. I have my own experiences about the subject, as well as some advice that might be helpful to those still considering being out at work. Librarianship is a profession that still mainly consists of women, and when most people think of the typical librarian, they think of a caricature of Nancy Pearl with glasses, making a shushing sound. This is our trademark. It is widely known that the general public tends to think of library science as a feminized field. I try every day to break this stereotype – not just as a man, but as a gay man helping to bring libraries into the future. I do this by being myself and proving my worth.

I work for a small, Southern, liberal arts university with a student population that is predominantly straight, white, and Christian. Even though this demographic is the makeup of my work environment, I have found that younger generations are more open to diversity, and more accepting of sexual differences. I am out at work, though I do not make a distinct point of letting others know about my sexuality. When people ask, I tell them; if they assume, I let them. My view is: I'm going to be as open as heterosexuals are regarding my personal life. This might not work for everyone, but it works for me.

I chose the library field after learning what librarians do. This career is more than a love for information; the idea of helping people sift through what they've found, and pointing them in the right direction is a good fit for me. I have worked in the library setting for over 10 years. I worked for two years in my high school library, and the male librarian there was a great guy who influenced my decision to join the field. He was a quiet, family man, and his trust in me regarding tasks and decisions gave me a much needed boost in confidence. In high school, I suffered from very low self-esteem and he made me feel important, not just personally, but to the school library as well.

Although I was not out in high school, when I went to college, I decided it would be easier to come out and be who I am. The Internet helped with this. It gave me a cloak of anonymity that I could hide behind and sort my feelings out. I quickly got a job working for the university's library where I shelved books and worked for the circulation department. As I became comfortable with my fellow student coworkers and classmates, I told a few of them about who I was dating and how my social life was going. One of my library coworker friends had a way of gossiping that was more endearing than annoying. This is how my first boss found out I was gay. Although I was embarrassed and felt awkward about the incident, she was very accepting about it and would often ask if I was dating someone or how things were going at home. She gave me some hope of acceptance in the work place. I started to feel that the library was a place where I could work and not be afraid of people knowing my sexual orientation. In high school, I felt that I had to lie to protect myself from bullying, while garnering what little acceptance I could. But in this academic environment, I was unknowingly gaining confidence and more self-esteem that would help me mature into the librarian I am today.

A few years after I graduated from college, a job became available at my old library, so I applied and was hired. I was working with the same people I had worked with as a student, but now I was a library paraprofessional. In order to move up in the library, I had to think about graduate school. It took me a few years to consider graduate school, and in the meantime, I was hiring and training student assistants to help me with interlibrary loan. Although I never hid my sexuality from them, and no one with whom I worked asked, occasionally I would out myself to them when I felt comfortable enough. People who did not know I am gay would see my partner visiting me at work, bringing me lunch, or simply talking with me in my office. Many coworkers assumed that I was gay based on that, though none of them came out and asked me point blank. I didn't mind, as I wasn't trying to hide anything. It is important to remember that most people use labels to explain something and to define a person based on their own comfort level. Although this seems terribly small-minded, people can be afraid of the unknown. For most gay and lesbian individuals, we deal with assumptions about ourselves every day, each and every time we interact with someone new.

When I completed my Master's of Library and Information Sciences degree, I had already been working for the same academic library for over four years. Because of my new degree and a need in my library, I was promoted to reference librarian within the same library. My responsibilities increased, and my interaction with students on campus increased as well. I was now teaching library instruction classes and working at the reference desk. My increased public visibility – being exposed to students more than I was before – caused me to consider how my own sexuality played into my job even more. Could a student watch me and pick up on cues that I am gay? I wondered. I mean, I don't dress as a flamboyant pseudo-cosmopolitan, speak with a lisp, or mince in a sassy way, but some people have the innate ability to pick up on small details that make them question whether a person is homosexual, even without thinking. We all have our own level of "outness." Even heterosexuals limit how much they'll disclose at the workplace. How a person acts around his or her family and friends is different than how he or she acts around strangers or professional relationships. As gay men and lesbians, we may dress a certain way, have an HRC sticker on our car, or maybe even wear a rainbow watch to show our pride. Yet, old stereotypes meet an incredibly hard death – for example, the idea that all librarians are all book-crazy, cheerless, and perhaps dowdy spinsters. As an academic librarian who teaches and encounters new people on a daily basis, I have been given the sage advice to rely on my expertise as an information professional, impress people and show them that I know, and am, more than what they initially perceive. I apply this to teaching students, training students, and interacting with coworkers.

In many library environments, students' labor is utilized in different ways, and good student workers can make the library operate very smoothly. Making the experience for them as positive as we can is very important – we might unknowingly be nurturing future librarians. Although I don't feel that my (or anyone's) sexuality is necessary information to divulge in the workplace, it does make it a bit easier to be open and not hide who I am. And as one befriends student workers and interacts with them more, it's natural for sexuality to come up. In this sense, coworkers are an important aspect of feeling emotionally healthy and comfortable on the job.

I have had a few students come out to me at work. Their comfort in approaching me with such a huge announcement has made an impact on me. I always say, "I've been there and I'm someone you can talk to if you need to." I offer support as a mentor if they need it. I don't force advice on them, but they know they can ask me. I simply put myself in their place: often, we librarians are as old as their parents, and they most likely cannot relate to us as much as we would like them to. Newly out students can feel conflicted with their family and religious beliefs, wondering how they fit in the world. With gay students, sometimes I'm engaged in a game of disclosure. As they disclose one clue about their sexuality, I might feel the need to disclose one myself. It is the normal part of any friendship to do this. I do not feel that disclosure of sexuality breaches the line between being professional and being too personal. If my being out can help any student I work with feel more comfortable in coming out or being gay, I feel I am helping.

Feeling comfortable with our sexuality at work depends on the comfort level the environment provides to us. When the extra dimension of students or those younger than ourselves is added, it is important to be aware that their feelings are not as mature as ours are. Not everyone has the same level of "outness" that we may have. I have encountered some students who are completely out and some who are still very conflicted. Being sensitive to that part of their current experience is important for their own emotional health, but it is equally important for me to behave professionally and ethically. Sometimes a student can become too familiar and disclose too much of his or her personal life. This happens with both straight and gay students (and coworkers too), and it can be embarrassing and uncomfortable. Sometimes students can push the limits of what is appropriate talk in the library. Student workers may try to coax similar levels of disclosure out of me as they do their own friends. Knowing my institution's policy on faculty/staff fraternization with the student population is necessarily important. Establishing a boundary in regards to what we feel is appropriate for student interaction and being consistent is crucial for both me and the students working along with me in the library.

Within the past five years, the popularity of social networking sites like Facebook, MySpace, and Twitter can out us without our knowing. Most sites have privacy settings that let us control how much information is shared. We can always leave information out if we are not comfortable with putting our partner's name or sexual orientation out there in cyberspace. I have used social networking sites to out myself to people, including students. I am typically mindful of what I am putting on the Internet. Many social networking sites allow for adding friends. Typically, this opens up new information about us based on our privacy settings. People who did not know we are gay can now see content such as pictures, comments, and other information that might allude to our orientation. It is important for all of us (not just gay people) to be aware of this and to figure out what we are comfortable with. Putting ourselves out in cyberspace opens up multiple doors we may not want opened, both personally and professionally.

Sexuality, Students, and Disclosure

If you think about it, this might help you with your own sexual disclosure in the work environment, with family, and with students.

Encountering a student through a social networking site can be very different than in person. Younger people can feel detached from the interaction. This is like being in a car and exhibiting road rage to someone in another car who has angered us. While in the vehicle, we feel detached and we might honk our horn, shake our fist, or flip them the bird. Being in the online environment can be the same as being in a vehicle – especially to less mature individuals. Things can be said that we or the student may regret later. As professionals, we should interact with the student as we would in person, at work, and as librarians. Some students become more familiar, due to their personality or genial nature. Most of the time, it is these students who will test our level of comfort when the topic of sexuality and our personal lives comes up. Students can be very curious about our personal lives, but it is up to us to be aware of what we are comfortable disclosing. The give-and-take of disclosure is just the natural part of any friendship.

Students and student workers will always be around in the academic library workplace. Every librarian has a duty to straight and gay students alike, to be supportive and pass on the knowledge we were taught. Those of us who have been there know that coming out can be scary, even with supportive peers. Our own "outness" can show to others that it is okay to be gay. The library environment can very well be the safe harbor a student needs to feel secure and safe. My commitment as a librarian is one that encompasses so much. If I have any impact on a student's choice to be out and proud, or just being someone to talk to, I feel I am truly making a difference. One day, a student may thank us for giving them the extra bit of courage to come out.

Girl meets girl. Girl works with girl. Girl falls in love with girl...

Brenda Linares and Emily Vardell

We follow office romances on television and cheer for the cute work couple in the movies. But how often does it happen in real life? According to a 2008 survey for CNN, 40% of workers have taken part in an office romance, and 29% of these couples get married (Haefner). The couples we see in the media and those represented in the CNN survey are most likely heterosexual. Same-sex couples have traditionally been underrepresented across the board in every situation, including surveys on office romances. By sharing our story, we hope to be a part of the growing visibility of same-sex couples and the diverse ways they meet, fall in love, and live their lives like any other couple.

We traveled two different paths to arrive in the same place. Emily grew up in Texas, graduated from Wellesley College in 2005, and lived for two years in Austria as a Fulbright Scholar. While in Austria, she completed her Masters of Library Science from Texas Woman's University and applied for the National Library of Medicine (NLM) Associate Fellowship Program. Brenda was born in Guatemala, immigrated to California when she was ten, graduated from California State University-Northridge in 2002, worked in the financial industry for a few years, completed her Masters of Library and Information Science from University of California Los Angeles, and applied for the National Library of Medicine Associate Fellowship Program. Luckily for us, we were both accepted into the program.

We met on September 4, 2007, the same day we met the other five Associates (as we're called for short). We were a diverse group, from across the United States (and one from Nigeria), and with a multitude of backgrounds. But we also had many things in common. We were all enthusiastic and ambitious new medical librarians and all newcomers to the Washington, D.C. area. Because we were all strangers in a new place, and perhaps because we had other similar interests, we spent quite a bit of time together outside of work and became a close-knit group. One would invite us all out to an Ethiopian restaurant she saw in Silver Spring, while another might suggest we walk to downtown Bethesda for drinks after work. In those first two months, our group spent about one night a week outside of work together, exploring our new city. Emily, who is a movie fanatic, often invited the group out to see one movie or another.

One Friday night about three weeks into the fellowship, Emily asked if anyone was interested in seeing "Across the Universe" that night. Most of the Associates had other plans, but Brenda said she would be interested in going. After work, we headed out to downtown Bethesda to a Mexican restaurant. This was one of the first times that it was just the two of us spending time together. We bonded over a fondness for Mexican food (having both grown up in areas rife with this cuisine), and shared stories about our families and growing up. We are both close with our families and, listening to each other's story, we could tell that we had many things in common.

After dinner, we headed to the theater and saw "Across the Universe," which we both enjoyed as musical buffs and Beatles fans. We grabbed a quick ice cream afterward, and Brenda realized she did not have enough cash on her so, of course, Emily offered to pay. When the cashier asked, "are you together?" Brenda hastily replied, "just for this!" The way she said it so quickly seemed to carry some hidden meaning behind it, though Emily wasn't sure what.

Emily's take:

As we walked back to the cars together, Brenda said, "I had a really great time tonight. We should do this again." I agreed, but when I got to my car I realized that was exactly the same thing you would say at the end of a first date. Did I just go on a date with Brenda? *I thought. I called my friends to talk through the night and they all encouraged me, saying, "you should pursue this!" This was the first time I had seriously contemplated such a thing. Although I had never dated either women or men, I had considered myself, perhaps as default, straight. But here was a person that I could talk with, who was interesting, smart, and with whom I had many things in common. I decided to continue spending time with Brenda and see how things proceeded.*

We continued to spend time together outside of work. Though we would always invite other Associates, many began to have busier schedules or simply didn't have the inclination to go out as often as we did. Brenda introduced Emily to Guatemalan food; Emily introduced Brenda to her grandmother who was visiting. The three of us spent an afternoon together at a fair and as we parted ways, Emily's grandmother said, "Brenda, take care of my granddaughter!" Little did she know her wish would soon come true. . . .

As with any relationship, it's hard to pinpoint the moment when you realized, *this is a person I could love*. It's always the little things – the innocent hugs or the sincere interest in what the other person is saying and feeling.

Emily's take:

I realized my attraction might be growing one evening when we saw the movie "The Jane Austen Book Club" (side note: somehow we kept seeing movies with gay women as supporting characters. What a coincidence!). I offered Brenda an Altoid and as Brenda took it from my hand, I felt a spark. I knew, somehow, that this was something special. Something to treasure.

Brenda's take:

I also felt a connection building with Emily as we spent more time together and learned about each other's values and interests. I felt an attraction towards Emily, but I was not sure if Emily was gay, and I myself was not out at work. I did not want to show any romantic feelings, because I really enjoyed Emily's company and did not want to lose a friend. This was someone I was building a friendship with and seeing every day at work.

On October 13, 2007, Emily got in the car to do some Saturday morning errands. As she was leaving a gas station, an elderly man unknowingly backed into her car. Though it was only a minor collision, it was still a little rattling. Her first thought was, *I wish Brenda were here*. Luckily, we had plans for later that night with one of our colleagues, and when Brenda called Emily to see what the plans were, Emily couldn't help but tell her all about the minor accident. Brenda asked if Emily needed help; Emily admitted she did; and Brenda promised to come quickly to her rescue! While waiting patiently at the mall for Brenda to come, Emily heard the Queen song "Somebody to Love," and wondered if this was the start of something wonderful.

Brenda showed up at the mall on Saturday afternoon and gave Emily a big hug. We walked around to clear our minds, and Brenda had her first Dairy Queen blizzard (the start of yet another tradition). After a while we headed to Emily's place so that she could take a quick shower and get ready for the evening. However, our friend called to say something had come up and she couldn't meet us. That left the whole evening to ourselves.

We decided to make a frozen pizza at home, watch a DVD, and just hang out. We enjoyed talking with each other and opened up even more than we had before. Brenda made little comments that made Emily start to think, *I'm pretty sure she is gay and maybe even is attracted to me*. But neither one of us ever confirmed it or said anything out loud. Brenda felt like she was letting her guard down and inviting Emily in. Eventually, Emily took a leap of faith and made the first move. She kissed Brenda, and Brenda kissed her back. And as they say, the rest is history!

At this point, neither Brenda nor Emily were out to each other or to anyone else at work. It was a government job in essence. We were only a month and a half into our fellowship. It was the start of our careers and neither one of us wanted to create extra obstacles or be labeled in some way that might negatively affect the rest of our career. Although the library world is a generally accepting and liberal world, as new professionals we wanted to play our cards right and be known for who we are as librarians, not who we are as gay women. As we looked around to see if there was someone at NLM with whom we could talk, and who was also from the GLBT community, we noticed that there were only a handful of staff and, thus, decided to keep quiet.

As Associate Fellows, the eyes of NLM were upon us. We were taken to important meetings and introduced. We had group seven-on-ones with the leaders of the library. It was an amazing experience, but also a bit of pressure to live up to the reputation as an Associate and to fulfill the promise expected of us. As with all of the other Associates, we kept our personal lives out of the office. However, during lunchtime and other times outside of work, our fellow Associates would talk about their husbands or ex-boyfriends. Neither of us said anything about our love lives – mainly because there was nothing to tell, as neither of us had ever been in a relationship. But we also kept quiet because it was a small group of seven – a group of seven women we had to spend 40 hours with every week for an entire year. We weren't interested in making things awkward or uncomfortable.

It was clear from the beginning that this relationship was not a one-time kind of thing. As we mentioned, this was a small group of seven people. Not the ideal situation for something casual. If we were going to go for it, we were going to be serious about it. We did not make it obvious at work, but we started spending much of our time outside of work with each other. Much as we had done before, we went to dinner together, to the movies, and generally enjoyed each other's company. It was a world with just the two of us there, and we were deliriously happy!

We still continued to hang out with our fellow Associates outside of work, but we never made it obvious that we were together. People knew we were close, but either did not think it was anything more than that, or did not say anything. We felt it was not something that needed to be shared with the entire library and that we would tell the Associates when it was appropriate.

The first work colleague we told was one of our fellow Associates. The three of us had bought tickets to see the Spice Girls before we were even together as a couple. The concert was in New York, however, so we had to plan out the details of traveling there together. We decided now was the time to tell one of the Associates with whom we were closest. She needed to know, as it would make the trip to New York as comfortable as possible. Luckily, she took the news well. She said she guessed there might be something going on and that she was happy to hear that we were happy. We were grateful she was so supportive.

At work we continued to act as we had before. We acted friendly in front of everyone, because they knew us as friends. We took the same leftovers for lunch and left people to make their own assumptions. We always maintained a professional atmosphere, even occasionally sitting apart. We did not want to make anyone uncomfortable, and we did not want to distract away from the purpose of the fellowship. We wanted to mold ourselves into outstanding medical librarians.

Having to deal with being in a relationship with a colleague in the same position, location, and library has its challenges. It seems to complicate matters even further when you are in a gay relationship, since there are many external issues involved. When straight couples begin dating at work, people often draw conclusions more quickly. As two women, we could often pass under the guise of a friendship. This has its positive and its negative side. Though we may not have to confront homophobia, we are not a visible presence and do not contribute to the visibility of gay colleagues in the workplace. This cycle seems to hold us back from being seen as a regular part of the professional community. It takes courageous people to step forward, come out, and show that sexuality is only one facet of a person.

It became more difficult as the year continued. We spent a lot of time with our mentors and other colleagues. We noticed how many people were casually open about their private lives, but we were not. We spoke about our families and friends, but we never brought our relationship into the conversation. We traveled on a few trips and when we would return, people would naturally ask about them. We would tell them that we traveled together, but we never mentioned that we were a couple or any details about our personal life. We figured they just thought we were very close friends and liked each other's company. Perhaps we were fortunate that we were never asked any personal questions. Sometimes we wondered if they knew, but were waiting for us to bring the topic up or open up to them. Since we were part of this special group, we decided that we would not say anything that year at NLM in order to keep attitudes and reputations professional. We did not want anyone to think that our relationship would interfere with our individual projects or with our relationships with the other Associates.

We focused on work, pursued projects in different areas, and built up connections with colleagues at the library and at other libraries across the country. We shared a room at the Medical Library Association (MLA) conference, but attended meetings and presentations individually. During our first year as medical librarians, we wanted to create our own, individual reputations. We also decided to join the MLA GLBT Special Interest Group. Here we found a group of supportive colleagues with whom we could network within an affirming environment. Being part of this group gave us an opportunity to share our story with our colleagues and to seek advice on what to do in our situation. They offered the advice that, as long as our relationship did not interfere with our work, we should not worry about making it public. This was, and is, a private and personal matter. So far, no one at work had said anything; and therefore, it seemed that if they knew we were together, they did not take issue with it, and perhaps assumed that when we felt comfortable enough we would be open about it.

The Associate Fellowship has an optional second year component. Associates can opt to spend a second year at a health sciences library somewhere in the United States. Different medical libraries compete to host an Associate at their library for a year to work on projects of the Associate's interest. Both of us were interested in taking part in this second year. We agreed, before we even read the proposals of the second year sites, that our professional development was important. If we had to move to two different places, we would make it work.

As we read the applications it became clear that our interests would take us in two different parts of the country. Emily is interested in public health librarianship, and the strong application from the University of North Carolina Chapel Hill appealed to her. Brenda is interested in outreach, and the projects proposed by the University of Miami were too good to turn down. We each visited these two libraries and realized they would be great fits for us in this next stage of our career.

We talked over our future plans carefully. We were used to seeing each other almost 24/7 – at work and at home. How would we manage living with several states between us? We turned to examples of family members and friends who had made the distance work. We knew we could do it.

In August of 2008, we packed up a Penske truck and hit the road. First stop? Chapel Hill, North Carolina. We unloaded Emily's things into the apartment she rented, jumped back in the Penske truck, and headed further South. We enjoyed the trip together, seeing friends and tourist stops along the way, including the gay pilgrimage site, the Whistle Stop Café from *Fried Green Tomatoes*! Once arriving in Miami, Emily helped unload Brenda's things and then hopped on a plane back to North Carolina.

In our second years in Chapel Hill and Miami, we were once again adamant that our professional reputation should come first. We wanted to be known first for our professional capabilities. Luckily for both us, we had gay colleagues who provided support.

Brenda's take:

I found fellow gay colleagues at the Calder Memorial Library at the University of Miami. I had always been self-conscious of being gay; therefore, being open to people about my sexuality was hard for me. Luckily in Miami, the work atmosphere was very welcoming and open. There were a couple of coworkers who were gay, and when I saw that they were open about their relationships, I felt comfortable enough to share with them that I had a girlfriend who was working in Chapel Hill.

The Calder Library has an annual Christmas party to which faculty and staff are invited to bring a guest. Brenda made the decision to invite Emily to the party. This was a big step in our relationship. It was the first time that we openly acknowledged our relationship in a professional environment. Brenda introduced Emily as "my girlfriend," and her colleagues could not have been more supportive. Luckily for us, there were at least three other gay couples present, so we seemed to fit in well. Everyone accepted Emily as part of the greater Calder family.

Emily's take:

In Chapel Hill, I had queer colleagues to whom I could turn for advice and support. Two of the three were out to anyone who cared to listen, and it seemed to be a non-issue. However, I was still hesitant. This was new: both being out and being a medical librarian. I noticed that most people at the library did not talk too much about their personal lives, so I followed suit and focused solely on my professional development.

In the spring, Brenda came to visit the Health Sciences Library in Chapel Hill as a part of her 2nd year fellowship. She met with many of the staff members and presented on her fellowship activities. Although everyone knew that we were close, I did not share that Brenda was my girlfriend. I wanted everyone to see Brenda in a professional context, and I felt awkward announcing this, having for so long not discussed personal matters. As time passed, however, and I was nearing the end of my second year, I became more comfortable with my colleagues and with my sexuality. More people became aware (not because I directly told them, but because they inferred from suggestions) of our relationship and were quietly supportive.

It soon became time to find permanent positions. The year apart was tough; the traveling and the distance had taken their toll. We now knew there was no question: we wanted to live in the same place. This also coincided with the worsening of the US economy, and resultant hiring freezes across the United States. As Associates, we were told we would have no problems finding a job, but that was when times were better. Fortunately, however, due to various circumstances and through a stroke of fate, two positions opened up at the Calder Library. Brenda was poised to take the position as the Financial Manager and Administrative Librarian. Her financial background and interest in library administration made her the perfect fit.

Emily wanted to support Brenda and this great opportunity, but she also wanted to continue to foster her own professional development. Luckily there was a position in Emily's interest areas available at Calder as well. This seemed too good to be true! Emily interviewed with the Executive Director and Director of Library Operations and met with the entire library faculty. Fortunately, she was offered the position. Beginning September 1, 2009, both Emily and Brenda were employees of the Calder Memorial Library.

Now we are back to being colleagues at the same library. We work in two very different areas, and continue to work at maintaining professional boundaries. We try not to visit each other too often or act too familiar with each other. We, of course, take our lunches together, but we make sure to include our coworkers in our conversations. We recently received the ultimate compliment from a colleague who told us we were handling working in the same place very well.

We feel we have come full circle. We started our professional careers shielding our personal lives from the professional goals we had. Our journeys have led us to continue to be goal-driven and focused on our professions, but also to be more comfortable being who we are and sharing our personal lives with our colleagues. As always, we continue to support each other in our professional endeavors, and we are there to be each other's rock when things are difficult, and a cheerleader when things are great.

Work Cited

Haefner, Rosemary. "Office romances rarely kept secret." *CNN News.* Turner Broadcasting System, Inc. 25 November 2008. Web. 11 August 2010.

It's Okay to *BE* Gay...
A Librarian's Journey to Acceptance and Activism[1]

Jason D. Phillips

One of the indirect consequences of library school is that I became a homosexual. That is a facetious statement, of course, but the truth is that my entry into the library profession was the first time that I felt accepted, encouraged, and supported as a gay individual. I finally felt the freedom to publicly speak out in support of GLBT issues outside of my immediate circle of friends. And while taking a summer course in Young Adult Services, I also found the inspiration and courage to come out to my family. As an academic librarian new to the profession, I have discovered allies, received support, faced challenges, and negotiated a professional identity in a conservative environment in a way that does not also compromise my status as an openly gay man. My two years at Mississippi State University Libraries gave me the opportunity to transform into the active GLBT advocate and researcher that I am today.

* * *

The journey to acceptance is a unique one for every GLBT individual, beset with its own obstacles. My own story begins in Southern suburbia, a place of growing affluence still clinging to conservative values. Taunts of "faggot," intermingled with my Southern Baptist upbringing, left me deeply

---

1. I spent two summers in Washington, D.C. working with high school students from around the country and the world. I taught them about diplomacy, foreign policy, international issues, and leadership skills. As part of our activities, we visited embassies in the D.C.-area. During one of these visits, an openly gay student asked an Egyptian diplomat if he could speak about Egypt's policy on homosexuals. The diplomat, obviously surprised by the question, responded by saying: "It's okay to BE gay ... as long as you don't ACT gay." These words elicited some chuckles from me at the time, but I have continued to ponder their meaning ever since.

fearful and ashamed for being uncontrollably different. Though I still felt extremely isolated and alone with the growing awareness of my blossoming sexual identity, I managed to carefully craft an acceptable "facsimile" that allowed me to blend in with my peers. Graduation from high school in 1997 led to a liberation of sorts.

I attended The University of Alabama (UA), a large university two hundred miles from my home in Mobile, where I knew less than a handful of people. In an effort to build my social circle and to fit into this microcosm, I pledged Chi Phi (a social fraternity) and perfected the mask I wore in public: scholar and party animal. So far from home, I finally felt some small measure of freedom to finally explore my sexuality, though I remained cautious and fearful of exposure. Interactions with openly gay men frightened me. Would they out me or would they know me for what I am? The constant fear of exposure, the heavy burden of self-loathing, and closeted clandestine activities continued until well into my final year of college.

In fall of 2002, I took a Women's Studies class that forever changed my perspective about myself and the world around me. Discussions in and outside of the classroom with my professor, Dr. Karma Chavez, opened my eyes to a possible future full of personal freedom and acceptance.[2] I began to accept that being gay is not just about sexual attraction, but it is also about a shared experience, community, and history. In secret, I began to watch GLBT films. In time, I came out to myself and accepted that I am gay and accepted myself for who I am: a gay man. I slowly, cautiously began to establish my identity throughout the rest of my life, and I began to tell my closest friends. It is important to note that while I may have accepted my identity as a gay man, I did not fully embrace it. I still feared the consequences of living openly as a homosexual in a conservative environment. I remained terrified of the possible rejection from my friends and loved ones if they discovered the truth.

This quiet lifestyle continued into graduate school at UA as I pursued a Master's degree in History. I finally found the courage to come out to a very close circle of friends, many of whom, as luck would have it, were also gay or bisexual. Behind closed-doors, we formed our own close-knit and supportive community and would occasionally venture out into the anonymity of the gay bar scene. I became stronger in my own self-confidence and identity. I eventually concluded that I did not want to pursue a

---

2. Karma and I spoke on a personal level about our personal and political views, but I never said to her "I am gay" – I shadow-danced around actually saying those words. I think she knew, but also recognized that I was struggling with my identity.

PhD in History, but instead wanted to continue working in the academic environment. My studies in History naturally drew me to archival work, so in the summer of 2005, I began my second Master's in Library and Information Studies at UA.

The first few weeks of library school were quite daunting and fraught with doubt in my still fragile sense of self and life purpose. My Organization of Information class, with its coverage of "content of bibliographic records in printed and machine-readable form, choice and form of access points, authority control, and verbal and classified systems of subject access," left me feeling bewildered and wondering if I had made the right choice.[3] However, my Collection Development class, taught by Dr. Charles Osburn, reaffirmed my decision to become a librarian. I learned that librarians are not only facilitators of information discovery, but also guardians of intellectual freedom. This awareness filled me with a sense of purpose and inspired me to continue along this career path.

What also made a lingering, life-changing impression was a classmate of mine, Josh Burford, who is openly and unabashedly gay. He spoke openly of his homosexuality and proudly incorporated his identity into librarianship, with the goals of providing services for the GLBT community – our community. The rest of the class welcomed his beliefs and views and provided an overwhelming sense of support that I had never experienced before outside of my close-knit circle of friends. This nurturing environment of discussion, debate, and acceptance of differing views helped me to discover my true voice as a gay professional.

My nascent identity as a gay professional continued to develop as I worked toward my degree. In addition to the aforementioned classmate, there were also two library school faculty members who became my role models and mentors: Drs. Annabel Stephens and Jamie C. Naidoo. Both are openly gay, and they provided the encouragement that was necessary for me to become an openly gay individual and professional. They shared with me books and articles about GLBT librarianship and mentored me through this transformative period. These books and articles introduced me to GLBT luminaries and pioneers in our profession like Carl Gough, Ellen Greenblatt, and Robert Ridinger. These efforts left me with a desire to improve services and provide resources for the GLBT community.

Every GLBT professional routinely faces societal challenges, and I experienced some of these common challenges as a student worker.

---

3. LS 500. "Organization of Information." *MLIS Course Descriptions.* The University of Alabama School of Library and Information Studies. December 30, 2009 <http://www.slis.ua.edu/Course_Des.html>.

Beginning in 2005, I worked as an archivist's assistant processing and cataloging the manuscript and rare book collections for the John C. Payne Special Collections department at the Bounds Law Library. My supervisors, Drs. David Durham and Paul Pruitt, were very encouraging and supportive; the work was edifying, and the other student coworkers became friends of mine on the social networking site Facebook.

After perusing my profile, one of these student coworkers discovered my homosexuality and questioned me. Initially, I was shaken, and quickly became fearful and unsure of how to handle the situation. Did I want to be "out" at work? I had already struggled with taking my first few steps to be an openly gay individual and professional, so I took a leap of faith and boldly confirmed his suspicions. Internally, I felt relieved, and was pleased that I had finally reached that personal milestone. Unfortunately, he gave me cause to soon regret my openness – he took my disclosure as an opportunity to ask questions I thought were too probing and uncomfortable. I developed the distinct impression that he might be questioning his own sexuality. The following week, he told me that he had spoken to our supervisors about my sexuality, disclosing it to them in a conversation. I was upset, not because I had been "outed" by an emotionally immature undergraduate, but because my sexuality is *my* truth to tell, no one else's. Fortunately, my supervisors were both very kind and open-minded individuals who did not care whether or not I was gay, as long as I continued to be a hard worker. From this, I learned two very valuable lessons that remain to this day: although we should never be ashamed of our identity, we should not put anything on social media websites that we are not comfortable sharing with the world; and we should be discrete and judicious when disclosing personal information to coworkers.

Though I may have had a taste of liberation upon graduating from high school and entering college, I experienced a virtual revolution during my first year of library school. The encouragement I received in the classroom and the support of my mentors gave me the courage to begin living freely, proudly, and openly as a gay man. Meeting and mingling with other GLBT individuals gave me that sense of community and acceptance that I craved. To reach my final milestone, all that was left for me to do was to come out to the rest of my friends and family. A Young Adult Services class was the very thing that gave me that last, much-needed final push.

The Young Adult Services class had a heavy reading load of books from every type of genre and subject for YA readers, and the professor, Dr. Naidoo, assigned me the GLBT-themed books. Each book, with its inspiring story of pain, courage, and triumph, chipped away at my fear and resistance to coming out. *The Full Spectrum,* an anthology of short stories by young GLBT writers, had a particularly profound impact.[4] I was personally acquainted with one if its authors, Matt Mayo, who attended a nearby university and agreed to come speak to our class about his short story and his coming-out experiences. I was struck by the profound courage of these young writers, who shared their fears, suffering, and ascendancy through their coming-out stories. Consequently, after garnering support from my GLBT friends and mentors, I sent letters to my family and came out to them as a gay man. Much to my surprise and relief, instead of experiencing the pain and rejection that I was sure would come, my family met the news with acceptance. My family and I still needed to work through the emotional upheaval inherent from a coming-out experience, but I took the last step toward accepting myself as a gay man.

Though my experiences in library school left an indelible mark on my development as an openly gay individual, I still needed to find a balance between an open lifestyle and my professional identity. My transition from student to professional librarian began in the fall of 2006 when I was hired as a paraprofessional copy cataloger at Gorgas Library, the main library at UA. Because of the close relationship between the library itself and the library school, I was already acquainted with many of the librarians, and many knew about and readily accepted my sexuality. Furthermore, my supervisor and I had been classmates, and we developed a supportive rapport that often included conversations about GLBT topics. Despite this relatively accepting and comfortable work environment, I was advised by other colleagues to maintain a low-key approach to my sexuality. So, in an effort to protect myself from workplace discrimination, I spoke openly to a few close colleagues, but I stayed silent on the subject of my sexuality with others. Although the injustice of forced silence proved painful, my low-key approach proved beneficial in avoiding any potential difficulties, especially in light of the fact that GLBT individuals did not yet have protection from discrimination in my place of employment, city, or state.

In 2007, the faculty and students at UA engaged in a very public debate about amending the non-discrimination policy to include sexual orientation and gender identity. This action was endorsed by the Faculty Senate and the Student Government Association, but the university's administration was initially reluctant to amend the policy. The administration eventually compromised. After the students left for the holidays, the

---

4. Levithan, David and Billy Merrell, eds. *The Full Spectrum: a New Generation of Writing about Gay, Lesbian, Bisexual, Transgender, Questioning, and Other Identities.* New York: Knopf, 2006.

administration made the quiet announcement that the university was extending its non-discrimination policy to include sexual orientation, but did not include gender identity.[5]

This debate heavily influenced my search for employment as an academic librarian. I made a point to research potential employers' non-discrimination policies. I also decided not to initially disclose my sexuality in my application materials. I omitted both my research interests and membership in the Gay, Lesbian, Bisexual, and Transgendered Round Table of the American Library Association (GLBTRT of ALA).[6] I agonized over this difficult decision, but decided that I did not want to suffer from any potential or latent discrimination during the search and interview process. This action, though legitimate, later proved to be unnecessary.

In March 2008, I interviewed for a position at Mississippi State University (MSU). During the interview with the search committee, Harry Llull – the Associate Dean for Public Services – asked me about my research interests. As planned, I only mentioned "safe" topics relevant to the position. But then he followed up by asking if I had any other interests. I paused, and made the fateful decision to disclose my interest in library services to the GLBT community. I could tell that he was surprised, but also approved. Immediately following my statement, Christine Fletcher – a Government Documents Reference Librarian and a lesbian – interjected and quoted the university's non-discrimination policy: Discrimination based upon sexual orientation or group affiliation is a violation of MSU policy and will not be tolerated.[7] This incident was *such* a welcome relief. I knew I had found the right place for me, especially in light of the recent debate at my alma mater.

I was very surprised to find GLBT individuals leading open lifestyles. MSU is located in Starkville, a small, college town in a rural, Southern state. It seems that this small community is welcoming and tolerant, with the proviso that its GLBT members are discrete. These individuals are an accepted and active part of the community, though there are no distinctly GLBT-themed public activities, nor is there a distinct sense of "community" amongst the gay population. Despite the close personal friendships I developed with other heterosexual individuals, the absence of this "community" created feelings of isolation and solitude at times, which was only somewhat alleviated by my work. The town's political and social climate

---

5. The University of Alabama's Office of Equal Opportunity Programs Policies & Laws: http://eop.ua.edu/law.html
6. GLBTRT website: http://www.ala.org/ala/mgrps/rts/glbtrt/index.cfm
7. MSU's Equal Opportunity Statement: http://www.msstate.edu/dept/audit/0302.html

does benefit from its proximity to the university, but it is still a largely conservative environment. And this "don't ask, don't tell" atmosphere was definitely reflected in the work environment of the library.

As I strove to negotiate my identity, I found myself walking a fine line that acknowledged the conservative environment I live in without compromising my identity as an openly gay man. In other words, I "kept one foot in the closet" while I was at work. I freely shared my research interests and professional activities, even going so far as to include them in e-mails to the library's faculty and staff, the library's directory, and my profile on LibGuides; however, I stopped short of discussing my *personal* life, except with a small number of close colleagues.

My first experience of interacting with another gay coworker, Lee Dempsey, illustrates this attitude of quasi-openness. A group of us were socializing one evening when I nonchalantly presented my own personal gay perspective on the present topic of discussion. In shock, Lee stated that he did not know that I was gay. I laughed and said, "The library doesn't pay me to be a GAY librarian!" So, though I continued to maintain a discrete professional persona, I do think that I was successful in pursuing my interests as a librarian who is also gay.

Although I had successfully begun to establish myself as both a gay professional *and* a gay man, the Library's very active presence in the 2.0 environment presented challenges to the balance I had so carefully cultivated. As part of my orientation, the importance of our organization's active presence on Facebook in promoting the Library's accessibility and services to patrons, though not mandatory, was strongly encouraged. I was reluctant to merge what had always been a very personal presence in social networking into a professional, and a very public, one. Would I have to censor myself? Would I have to hide my identity as a gay man? If I did expose my gay identity, would I be courting a backlash that would destroy my career? Despite my strong antipathy to self-censor, I still keenly felt the need for self-preservation, and promptly culled old postings and groups that may have been viewed as too controversial in this largely conservative community. Much to my relief, however, my initial fears again and again proved to be unfounded. My subsequent professional activities in the GLBT community, whether they were in the Library 2.0 arena or public services for GLBT students and faculty, were largely encouraged and embraced.

Social networking has proven to be an outstanding way for me, as a professional and a gay man, to serve the GLBT community. Patrons used Facebook to establish a connection with me and there have been a surprising number of students who have "friended" me after we interacted through virtual chat. In some instances, we have continued the reference transaction through Facebook messages. My membership in the group "Coalition of Southeastern LGBTQ Faculty, Staff, Students, and Allies" led to a student "friending" me and asking if there was a campus Spectrum group. I have been able to serve as a friend and counselor for him as he struggles with acceptance and his decision to come out, both to himself and to his family and friends. Members of the Spectrum group have also "friended" me on Facebook, which has given me further opportunity to converse with them about our library's resources, and has allowed me to discover what more I can do to assist their group and community. Despite – or perhaps due to – this ongoing discovery and interaction, I stopped censoring myself by masking my identity or tempering my status updates, posts, or comments.

There were many straight allies in my library who provided me with tremendous support during my tenure at MSU. I had colleagues, such as Susan Hall and Amanda N. Price, with whom I collaborated on GLBT-themed articles or projects. I was also given time at work to spend on this research and professional service. As mentioned earlier, I was able to focus most of my professional service activities with the GLBT Round Table. I also serve on two GLBRT committees, including the Stonewall Book Award Committee (BAC).[8] Furthermore, I received professional leave and financial support from the library to attend the 2010 ALA Midwinter Conference in Boston for my work on the Stonewall BAC. In April 2010, I was elected Secretary of the GLBTRT, an achievement that drew much praise from my colleagues across the library. This record of research and service led to other opportunities and interactions with students, faculty, and colleagues. I received questions and requests for assistance from other academic and public librarians in the state. At MSU, I was a member of the Gender Studies program, where I attended meetings and participated in program activities.[9] Additionally, I served as the program's liaison to the GLBT student group – Spectrum – by attending meetings and offering assistance as needed.

The chair of the Gender Studies program, Dr. Nicole Rader, recognized my service and activism on behalf of the GLBT community and gender equality by nominating me to serve on the (university) President's

---

8. Website for the Stonewall Book Awards:
   http://www.ala.org/ala/mgrps/rts/glbtrt/stonewall/stonewallbook.cfm
9. The Gender Studies Program has an open-door policy for faculty who have an interest in Gender Studies. They have graciously allowed a fellow librarian and me to participate in their meetings.

Commission on the Status of Women (PCSW). When I was asked to serve, Mary McLendon – the Chair of the PCSW – told me that I had the reputation of "having strong opinions about gender equality and that I am not afraid to articulate these opinions in a constructive fashion." It was her hope that I could represent the view of sexual minorities by giving them a voice on this important body that directly advises the university president on gender policy issues.

My brief service on the Commission opened my eyes to the vagaries of university politics, particularly the subtle tactics used by conservative homophobes to marginalize the GLBT community. The Commission is composed of faculty, various classifications of staff and administrators, and student representatives. The undergraduate representative is selected on a rotating basis from three different constituencies – one of them being a student from either Gender Studies or Spectrum. A vocal, but politically powerful minority on the Commission objected to this rotation – right before the student representative from Gender Studies/Spectrum was to be selected. Though they tried to be subtle with their arguments, it was clear to everyone in the room that they objected to a standing requirement calling for a representative from the GLBT community to serve on the Commission. The political stature of these individuals, both on-campus and in the state, gave the faculty members pause; fortunately, several courageous staff and administrators spoke in defense of this system of rotation and the importance of this "traditionally marginalized community to have a voice on the Commission." Much to my relief, the issue was tabled in the face of strong opposition from the Commission's other members.

I remained silent during the Commission's deliberations. Initially, I was shocked. I had never witnessed such an overt act of homophobia before in a professional setting. I am ashamed to say that when my shock subsided I let my concern for tenure sustain my silence; however, after the meeting, I immediately approached the officers to express my views. I lobbied them to continue with the rotation, and I recommended a student to serve as the undergraduate representative. I received assurances from them that the bylaws of the Commission were not going to be altered. This event taught me some important lessons: though they are a shrinking minority, there are still powerful forces seeking to exclude and disenfranchise the GLBT community; and there are a growing number of powerful forces who will stand up for our rights. I continue to wrestle with my decision to put my career first by remaining silent. Do we always have to be vocal advocates or can we also be effective by working behind-the-scenes?

Although I received a great deal of professional and personal support at MSU, one of the challenges that I faced was in the area of collection development. I conducted an assessment on the depth and breadth of the library's GLBT collection in the fall of 2009, and found some disconcerting results. I searched WorldCat using the following Library of Congress Subject Headings (LCSH): Homosexuality, Lesbians, and Gay men. I first counted the total number of books held by MSU with the aforementioned subject headings, and then I checked to see how many of those books were published from 2004–2009. Finally, I compared MSU's collection with the collections in other peer libraries.[10] The charts below show the total number of titles by LCSH in MSU's library's collection compared to the average number in each peer institution.

Total Number of Books with GLBT LCSH

	Homosexuality	Lesbians	Gay Men
Number in MSU Library	313	119	149
Average Number in Peer Libraries	1,006	420	613

Books with GLBT LCSH Published from 2004–2009

	Homosexuality	Lesbians	Gay Men
Number in MSU Library	42	8	15
Average Number in Peer Libraries	345	149	238

There is an obvious and regrettable gap between MSU's holdings and those of our peer-institutions. Upon examination of the traditional collection development practices, I learned several reasons for these discrepancies. MSU Library does not have any standing orders or a purchase plan for award-winning GLBT titles. It also does not specifically articulate the acquirement of GLBT materials in its collection development

---

10. These are peer land-grant and formerly Carnegie Research Extensive Institutions.

policy. Moreover, in recent years, MSU experienced a short-fall in funding, limiting the amount of monies available for book orders. Without a dedicated budget specific to GLBT materials, the collection has naturally fallen victim to funding shortfalls. Finally, the Gender Studies program has not recently received a book allocation due to the library's policy of only funding departments, not programs. Instead, they rely on faculty to specifically request GLBT titles.

Thankfully, I was able to make some progress towards remedying this situation. Last year, I requested two GLBT titles that were added to the Reference collection. Additionally, I donated all the books I received during my service on the Stonewall BAC to the library. Additionally, the Spectrum group plans to donate its private library of books and movies to the library, so that they can be accessible to the wider GLBT community.

Progress, however, was met with opposition. My attempts to recommend and purchase GLBT titles were met with some resistance. The library administration approved my request for the addition of the 2008 and 2009 Stonewall Book Award winners and honorees. I monitored the status of my request throughout the acquisitions process, so that I would know when the books were purchased and catalogued. A few months after I placed my request, a colleague followed behind me and requested the same number of books, except these books were of a conservative, religious, and homophobic bent.[11] I examined these titles in OCLC and found that many of them are located at private, religious schools and very few public universities have them in their collection. I received assurances from an administrator that these books would never be ordered and they were still supportive of adding GLBT titles to the collection, as funds were available.

The attempt to undermine my efforts towards building a meaningful GLBT collection demonstrates that there are librarians, even in academia, who are resistant to adding such titles to library collections. The incident also presented yet another unexpected challenge for me: how should I respond to situations such as this one in the future? Like most librarians,

---

11. A few examples of the requested titles: Dallas, Joe. *Desires in Conflict: Hope for Men Who Struggle with Sexual Identity.* Eugene, OR: Harvest House Publishers, 1991.; Konrad, J. A. *You Don't Have to Be Gay: Hope and Freedom for Males Struggling With Homosexuality or for Those Who Know of Someone Who Is.* Hilo, HI: Pacific Pub. House, 1992.; Nicolosi, Joseph and Linda Ames Nicolosi. *Parent's Guide to Preventing Homosexuality.* Downers Grove, IL: InterVarsity Press, 2002.; Dallas, Joe. *Gay Gospel?: How Pro-Gay Advocates Misread the Bible.* Eugene, OR: Harvest House Publishers, 2007.

I studied collection development in library school, and I know well the importance of a balanced collection. Though reconciling my professional obligations with my personal views can be a difficult task, I strongly believe that conservative-leaning titles have a place in collections so that all viewpoints are represented. It is fortunate that there are titles available that present a conservative view in a *scholarly* fashion.

I made what I consider to be tremendous strides with the general acceptance of my research and service interests, but I still wanted to improve the quality of service that MSU Libraries offered its GLBT patrons. The tolerant and permissive attitude toward my own activities did not include meaningful support for active GLBT outreach. So, how did I measure progress? I could feel impatient and frustrated by the glacial pace of progress and set-backs, or I could acknowledge the conservative environment in which I worked and lived and be thankful for any incremental steps forward that I've achieved. Each GLBT student I helped, every GLBT book I added to the collection, was one step forward. If I had stayed at MSU, perhaps, in the future, I would have had the opportunity to pursue outreach and programming for the GLBT community, but that would have been a goal I would have had to slowly and steadily work toward.

While at MSU Libraries, I had no appreciable barriers toward pursuing my research and professional service interests, and I was able to turn these interests into the foundation of a productive and active career. These activities and interests did not go unnoticed by the library's administration. MSU continues to increase their undergraduate enrollment and in response, the library's administration decided to create a new reference librarian position to provide additional reference services to the students and faculty. They had intended to transition me from my current assignment as a Government Documents & United Nations Reference Librarian to Social Sciences & United Nations Reference Librarian.[12] They also specifically referenced my research and activities with Gender Studies, the PCSW, and the GLBTRT as a factor in their decision. They believed that I could focus my outreach to these areas in which I already had an interest, particularly Political Science, Psychology, and Sociology. This would have been a tremendous opportunity, but, instead, I chose to accept

---

12. MSU Libraries had three Government Documents Librarians, so the loss of one would not overly diminish this area of library service. I would have kept my United Nations operational assignment because of my specialized expertise and experience with the United Nations and UN information, as well as the outreach efforts I made with MSU's Model United Nations organization.

an offer of employment from Georgetown University as a Government Information Reference Librarian & Bibliographer.

I found deep personal satisfaction from my work at MSU Libraries and many of my efforts toward networking had started bearing fruit; however, I still felt isolated living in rural Mississippi. I was highly productive in terms of my research and service, but I was beginning to burn out from working all the time in the absence of an appreciable gay community and other leisurely pursuits. Several of my friends who were aware of the situation would occasionally send me job announcements they thought I should pursue. The position at Georgetown was particularly attractive to me because of the potential in the position, the advancement in my career, and the quality of life that would come from living in the DC-area. So, I threw a Hail Mary and applied for the position.

In a marked difference from my previous experience applying for positions, I did not shy away from mentioning my numerous GLBT-related activities and publications in my application materials. My phone and on-site interviews focused primarily on my activities working with Government Information, reference, collection development, and instruction, so I did not have very many opportunities to discuss my research or service activities. My one-on-one meeting with John Buschman – the Associate University Librarian for Scholarly Resources & Services – addressed my concerns about being an openly gay librarian at a Jesuit university. He did not speak directly to my sexuality, but rather he addressed it indirectly. He, without prompting from me, discussed the progressive nature of the Jesuits, that the university offers full domestic-partnership benefits, and that the non-discrimination policy includes sexual orientation and gender identity. I also learned that, beginning in 2007, Georgetown University made a substantial commitment to outreach and inclusion efforts with its GLBT community, which culminated in the creation of its LGBTQ Resource Center, "the first such Center of its kind at a Catholic/Jesuit institution in the country."[13] This information allayed my fears.

I initially struggled with my decision to leave MSU. As I previously stated, my hard work was beginning to pay-off and I was about to move in a position that would allow me to focus my activities to the benefit of MSU's GLBT community. I felt like I was leaving unfinished work in a place that really needs a strong and active GLBT advocate. Efforts for greater GLBT inclusion and visibility are at a nascent stage, where progress is incremental and faces powerful conservative opposition.

---

13. Georgetown University's LGBTQ Resource Center: http://lgbtq.georgetown.edu/about.html

Ultimately, the decision to leave was a personal one: I am furthering my career by going to Georgetown and I will be able to live in a vital and active GLBT community. I do not know if my position and duties will allow me to be actively involved with their LGBTQ Center or their Women's and Gender Studies Program; however, I can be an active GLBT advocate in the library, continue my research, and will have the resources to increase my professional service activities. There is also the added advantage of working in a decidedly GLBT-friendly environment that offers domestic partnership benefits. It is my hope that once I have become acclimated in my position, I will have the opportunities and ability to become an active advocate on-campus.[14]

These professional triumphs and challenges speak to my continued development as a gay librarian; however, I still seem to have miles to go as a gay person. I greeted the call to contribute chapters to this book with enthusiasm. I believed that my story of how library school inspired me to come out to my friends and family, along with my experiences working in the profession, might benefit others. Yet, when it came time to articulate my fears and sense of isolation due to living in a conservative community, I found myself feeling reticent. At first draft, I found that verbalizing my challenges and triumphs at work came easily. But the professional persona of always having "one foot in the closet" is one with which I have become very comfortable (perhaps too comfortable), and I inadvertently adopted a crisp, cold professional tone, even unconsciously continuing to practice self-censorship. Then I took a step back and asked myself: Why did I do this?

At the core of my reticence is the teenager who desperately tried to fit in with the heterosexual crowd. Dormant memories of abuse and fears of rejection still cast a long shadow that impedes my ability to freely speak in candid terms about my past, sexuality, and road to acceptance. Living openly as a gay man is something that I chose to do. We are not really living if we are dying on the inside, and that is what I was doing by living a life in the closet, based on lies and fears. The unfortunate side-effect of spending years living in a closeted, conservative environment is that it has conditioned me to be taciturn when sharing things of a personal nature, even with those to whom I am closest, much-less you good readers!

It is my good fortune that my close friend and colleague, Amanda N. Price, assisted me with this effort. Amanda reminded me that creative and confessional writing is so much harder than professional writing,

---

14. My employment at MSU ended in June 2010 and I began working at Georgetown in August 2010, after the deadline for chapter submission.

especially for guarded individuals like me. It is really hard for me to show my inner-self – it almost seems like weakness; however, she reminded me that this chapter is an opportunity to reach out to you, the readers, who are members of my community, to offer you hope and comfort, to identify with you, and to let you identify with me. Through her gentle persuasion, long conversations, and humorous brow-beatings, my words took on more of a personal tone, so that you can now see the person behind the words and not just the librarian.

* * *

So, to amend my opening sentence: one of the indirect consequences of library school is that I experienced a transformation. I transcended from the life of a closeted, self-loathing outcast to one where I live openly and proudly as a homosexual. I have become an active member in the GLBT Round Table of ALA; I am encouraged to pursue research and writing opportunities of a GLBT-nature; and I have become a visible advocate for GLBT issues in the library and on-campus. I will continue to face challenges and obstacles as both a gay librarian and advocate for the GLBT community, counting every victory – great or small. And perhaps, one day, I can speak openly, candidly, and comfortably about personal matters without feeling the anticipation one experiences before plunging into cold water.

Out of the Frying Pan:
Coming Out As a Culinary School Librarian

Rachel Wexelbaum

There are many similarities between the culinary industry and the library profession. Both require a commitment to service, passion for one's subject, and an obsessive nature. Chefs and librarians both learn taste. While chefs must know how to identify every ingredient, down to their varietals, librarians must develop an appreciation of literature and know how to locate and evaluate appropriate resources for research. The tricks that they learn – be they with fire or Google – are as much an art as they are a science.

People who become chefs or librarians are not so different. Peel us like onions, and you will find a damaged core. Memoirs of brilliant chefs will often reveal painful childhoods due to extreme dyslexia, poverty, or dysfunctional family dynamics, their lives brought to order in the kitchen. While few written memoirs of librarians exist, many who entered the stacks as youngsters found refuge from pain there, and never left.

What I've never understood is the snobbery among librarians who work in different library environments. Many times I have encountered academic librarians who look down on public librarians, and academic and public librarians who look down on school media specialists. This type of snobbery does not exist among chefs; to build street credentials in the culinary world, one must work anywhere and everywhere to keep one's knives sharp. Even the great Marco Pierre White, master chef and mega-restaurant owner, mentor of Gordon Ramsay, Mario Batali, and Heston Blumenthal, will still take catering gigs for weddings and holiday parties, something that his disciples now refuse. At some point in their careers, every chef has done what the unsophisticated would consider a dirty cooking job: flipping burgers, manning the deep fat fryer, cleaning and fabricating animals that had been bleating, clucking, or crawling minutes ago. Without that experience, they never would have learned what food is all about, nor would they have learned how to run the stations of a kitchen.

Some librarians have worked in only one type of library throughout their entire career. Many have only worked *in one area of librarianship* throughout their entire career. How do these librarians truly learn what libraries are all about?

Prior to my current position, I had worked in a culinary school library for eight years. When I would share this fact at library conferences, my academic librarian colleagues would look at me quite strangely. "I didn't know that culinary schools *had* libraries," they'd confess. "Do the culinary students really read and write?" I would feel these librarians looking deep into my soul, contemplating whether or not I was truly a member of their tribe. Even worse were the foodie librarians, who would flock to me to schedule tours and reservations at our student-run restaurant, as well as the fawning library school students who begged for internship hours at my library.

"I would *love* to work with your collection!" they would squeal. "I *love* cookbooks!"

A few library school students repeatedly asked me if there would ever be a position open at my library. One went so far as to treat me to lunch any time she stopped over. Once she wore a revealing outfit. *Ma'am, I'm on duty,* I felt like telling her, *and no, there are no openings for women who wear revealing suits in my library.*

Still … what a rush from that experience! How did I achieve a position of power, where women would offer themselves to me for a few hours of library work?

Some people become librarians because they love books. Although I had been an active library user since I was two years old, I had never envisioned myself as a librarian. The first librarian I had ever met as a child was George the Adult Reference Librarian. My father and two older brothers often described George as "fruity" because of the way he talked and used his hands. Because of his mannerisms, I too assumed that George was gay. All day long, George would answer questions about books, and he would talk at great length about the books he had read. I was a little afraid to approach him, but I enjoyed listening to him even more than the storytime librarian, because George knew every book in the library. He would become very excited about some titles, waving his hands and rolling his eyes as he recalled their plots, and later, I would quietly look up those titles in the card catalog to read myself.

I never approached school librarians for anything as a high school student. I wanted to be an artist or an activist; I had no idea what librarians at my school did. Unlike good old gay George the Adult Reference Librarian, in my adolescent opinion, school librarians were only good for screaming at kids who could not be quiet or did not return their library books on time. I would watch some of my classmates working as library assistants, alphabetizing and shelving, adding new cards to the card catalog, putting up holiday decorations. Teachers did not take Honors/Advanced Placement students to the library for special library instruction; it was our responsibility to figure out how to do research ourselves. As I rarely saw other kids in the school library looking for books, I decided to bypass the school librarian altogether by jumping our clunky security gate, taking the books that I liked home, and never returning them. Due to the hours I spent there, and the fact that I had read a good deal of the collection, I truly believed that my high school library belonged to me.

The three librarians of my elementary school, middle school, and high school all identified as "Ms.," neither "Miss" due to their age nor "Mrs." to imply that they were married. They all had short hair, short fingernails, and didn't talk much. I wondered about them, too. All of my female English teachers were ex-nuns, perpetually single, or lesbians, so as a teenager it made sense to me that librarians who loved books even more than English teachers could be lesbians, too.

I have no idea how I knew who was gay or lesbian when I was a kid. I grew up during the 1970s and 1980s, when Elton John, Queen, and Boy George ruled Top 40 radio and MTV. I do not remember the gay kids being teased where I went to school, but I knew who the gay kids were. I felt myself staring at them sometimes, in the hope of connecting in some way. It was extremely difficult for me to make friends with anyone my age when I was growing up. While they talked about Benetton sweatshirts, I talked about André Breton. From 6th through 12th grade, I was taken out of class upon request of my teachers to speak to the school psychologist. *Honors student*, they would scribble in their pads, *active participant in many after school activities, lives for art and writing, no friends.* I think they were making sure that I was not a danger to myself or society, long before teen suicide or Columbine killers became headline news. The school psychologists did not understand me either. Instead of helping me learn how to make friends, they assumed that my problem was low self-esteem. They told me that I was smarter than anyone else and that all of these other kids would be scrabbling for clerical jobs while I went to college and became... *someone*.

I spent a lot of time in the library to escape from the people who hurt and confused me. I would cut gym class, curl up in the Oversize section, and read whatever caught my interest at the time. At 15 years old, I discovered Nancy Garden's *Annie on My Mind* in the young adult section of my public library. I will always be touched by this story because it is about two girls who meet in the Metropolitan Museum of Art in New York City and fall in love. That is the only romance novel that ever made sense to me, but it still took me a few years to figure out that I was a lesbian.

I went to college, and my world blossomed. I also got my first library job. As the main university library had a huge office just for hiring student employees, I equated that big office with many job opportunities. I had no idea what I was going to do once they hired me, but I figured if I was an expert library user, the library *had* to hire me. Sure enough, right after I filled out my application, I was directed to sit before a white-haired old lady with glasses and a bun (the oldest, most powerful librarian in the university, I thought at the time) who gave me a job. "There's a position open at the Chemistry Library," she informed me in a gravelly Brooklyn accent. "When you get there, talk to a guy named Mark to set up your hours."

I was a bit nervous at first. Chemistry Library? I ran through everything I remembered from my 11th grade Chemistry class, and I hoped that it would be enough to work at the Chemistry Library. But when I met Mark, my supervisor, I sensed that everything would be OK. Mark was as gay as Gay George the Adult Reference Librarian. He gave me a tour of the library, and explained my duties. From Mark, I learned how to work at the Circulation Desk and how to shelve bound journals. I learned how to take inventory, and how to show people how to use our online catalog. I learned all about reserve books and interlibrary loan. I also learned that Mark was not a librarian; he was a circulation supervisor, and his job was to supervise student employees who did all of the circulation work. "Whatever you do," he whispered to me one day, "do *not* make Janet come out of her office." Janet was the "real" librarian, the head of the Chemistry Library. She always dressed in plaid suits, smelled like lamb chops, and would shout at Mark if something didn't go right.

I loved my Chemistry Library job. I walked through snowdrifts with a broken toe to be on time. I made sure that every book and journal was neatly shelved, in call number order, because anything less would have embarrassed me. I met graduate students and faculty from all over the world, who would come to the circulation desk to check out materials or pick up their reserve books. I gave tours of our library to visiting scholars, and saw firsthand how important this library was to the chemistry professors and graduate students. Every day, the graduate students would pick a table, remove nine or ten bound journals from the shelf, take their notes, and leave them for me to clean up. I made sure those bound journals were shelved in the right place, because sure enough the students would return for them. Most of all, I enjoyed my Chemistry Library job because of the conversations I had with Mark, crazy Janet, and Anna, the Slavic language cataloging librarian who worked in our library because she was allergic to the dust in the university library cataloging room.

I never had a "coming out" process. "Coming out" implies that a person had previously been in the closet. I had nothing to hide. If I had not apologized at that point for my curly hair, my Jewish ancestry, and my family background, I would feel no shame about my sexual orientation. I told everyone about it. Mark, my gay circulation supervisor, was a font of knowledge. We talked about dating, homosexuality, spirituality, and being out to people. I wish I knew where Mark was today; not only was he responsible for teaching me about library work, but he was also responsible

for teaching me a lot about being gay, and I owe him a great deal for all that he has taught me. I slowly met other LGBT faculty, staff, and students on campus, including a lesbian classmate whose girlfriend was a public librarian. I began to connect the dots – gay and lesbian people work in libraries!

But I became an English teacher instead.

If I could live my life over again, I would run away from home during my senior year of high school and go to art school. When I told my art teachers that I was accepted to the Honors Program at a state university and planned to become an English teacher, they looked at me as if I'd just said I was checking into an institution for a lobotomy. They told me I could get a partial or full scholarship to any art college I wanted to attend, and I was giving up a big opportunity. My parents told me that I was going to college to become an English teacher, and that I could do my art and writing as a hobby. The same girl who told her parents point blank that if they didn't like her as a lesbian they didn't have to see her again, bought that "art as hobby" story because I knew no better. No one in my family had finished college except for my cousin, who became a college professor, and I figured I should do what she did – especially since she was never happy with men. I still did not picture myself working as a librarian, even though I saw gay and lesbian folks working in all different capacities in libraries.

During the 1990s, openly gay and lesbian people still had a very hard time working in public schools. After college I joined a lesbian support group; quite a few women in the group worked as public school teachers. All were afraid to reveal their orientation to anyone, for fear of losing their jobs. I heard their stories, but did not take heed. I thought, duh, everyone knows that female gym teachers are lesbians and it's a non-issue. I was going to be an English teacher, and I knew that some of my English teachers had been lesbians. I was also pretty confident in my teaching abilities. I ran my own tutoring business and worked as a substitute teacher for all subjects, as well as a substitute middle school librarian. Naively, I thought that good teachers would not have to worry about getting fired as long as they did not do anything illegal. *I was not listening.* To make a long story short, I was a great English teacher, but was forced to resign because of my sexual orientation. I was basically told that I was not fit to be an English teacher because I was not like the other public school teachers.

If I had been older and wiser, I could have hired a lawyer and fought for my job, especially since Connecticut, the state in which I was living at the time, had a non-discrimination policy. But I was too intimidated by the process, and did not think that I could afford a lawyer. I was young and scared, living all by myself in a small town full of people who felt completely comfortable telling you how they thought God should kill off the gay people while you sat together at the mechanic's waiting for an oil change. I fell into a deep depression and did not leave my dingy apartment for three months. I remember standing in front of the living room mirror and cutting the hair off the back of my head with kitchen scissors because I no longer had my English teaching job and I wanted to die.

What kept me afloat was my lesbian support group and an Internet connection. I was chatting with a lot of people online, including the woman who is now my partner. I could chat with up to nine people online at a time while playing a video game or typing a story. My typing and computer skills helped keep me from going into debt. My shrinking savings account motivated me to sign up with temp agencies for clerical jobs. These were the type of jobs that the school psychologist told me the "other kids" would have. I kicked that voice out of my head. I worked for Parking Enforcement, a Frito Lay packing plant, a mortgage department in a bank, and finally the bingo hall of a tribal casino. My coworkers at the casino had told me yes, if I was working in the Bingo Paper Sales booth, I had indeed hit rock bottom. There would be no fancy jobs for me, no fancy goals, for a lonely lesbian in a depressed New England town. Every day I went to work, I heard one or more of my coworkers spit the words "dyke" or "faggot" behind the backs of customers or coworkers. One woman insisted on telling me, at least once during every shift, that she "liked dick," because she knew that I was a lesbian, and we worked in close quarters together. Apparently, the word "dick" was a protective talisman that would keep lesbians away.

One day I realized that I had options. I had a girlfriend in California who was begging me to move in with her. I had varied and extensive work experience, from culinary to educational to clerical. One day I got fed up with the coworker who kept shoving dick in my face, packed up my stuff, called my girlfriend, and we enjoyed a Ryder truck road trip across the country to the queer Mecca of Los Angeles.

I had a lot of rough edges as a 20-something lesbian. I was loud, aggressive, and had a New York accent. This made my job search in California a bit difficult. When I interviewed for an assistant editor position at a publishing company, I almost got the job, but was turned down because one of the people on the hiring committee thought I had an anger management problem, and would not be a good fit in their calm, quiet office. I held back my choice words for this company and sent them a brief, polite thank you letter.

Out of the Frying Pan: Coming Out As a Culinary School Librarian

One week before my unemployment checks ran out, I discovered a tiny advertisement in our local newspaper for a library assistant position. As there was a small public library not far away, I thought it was for a job there. It was only $8.00 an hour, for 20 hours a week, but I did not care. Warm memories of my college job at the Chemistry Library bubbled up inside of me. I called the number and asked if the position was still available. A friendly voice responded that yes, the position was indeed available, and that my duties would be data entry, shelving, and assisting students with homework and research. Was that something I thought I could do? Absolutely, I responded.

"By the way," the friendly office manager said, "we're a culinary school. Is that still OK with you?"

Books, food, chefs. What *wouldn't* be OK with this position? I told the office manager that I would be very happy to work at a culinary school, and I was invited to come for an interview the same day. I met the librarian and my two fellow library assistants, and was given a tour of the school. At that time, the library was a small room with only a few shelves of books, a magazine rack, a worktable, and six computers. None of the books were catalogued, as the librarian and her assistants had just put the shelving together. The books were arranged by color-coded label, by subject. While the morning class cooked and baked, the afternoon students came in and out of the library to check email, to find recipes, to do homework. I saw right away that there was a lot of work to be done in that small room. I told the librarian that I was interested in the position, and that I would also like 40 hours per week. I owe a lot to that librarian for looking into giving me more hours, realizing that I needed and deserved them.

I quickly filled my time. Not only did I complete the entire database for the collection (we did not have an OPAC yet), I selected books for the collection, became acquainted with the culinary curriculum, and learned that the students needed a lot of help with math and computers. I asked if there was a tutoring program for the students, and as there was none, I established one. I trained the other library assistants to tutor the culinary students in any subject covered at the school, and I worked with the math – and computer-phobic. I designed all of the instructional materials and flyers to advertise our tutoring program and computer assistance. I became a favorite with the chef instructors and the administration, and the students would bring me breakfast and treats every week because of the service and quiet, contemplative library environment that I provided for them.

No one at the culinary school cared that I was a lesbian. In fact, one of the head chefs was a lesbian, and at least two other chefs were gay. All three of them were popular instructors, and they welcomed me into the fold. The librarian would regularly ask how my partner was doing, and would invite us both to holiday parties. My fellow library assistants were more fascinated by my knowledge and talents than my sexual orientation. I built my reputation like a stone fortress, and no one would dare knock it down. I loved the library that I helped build, I was grateful for my coworkers, and I cared deeply about the culinary students who worked so hard to achieve their dreams. I decorated the library with posters that I drew and colored myself, and when word got out about me being an artist, I was asked to do comics for the school newsletter, then asked to take over as faculty advisor of that newsletter. Within one year, I became a celebrity at work.

After my first year, the librarian decided that she wanted to retire. I ran the library for a short time until the administration decided to hire a library director with a Master of Library and Information Science for accreditation purposes. For the first time, I had the opportunity to choose my boss. I got to read the resumes of various librarians, and to interview them. One candidate with a PhD reviewed the shelves with her back to me during most of her interview. Another candidate admitted to me that she was afraid of the kitchen. Not only was I choosing a librarian that I thought I could work with, I was also choosing someone who would understand the chef instructors and culinary students. After three lemons, the perfect candidate showed up. She had over 30 years of library experience in many different types of libraries. She was also an East Coast transplant from New Jersey who had her own rough edges. We looked each other in the eyes, and I told administration that she was the best candidate. We worked together for eight years, building and modernizing the library as the culinary school grew.

One year after I started working at the culinary school, with my new boss as a mentor, I went to library school. My first class, *Introduction to Libraries,* brought two important things to light for me. First, there are many different types of librarians, and many types of libraries. I wanted to taste them all. Second, all different types of people use libraries, and it is the librarian's job to serve their information needs. We learned about the information needs of the disabled, of senior citizens, of immigrants. Although we were a library school program in California, not a single article in the Special Populations unit addressed the information needs of lesbian, gay, bisexual, or transgender people. Finally, after reviewing an article about the information needs of blind Asian American senior citizens, I stood up. "Hey," I shouted, "what about the gay people? Why is there not a single article in our packet about what libraries have to do for gay people?"

In other states, perhaps I would have been told to sit down, or to leave the room. In California, our *Introduction to Libraries* professor actually apologized to the class, and humbly admitted that she had not thought about gay people as library users, although she knew many gay librarians. She asked me to look into it. Not only did I find many articles, but I took my library school's class on *LGBTIQ Library Resources and Services* (taught by Ellen Greenblatt herself) and wrote a lot of papers – including a Master's thesis – in library school on LGBTIQ resources, users, and librarianship.

I was fortunate in that everything I learned in library school I was able to use at work. I learned how to catalog everything in the collection, and wrote a cataloging manual for it. I trained the student employees on how to provide good reference and customer service. I analyzed our collection and recorded its history. I developed a bibliographic instruction program for our students. We addressed copyright issues, accreditation issues, ADA issues. I worked in a small library, and had the privileged opportunity to learn how to do all of these things.

The library director recognized something in me. She saw that, at the rate I was going, I would soon outgrow my current position. We would participate in events for academic and special libraries together, and talk about what we learned. Some things that interested me, I realized, I would not have an opportunity to explore at the culinary school. Our programs were too specialized, and our users had very specific, but simple needs. Soon I would finish library school, and my boss said that she was not kicking me out the door, but she encouraged me to visit as many libraries as possible and apply for open positions at libraries that interested me.

At first I did not like hearing this. The culinary school library had become my comfort zone; it was the best job I'd ever had, a job that I had created in an institution that I had built, with collegial coworkers who did not care that I was a lesbian. At the same time, I had done practicum hours at an academic library and an archive, and decided to apply for academic librarian positions.

I felt quite fortunate because I was looking for a position while I already had a job. I did not understand why I received so many rejection letters, but I did not take them to heart. I knew that many times libraries hired from within, or, due to budget cuts, could not fill a position they had advertised. I also knew that my CV, while full of valid library work experience, threw many Human Resources Departments for a loop. I identified myself as a culinary school librarian, and people interpreted this in different ways. Few people understood that our library was an academic collection, as well as a special collection. I kept fine-tuning this point in my CV – that I had many years of academic library experience under my belt with progressive levels of responsibility. I stressed that I was considered faculty at my institution, as I taught courses and engaged in research. In fact, I had a letter from our Vice President of Education stating this fact, so that I could get a library card from UCLA to do more in-depth research. I indicated the title of my Master's thesis on my CV, however, as well as the relevant LGBT-related work experience and publishing record that I had accumulated. As I did not send out applications to any institution without an LGBT Resource Center or LGBT Faculty/Staff organization, I did not see my LGBT affiliations as an issue on my CV. I was simply an odd duck, coming from a non-traditional library.

One day, I learned of a position announcement for a Collection Management Librarian at Saint Cloud State University in Minnesota. I read the job description, and could match it point-by-point with my own experience. I also did some research on the city, and discovered that it had hosted a GLBTA Film Festival for the past seven years. My partner and I had a long talk about the position; I told her that the job opportunities for academic librarians in California were drying up due to the state budget cuts, and that this position – though far away – would be an excellent opportunity in a potentially gay-friendly area. If I got the position, great. If not, I would still have a job.

I came a long way. Not so long ago, I was getting dick shoved in my face at work in a bingo hall. Thanks to librarians and chefs who believed in me and gave me the opportunity to rise to a position of power, I regained my confidence. I spent three days in St. Cloud to get a feel for the place; I not only got to know my potential coworkers, but also the local Jewish community and GLBTA community. Every day, the city and the people grew on me. On my last day, when asked if I had any questions or concerns, I briefly recounted my forced resignation as a high school English teacher in a small town, and told everyone straight up that if they had a problem with me as a lesbian, then I could not accept the position. I was hired, not as a token, but as a potential asset to the library, the university, and the community. They were not wrong.

Part Two:
Sex and the Institution

Gay Librarians on the Tenure Track: Following the Yellow Brick Road?

Paul Blobaum

Outside of the pressing issues of salary, job responsibilities, and location, the issue of being gay and out is a significant factor in making career decisions. When contemplating career options, librarians may find themselves considering positions in academic libraries.

I came to tenure-track librarianship by accident. As in Dorothy's journey in Oz, my career in libraries unfolded following tornado-like personal and career crises. While studying in a M.Div. Program, I woke up one day and found my world had changed from black and white to Technicolor. Continuing to study for a church ministry became impossible after I failed all of my courses my last semester of divinity school. And unlike Dorothy, I did not have a Good Witch to show me the yellow brick road back to Kansas.

It is said that "opportunity comes disguised as hard work." Following seminary, there was plenty of hard work, both to pay the bills, and to put my life back together. I worked first for a temp agency making cattle prods and roller blades, and later did a stint at an IRS Tax Form Distribution Center as an order clerk. I also worked in a greenhouse and worked at three different church camps as a staff person. On the urging of a friend, I got on a civil service hiring list at the University of Illinois at Urbana-Champaign Library, and landed a job as a Circulation Clerk in a departmental library. Later, thanks to the prodding of my boss, I applied to library school and was hired as a graduate assistant in the same place. Upon completing my MSLS, I took the first job offer I was given at a teaching hospital library in the Chicago region. All this while I was in the closet to my coworkers at work. I felt it was a private matter that wasn't necessarily anyone else's business in the workplace.

Fast-forward 10 years. My 2nd professional medical librarian position, a one FTE library in a community hospital, was being reduced from full-time to part-time. I was growing weary of fighting to keep my position as a full-time FTE, and also being a pawn in the middle of a battle between the physicians and hospital over how the library was to be funded. At the same time, the health science librarian from the state university library near my home in the Chicago suburbs, a professional friend of mine, told me she was leaving her job as Head of Circulation, and asked if I was interested. I had applied for that position two years previously, but she had been the one hired instead.

The position was on the tenure-track, a probationary employment arrangement with the possibility of permanence. Part of the reason I was still interested in the job after several years was that I perceived a public university library as being a workplace where I might have some job security. I had always worried about what the effect of being perceived as gay might have on my career, and in the back of my mind wondered if that was a factor in having my position reduced to half-time. After all, I didn't play golf with the others in the leadership at work, and I didn't otherwise pal around with coworkers. I had not been openly "out" at work due to not only the privacy issue, but also fear. I had come out to only a few people in a professional context, and these were contacts I had made with the LGBTQ Special Interest Group of the Medical Library Association. So, I interviewed for the university library position and accepted the offer to be Head of Access Services.

There are typically six years on the tenure track, usually beginning with an appointment at the rank of Assistant Professor. At my university, library faculty must have a 2nd master's degree, and so my seminary degree was an asset. On the tenure track, job performance is evaluated by peers as well as superiors. A portfolio is assembled annually and organized according to primary duties, research, service, and a comprehensive self-evaluation is prepared and submitted to the unit's faculty personnel committee. In the final three years, the portfolio goes before the University Faculty Personnel Committee, who makes recommendations to the Provost and President. On the 6th year, the President makes a decision to grant tenure, and promotion is granted at the same time to Associate Professor rank.

One of my early challenges while on tenure track was making an unwanted transition from Head of Circulation to the Reference Department less than a year after my hire. Being reassigned was devastating to my self-esteem and professional career. I became convinced that I was being discriminated against or treated unfairly due to the perception of my sexual orientation, but there was no way to prove it. This decision was made by a new interim director just a few weeks after the director who hired me left. Since I couldn't just walk away from a new job and needed to pay the mortgage, I decided to make the best of the situation. Even if Illinois would have had an LGBTQ non-discrimination employment law in 2001 (it was not to be enacted until 2006), I was too timid to push the matter, and didn't really know my rights under the union contract. Thus, although it was neither my plan, nor the reason I was hired, over the subsequent years, I eventually became a medical librarian again. As library faculty retired, I was assigned to serve as a liaison to the Health Professions programs.

Clearly, the tenure track, which offers the promise of a lifetime position on the faculty of a college or university, as well as the protections of academic freedom, is not for the faint of heart. Early on at the university, I was counseled to not make enemies of anyone on my tenure committee, to keep my head low, and to be careful of whom I might upset. Despite a commitment to the values of academic freedom and freedom of thought, there is plenty of political intrigue and hijinx in higher education. Grudges against faculty colleagues and administrators are nurtured until the opportunity to pounce presents itself; petty matters get blown out of proportion and wind up in personnel files. Retaliation is real and sometimes difficult to prove.

I eventually decided that my success in earning tenure would depend on my excellent accomplishments, not because of whether or not I was gay. Still, I decided to choose my research interests and service activities carefully: they would be related to my academic credentials (music major bachelor's, master's in theology) or to my librarian responsibilities. If the closet door were to open at work, it would do so ever-so-slowly and cautiously.

When I started working at the university, there was a newly minted LGBTQ faculty/staff/student group on campus that met informally at lunch time, and I made acquaintance of several participants. When the faculty advisor retired toward the end of my first year, he asked if I would take over. I begged off, mostly because I was worried how it would affect my tenure prospects. I agonized over the decision, but in the end, I felt I did not have the time or support to be an advisor to the group. This LGBTQ group fell apart after the outgoing advisor's retirement.

Interesting opportunities came along that were related both to my interest in LGBTQ issues and my professional responsibilities, which involved grant writing and scholarly presentations. In concordance with my university's Health Professions programs' research focus on health disparities, I wrote two grants. The first, a $50,000 NLM HIV/AIDS information outreach grant, was unsuccessful. The second was a $3,000 ICCMP grant (a state academic library cooperative collection management program) entitled, "Research and Support of Health Care Information Needs of LGBT Persons and Caregivers," and which was successful. I also wrote another successful ICCMP grant proposal for resources for health disparities research. Based on my collection development work with the LGBTQ grant, I gave a presentation to a national meeting of the Medical Library Association, and another related proposal was accepted for presentation at an international conference. This paper, "Collection Development Strategies for Health Care of Lesbian, Gay, Bisexual, and Transgendered People," was presented in 2006 at the 1st International GLBT ALMS (Archives, Libraries, Museums, Special Collections and Collectors) Conference, at the University of Minnesota, Minneapolis. These were wonderful experiences that I enjoyed, and which were intellectually interesting.

The energy I spent worrying over how being gay would affect my job helped me focus on doing scholarly projects that were closely related to my professional assignment and above criticism for being just "gay research." I am now the de-facto contact person for LGBTQ issues in the library and find myself pretty much out of the closet. This essay is a good example: my dean forwarded me the request for proposals for *Out Behind the Desk* from one of her listservs, with this note, "I don't want to assume anything but would this be something you would be interested in writing for?" Far from being offended, I appreciate her thoughtfulness about forwarding on an announcement of a writing opportunity.

Being out as a faculty member has been good for me, although I am sure not everyone knows. I have gone on to serve as President of my university's Faculty Senate, and received two faculty excellence awards.

Perhaps it comes with the wisdom of maturity, but the older I get, the less I care what other people think about me or what I do, although others' prejudices and bigotry can still be sources of aggravation. I am shocked that bigotry and homophobia still exist on university campuses. I have heard jokes directed at LGBTQ persons. During a Faculty Senate meeting, a senator mentioned that due to a forthcoming trip to San Francisco to do research, he would miss the next meeting. One of my colleagues (who is mostly respected and admired, but is known for sometimes making outrageous provocative comments) leaned over to me and whispered, "So he can do his research in the baths!" I informed him that Senator So-and-

So had done graduate research on the smoking industry in San Francisco, and for his information, the tobacco industry legal settlement (making the industry pay for health costs due to smoking) resulted in a huge archive of the industry's primary source documents being archived at the library at the University of California, San Francisco, and, furthermore, libraries were still places where legitimate research was conducted (although I've never seen the bigot I was talking to darken the door of the library!). I doubt I changed my colleague's proclivity for outrageous comments, but my silence would have implied agreement.

    I have had tenure for almost three years, and I certainly think that the struggle and work involved in getting it was worth it. I feel more freedom to say "no" to those things that I am not interested in doing, and I feel free to pursue those that I am passionate about, without fear of losing my job. Retaliation, bigotry, and sexism do exist in academia, despite the high-minded ideals and legal protections. Still, academic librarianship is not a bad place to be. It provides opportunities for professional growth, personal development, and a wider impact on matters that are important to LGBT people than we would find in any other type of librarianship.

Out All Over:
Giving Voice to LGBTs on Campus

Donna Braquet and Roger Weaver

It all started with the Commission. On December 5, 2005, two tenure track faculty members and an administrator met with the Chancellor of the University of Tennessee to discuss strategies for improving the campus climate for LGBT faculty, staff, and students. Coincidentally, all three, one of the authors included, were "out" Library and Information Science professionals: a librarian at the campus' main library, a professor in the library school, and a librarian turned director of the university's distance education programs. Nearly one year later, on November 7, 2006, the Chancellor established the Commission for Lesbian, Gay, Bisexual, and Transgender People. The formation of this commission followed in the footsteps of the Chancellor's Commission for Women and Commission for Blacks. Mehra and Braquet further detail the formation of the Commission (557).[1]

The Commission signaled the first official acknowledgment by the university administration of LGBT concerns on campus. Its mission is to advise on planning, implementation, and evaluation of university programs, policies, and services designed to improve the status of lesbian, gay, bisexual, and transgender people on the Knoxville Campus. In its role as an advocacy group, the Commission is committed to the protection and advancement of LGBT students, faculty, and staff at the University of Tennessee, Knoxville. At its inception the Commission consisted of five committees: the Executive Committee, comprised of the leadership and committee chairs; the Equity Committee; the Research Committee; the Membership Committee; and the Communications Committee.

---

1. http://muse.jhu.edu/journals/library_trends/v056/

The authors were appointed co-chairs of the Communications Committee in January 2007. This committee's mission is to increase the visibility of the Commission and LGBT issues on campus through media, special events, and programming, and to provide support for the Commission's internal communication as needed. We used our skills and expertise as librarians to bring LGBT issues out of the shadows on campus; until then, the campus offered very little in the way of LGBT resources for students, faculty, or staff. We developed the commission's public website, a virtual resource center, and a Blackboard site to archive the Commission's documents. Perhaps most important to fulfilling the mission of increasing visibility on campus was the committee's programming efforts.

Under our leadership, the committee offered the campus meaningful events centered on current issues, such as queer politics, policy, and identity. Realizing that the success of our events depended greatly on cooperation from departments, units, and individuals not serving on the Commission, we involved members of the campus community whenever possible. Faculty were invited to present their LGBT-related research as part of the Faculty Brown Bag Series. Using the University Libraries' auditorium and media collection, the committee held an LGBT Documentary Series each semester. Two forums were sponsored: "OUT on Campus: What is it like to be gay at UTK?" and a second in January 2009 called "LGBT Political Issues: A New President, Prop 8, and More!" The Communications Committee planned one public lecture each year to be showcased during LGBT History Month. In October 2007, community activist, writer, and lesbian, Suzanne Pharr spoke about the intersections of homophobia, racism, and sexism. In 2008, writers Pat Gozemba and Karen Kahn spoke about their book, *Courting Equality: A Documentary History of America's First Same-Sex Marriages,* and in 2009, author Dorothy Allison spoke on being out in the South ("Past Events by Type.").[2]

In this two-year period, the University of Tennessee saw the most LGBT events ever held on campus. At times, we felt hesitant to be so vocal about LGBT issues on campus, yet we were encouraged by the University's recent commitment to diversity through its Intercultural/International Quality Enhancement Plan, which was later branded *Ready for the World*. The plan called for UT's students to possess "a worldview that recognizes, understands, and celebrates the complexity of cultures and peoples" and "the capacity to think critically about international and intercultural issues [...] and gain the ability to recognize their own cultural preconceptions and stereotypes" (Crabtree).[3] The programming that we developed

---

2. http://lgbt.utk.edu/pastevents.html
3. http://www.utk.edu/readyfortheworld/about.php

through the work of the Communications Committee addressed these two important goals of the *Ready for the World* initiative, and we felt secure in having this initiative to reference, should our LGBT-focused endeavors be questioned.

Anyone who is charged with producing events knows that, even when given equal effort, some are resounding successes, while others want for attendance. The impact of programming can be elusive and fleeting. The authors brainstormed about a project that could have lasting impact on campus. Our answer is *Voices of Diversity*, an online archive of stories by LGBT faculty, staff, students, and alumni.

A Brief History of Voices of Diversity

The concept of *Voices of Diversity* originated in early 2007. It has its origin in a news story on NPR's *All Things Considered*, which focused on NPR's StoryCorps project. StoryCorps' mission is to honor and celebrate each other's lives through sharing and listening ("StoryCorps").[4] StoryCorps travels the country collecting the stories of everyday people. Upon hearing this newscast and reflecting back upon conversations within the Commission concerning the need for visibility on campus for LGBT people, Roger Weaver began to consider how personal stories of LGBT people on campus might contribute to LGBT visibility and, thus, foster overall diversity efforts.

There is power in the personal story. Storytelling uses our individual experiences as a tool to link us together. The listener is able to relate with the storyteller through similar shared experiences, creating empathy and leading to better understanding. Stories are the ultimate teaching tool because they teach by bonding the listener's experiences to those of the storyteller. How to best harness the power of the personal story became the topic of many discussions between the authors. During our discussions we established five overriding goals for *Voices of Diversity*.

First, *Voices of Diversity* serves as a way for students, faculty, staff, alumni, and allies to share their experiences with others. **Second,** *Voices of Diversity* helps other LGBT individuals on campus realize that they are not alone. **Third,** the project provides much needed visibility to LGBT issues and raises awareness among non-LGBT students, faculty, staff, and alumni. **Fourth,** *Voices* plays a role in developing a supportive learning environment for LGBT students by giving out faculty, students, and administrators an opportunity to serve as positive role models. **Finally,** the

---

4. http://storycorps.org/

Voices of Diversity

An Online LGBT Story Archive at the University of Tennessee Knoxville Campus

About Voices of Diversity

In a college or university environment, diversity should be regarded and celebrated in all its forms. Intellectual and social growth is best fostered in a campus community comprised of individuals with varying backgrounds, perspectives, interests, talents, and values. The personal story serves as a powerful tool in aiding the creation of a diverse campus environment by spreading ideas, highlighting differing viewpoints and emphasizing unique personal experiences.

Voices of Diversity is a collection of stories created by students, faculty, staff, alumni and allies at the University of Tennessee as they relate to the lesbian, gay, bisexual and transgender (LGBT) experience on the Knoxville campus. The stories range from the simple narrative to multi-media productions, all accessible through the Internet.

This project is sponsored by the University of Tennessee Commission for LGBT People and has been approved by the University's Institutional Review Board.

Who Can Participate

All lesbian, gay, bisexual, transgendered or ally students, faculty, staff and alumni may participate. Authors have the right to withhold or remove all personally identifying information from their stories before they are made accessible to the public. Visit our web site for more information: lgbt.utk.edu/vod.

The Goals and Objectives of Voices of Diversity

1. Voices of Diversity serves as a way for students, faculty, staff and alumni to share their experiences with others, be they stories of identity and community or stories of acceptance and discrimination.

2. Voices of Diversity helps other LGBT individuals on campus realize that they are not alone.

3. Voices of Diversity brings much needed visibility to LGBT issues and raises awareness among non-LGBT students, faculty, staff, and alumni through the simple, yet profound, vehicle of the personal story.

4. Voices of Diversity plays a role in developing a supportive learning environment for LGBT students by giving 'out' faculty, students, and staff an opportunity to serve as positive role models.

5. Voices of Diversity serves as a living historical archive of LGBT experiences on the Knoxville campus. The stories will serve as an invaluable resource for future students and researchers.

**Add Your Voice
Tell Your Story
at
lgbt.utk.edu/vod**

About the Commission

The UT Commission for LGBT People is a body appointed by the Chancellor to advise on planning, implementation, and evaluation of University programs, policies, and services designed to improve the status of lesbian, gay, bisexual, and transgender people on the Knoxville Campus. The Commission, in its role as an advocacy group, is committed to the protection and advancement of LGBT students, faculty and staff at the University of Tennessee, Knoxville.

Commission members are appointed by the Chancellor. The Commission for LGBT People at UT Knoxville is comprised of LGBT faculty, staff and students, as well as LGBT allies. Those interested in serving on the Commission or non-members interested in service opportunities may contact the Commission at lgbtcom@utk.edu.

Additional information about the Commission, including LGBT campus resources and events, is available on the Commission's web page at lgbt.utk.edu.

For More Information, Contact:

Donna Braquet
Research Librarian
dbraquet@utk.edu
(865) 974-0016

Or

Roger Weaver
Library Trainer
jweaver2@utk.edu
(865) 946-2117

Flyer-General-120508

archive serves as a living historical collection of LGBT experiences on the Knoxville campus.

With the establishment of these goals, we announced the creation of the *Voices of Diversity* project at the September 2007 meeting of the Commission. What followed was a series of meetings to plan how best to market the project in order to generate a high level of participation. We also began discussions on how best to capture and present the stories.

The marketing and outreach discussions were relatively easy and straightforward. Multiple avenues already existed on campus for outreach. The membership of the Commission consisted of various individuals from multiple departments and organizations across campus. From within the Commission we had direct access to students via representatives from housing, health services, and Lambda Student Union, the campus' LGBT student organization. We also had direct access to faculty and staff from many departments and schools on campus, including Social Work, History, and Information Science. We were familiar with, and had contacts for, various campus publications, such as the campus newspaper and various newsletters and calendars, both print and electronic. Thus, our efforts consisted primarily of utilizing existing contacts and relationships to build a communications network. Additionally, we also prepared various informational materials, such as flyers, brochures, and a website. These were distributed through the network and placed on bulletin boards, discussion lists, in residence halls, and at Commission events.

Discussions on capturing and presenting the stories led to the realization that it might be necessary to seek Institutional Review Board (IRB) approval. IRB is necessary in situations involving human subjects in research. Its purpose is to protect the rights and welfare of research subjects. We could already envision how the interviews, the associated data, and the process of creating *Voices of Diversity* might be of interest to others and, thus, could lead to further research endeavors. We therefore felt it necessary to go through the IRB process. Some members of the Commission, however, felt that it was more important to get the project up and running quickly and did not see the need for IRB approval.

Ultimately, we did elect to go through the IRB process. As a result, the project was delayed for several months while we prepared the required IRB Form B and all of the accompanying documents. Because we would be interviewing individuals of a potentially "at risk" population and making their stories public, we received several recommendations from the reviewers regarding ways to ensure protection of the participants. One of these suggestions was to prepare a list of campus and local LGBT resources to give to participants during the initial meeting. A second suggestion was to create a Deed of Gift form, whereby the participant gives permission for the story to be posted in final form. Lastly, the informed consent form explicitly states that a story can be removed at the request of the participant, though removal by search engines and Internet archiving services can not be guaranteed. The revised documents were submitted in February 2008, and we received IRB approval on April 10, 2008.

The resulting procedure to submit a story to *Voices of Diversity* consists of two meetings with the participant. The first meeting includes:

- An overview of *Voices of Diversity*
- An explanation of the Informed Consent Form
- A discussion of requirements
  - Must be 18 years of age or older
  - Read and sign an informed consent statement
  - Complete a submission form
  - Stories cannot threaten violence, contain copyrighted content, contain identifying information of others without their permission, or be sexually explicit
- Clarification of any questions or concerns
- A discussion of the options available for submitting a story
  - Stories can be written or typed text, audio, video, photographic essays, or combinations thereof
  - Submit a prepared story at the first meeting
  - Submit a prepared story at a later date
  - Be interviewed at the first meeting
  - Be interviewed at a later date

After a participant submits a story we review it and, if necessary, convert it to an appropriate format for archiving and for presentation. A subsequent meeting with the participant includes:

- A review of the story
- Agreement from the participant to accept the story. Should someone not accept the story, additional changes can be made until the storyteller is satisfied
- Signature of the Deed of Gift transferring the story to the archive

The story is then placed in the archive with the associated metadata to enable searching and retrieval.

Our first interview occurred April 25, 2008, and we continue to collect stories to the present day. To date, the stories in *Voices of Diversity*

Out All Over: Giving Voice to LGBTs on Campus 75

What is Campus Like? • **Have You Ever Been Afraid on Campus?**

LESBIAN, GAY, BISEXUAL, TRANSGENDER PEOPLE

Share Your Story

Are you a gay, lesbian, bisexual or transgender student, faculty, staff, alumni or ally on the University of Tennessee Knoxville Campus?

Do you have a story to tell about your experiences on our campus?

You are Invited to Participate in Voices of Diversity

Voices of Diversity is an online multimedia archive of stories submitted by GLBT students, faculty, staff, alumni and allies on the Knoxville Campus of the University of Tennessee. We are collecting stories that are handwritten or typed text, video, audio, photographic essays, or a combination thereof. You may submit a story, or request an interview. Anonymous participation is welcomed.

For Information Contact

Donna Braquet
Reference Librarian
University of Tennessee
John C. Hodges Library
dbraquet@utk.edu

Roger Weaver
Library Trainer
University of Tennessee
John C. Hodges Library
jweaver2@utk.edu

For More Information

lgbt.utk.edu/vod

Sponsored by the University of Tennessee Commission for LGBT People

This project has been approved by the University's Institutional Review Board for research including human subjects. To find out more, visit our website at http://lgbt.utk.edu/vod

Share Your Coming Out Story • How Do You Feel About Being GLBT? On Campus?

What has Your Campus Experience Been Like?

Do You Share Your Life Story With Others? • **Are Things Changing?**

consist of audio interviews and several typewritten poems. The consent form, list of resources, list of potential interview questions, submission form, and the Deed of Gift are available on the *Voices* website ("Voices of Diversity").[5]

The Opportunities Along the Way

As librarians, it is second nature to collect and preserve. As a science librarian, Donna Braquet collects and preserves books and journals. As an institutional repository librarian, Roger collects and preserves the university's intellectual output. As out librarians, we strive to collect and preserve the experiences of LGBT students, faculty, staff, and alumni. In doing so, we document the history of LGBT progress at our university.

While working on the development phase of *Voices of Diversity,* we were able to attend the GLBT Archives, Libraries, Museums, and Special Collections (ALMS) Conference in New York, with support from the University Libraries, the University *Ready for the World* fund, and the Commission for LGBT People. This was our first opportunity to share our project with the profession. To our surprise and delight, this served as an excellent opportunity to discover and network with librarians who were also involved in similar projects, including Heather Mitchell at The Ohio State University, Santi Thompson at the University of South Carolina Libraries, and Tami Albin at the University of Kansas Libraries.

The Challenges Along the Way

How do we know if we are successful? How we overcome challenges is one way to measure success. *Voices of Diversity* presented a unique set of challenges to overcome, and as it evolves, it continues to challenge us in unexpected ways. Early on, we realized that the politically and culturally conservative environment on our campus would be a challenge to the project, one being a limitation on our sources of funding and resources. The campus administration, although verbally supportive, provided no financial support beyond the minimal operating funds of the Commission to get the project started. Enthusiasm was tempered as few campus entities were willing to fully support or help fund a project focusing on LGBT issues. As a result, we are forced to be creative and use available resources whenever possible. Working at the University Libraries proved to be helpful in having access to technical expertise and audio/visual equipment and

---

5. http://lgbt.utk.edu/vod/

editing software. Our one large expense was a high quality digital audio recorder and microphone, which were purchased by the Commission.

Finding secure and permanent server space was perhaps the most challenging problem we faced. We approached the Library Dean with our project proposal and a request for the University Libraries to host the project, but our request was denied, due to the Libraries' own priorities and the uncertainty of its financial and computing resources. The campus' Office of Information Technology was willing to provide space for an annual fee, but we have no ongoing funding for the project. We started the *Voices of Diversity* using the limited free space allotted to the Commission's website, realizing that project files would rapidly exceed the limit. In less than a year we did, in fact, outgrow the fixed space.

Luckily, the University Libraries had begun a pilot project for an institutional repository utilizing server space hosted by the repository provider. We offered *Voices'* digital content to the Scholarly Communications Librarian, who was in charge of the institutional repository, to use as a test case. As of this writing, *Voices of Diversity's* content has been migrated to the repository and we now have unlimited space to acquire additional stories. This serendipitous solution was greatly welcomed; however, it may not be a permanent solution. There is no guarantee of server space beyond the two year contract the library has with the repository vendor. Additionally, as the library develops its plans for the repository, there is no guarantee that the space will remain free, and for the foreseeable future the struggle to acquire steady funding and resources will continue.

Another challenge associated with the conservative environment at UT is the unwillingness of people to associate with our project. In an environment where many are still uncomfortable with being out for fear of losing their jobs, being denied tenure, or endangering their personal safety, it is no surprise that some are not willing to tell their story. We attempted to compensate for this by allowing for anonymous submission of stories; we wish that we could say that this obstacle has been overcome, but it simply has not. Beyond a few members of the Commission, there has been little participation. And even among those willing to be on the Commission for LGBT People, there are many members who have yet to participate. The unwillingness or inability of those in our LGBT community to associate with the project remains an ongoing challenge. So, if we were to summarize our challenges in one word, it would be – sustainability.

We have not given up, however, and following several brainstorming meetings, we now have quite a few concrete ideas to remedy the low participation rate. Emphasis on continued development and strengthening of the communications network, as well as persistent marketing and outreach are key. The utmost importance must be placed on the creation of a trusting relationship with each potential participant. We have decided to ask each storyteller who has contributed to *Voices* to encourage their colleagues and friends to participate. Additionally, we will ask past participants to speak to groups of potential participants detailing what the process of their storytelling meant to them. As more stories are added to the archive, with little-to-no adverse effects on those submitting them, the community will become more willing to participate. Having participants who have been through the process provide assurance to potential storytellers may lessen wariness of the detailed and somewhat daunting procedures.

That being said, the authors are aware of the complex and time intensive procedures that the *Voices* project requires of its participants. In an effort to streamline the process and make it easier and more accessible, we plan to hold LGBT Story Days. These would be events in themselves, where those interested could stop in to gather more information, ask questions, or even submit a story on the spot. These events, we hope, will create interest and momentum in contributing stories, and possibly encourage those with intentions of contributing, but who have not yet contacted us. Making these story days a component of nationally recognized events, such as National Coming Out Day, Day of Silence, LGBT History Month, Pride Month, and even StoryCorps' National Day of Listening, may show potential participants how *their* stories are a valid and important part of the larger American narrative.

Our final idea to increase participation in the *Voices* project is to point to how the stories can make a difference in the campus experience for members of the LGBT community, our allies, and the campus at large. We plan to invite professors to use the interviews, poetry, and other submissions as class discussion topics or as assigned readings. Another idea to show the importance of each person's story, would be to select quotes from the interviews or pieces of art to showcase on the Commission's website, in Commission reports, on the *Ready for the World* website, or on the University of Tennessee's Diversity website. These publicity ideas, which will use *Voices'* stories for promotional, curricular, and research purposes are within the range of acceptable uses outlined in the IRB proposal. We are quite pleased that we were proactive in seeking approval from IRB, which now allows us greater flexibility in how we use the archive.

Personal Perspectives

Roger

Providing a personal perspective on *Voices of Diversity* and its impact upon my life and career has proven difficult. It is easy to write about history, process, and planning, but writing about the personal presents unexpected challenges and concerns. I will begin by stating that my own primary personal concern with participating in *Voices of Diversity* was that it would not be perceived as a legitimate professional activity by my colleagues, and that the scholarly nature of *Voices of Diversity* would be questioned. To be blunt, I was afraid that the personal prejudices of some of my colleagues toward LGBT persons would be used as a tool to attack me both personally and professionally.

Many questions arose in my mind. Will I be able to get a job? Will I be able to get tenure? Will I be taken seriously? Will I be safe? Will this have a negative impact on my partner? Is this project worth the risk? Ultimately, I decided that yes, *Voices of Diversity* was worth the risk. I have never been one to shy away from a challenge. I made the decision early on in my life to always be out. I believe that being out is the best way to demonstrate that LGBT people are no different than everyone else. I also believe that being out on campus provides much needed positive role models to the students. In the end, I saw *Voices of Diversity* as just another way of being out, and as a result, another way to have a positive impact on others.

This is not to say that my concerns were not legitimate. A few colleagues have questioned the scholarly nature of my work with the *Voices* project, and I have been accused of using what was phrased as "illegitimate research" as a way of advancing my personal political agenda. However, aside from these few and isolated bigoted comments, on the whole, my colleagues' reactions have been quite positive. In fact, I believe the experience that I have gained from *Voices of Diversity* played a contributing factor in successfully finding a new professional position as an Institutional Repository Librarian.

I have also been battling a growing feeling of personal disappointment in my LGBT colleagues on campus, particularly those who serve on the Commission, but who continue to refuse to share their stories. I, frankly, do not understand why they will not participate; many are tenured, or in similarly safe positions. When asked repeatedly, they agree that they should participate, but never actually come through. Their positions on the Commission place them in leadership roles on campus, but they do not lead through action. I am reminded of a statement by Frederick Douglas:

> *If there is no struggle, there is no progress. Those who profess to favor freedom, and yet depreciate agitation, are men who want crops without plowing up the ground. They want rain without thunder and lightning. They want the ocean without the awful roar of its many waters. This struggle may be a moral one; or it may be a physical one; or it may be both moral and physical; but it must be a struggle.*

This statement has been a guiding principle for me through my adult life. It codifies my belief that change can only come through persistent actions.

This disappointment aside, I am glad to have been involved in *Voices of Diversity*. I have achieved a personal sense of satisfaction in bringing the project from a vague thought to a fully functional reality. I have gained experience and insight. I have had the pleasure of meeting interesting, caring, and thoughtful people. I have had the unique opportunity to work with Donna Braquet, the most dedicated, concerned, and caring librarian I know. I am proud to count her among my dearest friends, and I look forward to our continued collaboration on *Voices of Diversity*.

Donna

When I accepted my position in 2004 as Life Sciences Librarian at the University Libraries, I had no intention of being a leader on campus for lesbian, gay, bisexual, and transgender equality. I had come out in college ten years earlier, and had been active in the student-led Gay and Lesbian Alliance. My days of involvement in gay organizations on campus were long gone, or so I thought. During library school and my first few years as a librarian, I had little reason to be out. That changed, however, when I joined the faculty at University of Tennessee. Knoxville and Tennessee's flagship university lacked the level of institutional commitment to diversity, especially regarding LGBT issues, that many other major universities had come to embrace.

For me, the road to the *Voices of Diversity* project was a progressive one. In 2005, I joined forces with Bharat Mehra in researching ways for LIS professionals to support LGBTQ individuals. During 2006, I joined Mehra and an out, long-time administrator to lobby for the creation of an organization that could advocate for positive change in support of LGBT students, faculty, and staff. In 2007, I took a leadership role in the newly created Commission for LGBT People, and *Voices* began accepting stories in 2008.

Being in a campus climate less than optimal for LGBT faculty, staff, and students, I often worried about the cost of my increasing outness. This was especially significant as I am in a tenure-track position. I, like Roger, was concerned that my colleagues would see *Voices* as a superfluous and political – if not an activist – type of activity. Other questions concerned me as I considered such a public project like *Voices of Diversity*: How would the biology faculty and students react if they discovered I was promoting a queer archive? Would the Libraries welcome the attention garnered by one of its librarians being so visible on campus? Would the work involved in the project be counted toward my tenure portfolio? If the stories were critical of the university or administration, would the project (or would I) face negative consequences? Would conservative members of the Board of Trustees refuse to grant my tenure? Was I foolishly putting my job at stake?

One of the most damaging outcomes of institutionalized homophobia and heterosexism is fear. The fear of what *might* happen can be crippling. But, I can personally attest that working through the process of developing and promoting *Voices* dispelled my fears. And it is my sincere hope that *Voices* has helped purge the fear of those who have shared their stories. Indeed, I truly believe that it will help eradicate the fear of others on campus, both LGBT people who are afraid to come out, and also those who – for one reason or another – fear lesbians, gays, bisexuals, and transgender people.

Voices offered me a chance to use my expertise as a librarian to bring forth the stories of those who are too often unheard. I feel honored to have been entrusted by those who have shared their stories. I learn something new from each participant. I treasure the relationship that Roger and I have forged through the development of this project. I enjoy the variety of work that *Voices* allows me outside of my science librarian responsibilities. I submitted my tenure dossier in September; I look forward to being an Associate Professor next fall.

Conclusion

Building the archive and planning for long-term sustainability is a slow and methodical process, requiring persistence, patience, and dedication. The authors envision a day when there are countless stories in the *Voices* archive. Ultimately, though, we feel *Voices of Diversity*'s success is best measured by the significance gained by those who share their stories with the world, no matter how many, and the change that occurs within each listener, no matter how small.

Works Cited

Crabtree, Loren. "About *Ready for the World.*" *Ready for the World.* U of Tennessee, 1 Jan. 2005. Web. 7 July 2010.

Douglass, Frederick. "West India Emancipation." Canadaigua, NY. 3 Aug. 1857. Address.

Mehra, Bharat and Donna Braquet. "Library and Information Science Professionals as Community Action Researchers in an Academic Setting: Top Ten Directions to Further Institutional Change for People of Diverse Sexual Orientations and Gender Identities." *Library Trends* 56.2 (2007): 542-565. Print.

"Past Events by Type." *Commission for LGBT People.* U of Tennessee, n.d. Web. 7 July 2010.

"StoryCorps: The Conversation of a Lifetime." *StoryCorps.* National Public Radio, n.d. Web. 7 July 2010.

"Voices of Diversity: An Online LGBT Story Archive." *Voices of Diversity.* U of Tennessee, n.d. Web. 7 July 2010.

Managing Outside the Closet: On Being an Openly Gay Library Administrator

Matthew P. Ciszek

Library administrators face many challenges at work, including balancing shrinking budgets, motivating staff, and ensuring that library operations run smoothly and efficiently. Being an openly gay, lesbian, bisexual, or transgender (GLBT) administrator adds to these challenges and redefines them in many ways. As an openly gay man and a library administrator, I will share experiences and situations that I have faced, explain how I handled these, and discuss the lessons I learned along the way. I will also provide advice and counsel for GLBT persons in library administration positions, and ways that they can manage from "outside the closet."

Current research illustrates that "disclosing one's sexual orientation is one of the toughest issues" that GLBT people face, and "those who remain closeted report lower levels of psychological well-being and life satisfaction, increased health risks, and extensive energy-draining activities focused on covering up their stigmatized identity" (Griffth and Hebl 1191). Since administrators are often called upon to be the leaders and role models of an organization, it becomes increasingly important that GLBT administrators live a work life "out of the closet," in which their personal relationships are known among their coworkers and the staff that they supervise. Not only is this process beneficial to the well-being of the administrator, but it also establishes a work environment built on honesty and trust. Personal relationships are "frequently assets in the politics of the work environment" (Day and Schoenrade, "Staying" 148), and allow administrators and the staff that they supervise to "establish closer and more honest relationships" (Griffith and Hebl 1192). As administrators, we must create programs and practices that provide equal opportunities for all staff, without "alienating conservative" staff and patrons (Day and

Schoenrade, "Relationship" 360). This is the delicate balance that openly GLBT library administrators must strike.

Before discussing the specifics of how to "manage from outside the closet," I want to provide some background information about myself. I came out to family and friends in 1995 when I started library school, and have lived my entire professional career out of the closet. In each position that I have held, I have tried to be as open as possible with my coworkers, supervisors, and subordinates with respect to my personal life and my relationships. Throughout most of my career as a librarian, I have been in a committed relationship with another man, and have made no distinction, whether privately or publicly, between this relationship and those of my heterosexual colleagues. I have made a conscious decision to live openly as a gay man, and have enjoyed the benefits and faced the consequences of this decision. I hope that all in the field of librarianship can learn from my experiences, and that GLBT persons in librarianship who are considering coming out of the closet will find this information useful, especially if they are in an administrative or supervisory position.

Coming Out of the Closet to Perfect Strangers

Friends and family are often the first group of people to which a GLBT person comes out, and this can be a difficult process under the best of circumstances. This process can also be complicated for an administrator who makes the decision to come out to his or her subordinates. Even though a library or institution may be welcoming and supportive of GLBT persons, and have well-crafted policies and procedures protecting against discrimination and promoting diversity, opening up to staff about one's personal life is a decision over which a GLBT person may agonize for many hours. Ultimately, though, being open and honest about one's life outside the office can build a culture of honesty and trust that will benefit the entire office environment.

Personally, I have strived to be as open and upfront as possible about my non-work life with my staff, and this began from the moment I interviewed. During the interview process of my last three positions, there was an opportunity – usually at lunch – to talk casually with those whom I would be supervising. I felt that in order to begin my relationship with them on the right foot and build trust from the start, I would be honest with them when questions turned toward my family life, my marital status, and the like. The response from my "future staff" has always been positive, and I have felt that it was a great way to judge the climate of the institution. If the response had not been positive, or if I got the feeling that my sexuality was a major problem for staff, coworkers, or those to whom I would report, I would then know that this work environment would not be one in which I would feel comfortable and be able to thrive as an administrator. Honesty and openness is indeed the best policy, and can prevent problems further down the road.

I advise GLBT administrators to be honest and straightforward from the beginning of the relationship with their staff. One need not waive the rainbow flag and start a GLBT support group the first day in a new position, but there are many ways that one's personal life can be worked into casual conversations around the office, and staff and subordinates will appreciate this honest and open attitude from day one. Staff members seek information about their supervisors by asking subtle questions soon after arrival, and GLBT administrators should expect questions about what they did last weekend, how house-hunting is coming along, or how their wife/husband/spouse is adjusting to the move. These questions provide an excellent opportunity for the GLBT administrator to come out to their subordinates in a casual, non-forced way and begin to form a relationship between supervisor and staff that is built on trust and honesty.

The Significance of a Significant Other

Coming out at work can be a difficult and trying process for any GLBT person. Developing a support system is essential to ensure that a new administrator has an outlet to talk about the emotional, social, and physical stresses that he or she is going through during this process. GLBT persons may find this support from friends and family, and those with significant others (SO) often rely upon them for support. Although I came out at my first professional position during a period where I had no SO, I have had a partner throughout the last five years in which I have been a library administrator. While I believe that any GLBT person should come out at work as he or she is comfortable, having a partner has made this process simpler and more straightforward. My partner has provided me with immeasurable support in my work life, and at the same time has provided me with topics in which to engage those whom I supervise in casual conversation.

Casual conversation in the workplace often revolves around spouses, children, and family life. The family is viewed as the quintessential social relationship in American society, and much emphasis is placed on family and relationships, even in the workplace. Oftentimes, GLBT persons feel left out of these conversations, fearing that their "family" or relationships may not be accepted as part of the conversation. I feel that opening up about my own relationships and family life has allowed my staff to understand me better, and has fostered an open and communicative environment.

My advice to GLBT administrators with SOs is to introduce them to your staff and subordinates as you would a spouse or boyfriend/girlfriend, and to include pictures of them and effects of your relationship together in your office. When casual conversations turn towards spouses and families, do not shy away from discussing your SO. Additionally, if you have children with your SO, include them in work-sponsored activities designed for families, and ensure that your SO is invited to work-related functions to which other spouses, partners, and boyfriends/girlfriends would normally be invited. My goal has been to include my partner as any other heterosexual coworkers or employees would their spouse, and to make sure that my partner is considered in the same context as others' spouses.

I also recommend that GLBT administrators make clear to colleagues and staff what name or title should be used when referring to his or her SO. In a previous position, I had an employee that continually referred to my partner as my "special friend." I went along with this for a while out of respect for the staff member, who was quite a bit older than me, and was possibly coming to terms with how to frame my relationship in her own mind. After a while, I did ask her to refer to my partner either as "partner" or by his first name. This prevented others from using this turn of phrase, but also put her mind at ease on the issue, and allowed me to define how my partner should be referred to in casual office communication.

Being the Odd Man Out

GLBT persons can often feel like an "odd man out," especially in work situations. Libraries and workplaces, in general, tend to be fairly homogeneous environments. An "odd man out" is anyone who exhibits characteristics contrary to this homogeneous environment. This feeling can be further intensified when one is a GLBT person and also responsible for leading a group of employees, most of whom are not GLBT. Additionally, most administrators and supervisors employ some form of team-based leadership, and it may be difficult to lead a work team when there is some type of difference between the administrator and the staff that he or she is supervising. There are many ways to combat these feelings, and to educate and enlighten your staff along the way.

To avoid being the "odd man out," many GLBT administrators avoid being the "poster child" for all GLBT persons, but as an openly GLBT administrator, I welcome questions on GLBT topics. Encouraging open dialog among my staff contributes to a receptive and welcoming environment for everyone, and helps to bridge the understanding gap, as well as provide education on the significance and struggles of being an openly GLBT person in modern society. Being open to questions about an area of life that many GLBT persons choose to conceal may feel strange at first, but willingness to entertain questions with an open mind and attitude helps overcome this feeling in due time.

Another approach in preventing the feelings of the "odd man out" is to build support networks at work. One way to build a support network is to find a "staff ally," or an employee that is supportive, understanding, and sensitive to your status as an openly GLBT person. In my experiences, there has always been an employee with a gay son, or a lesbian best friend, or the like who can empathize with how you are feeling and who can provide support, especially if issues and situations arise due to your status. An openly GLBT administrator will be able to thrive without a staff ally by seeking support outside the workplace, but having a staff ally can build bridges among your staff and make a transition to a new position much easier.

Finally, I want to stress the importance of finding other GLBT colleagues, both locally and nationally. Often the only people who can truly understand what it is like to be out of the closet in our work lives are others in the same situations. Most colleges and universities, and many larger public library systems, have GLBT groups that would welcome our involvement. There are also local, regional, and national GLBT organizations, both library-related and otherwise, that can serve as resources and support for GLBT persons in their work lives. Having a support network is critically important, and my advice to the GLBT administrator is to find this support as soon as possible.

Should I Draw You a Diagram?

My management style is based upon the "open door policy." I welcome feedback, questions, and interaction with those that I supervise, and strive to build an honest relationship with my employees based upon trust. This open relationship with my staff has led to some interesting situations, and the need to establish work/life boundaries. Being a resource for staff with questions about GLBT persons, while keeping certain aspects of life private, proves to be a delicate balancing act.

Every individual has a comfort level with the amount of personal information that he or she is willing to share with work colleagues and employees. I have worked with employees and coworkers who are very guarded about their non-work life, and others who share a little too much information. Personally, I feel that fostering open communication requires that GLBT persons share some aspects of their personal lives, especially those that seek to live outside of the closet. GLBT administrators must find the right balance, and this often comes after months or years of working in an institution.

Inevitably, an openly GLBT administrator will be asked a question, or asked to explain a situation, about his or her orientation, gender identity, or the inner workings of GLBT relationships. One example from my personal experience is a question I had from an employee who asked "who was the woman" in my relationship with my partner. This was a perfect opportunity for me to draw boundaries around what was acceptable material for discussion in a work context, while also educating the employee. I had worked with her for some time and knew that her question was an honest one, so I simply explained that in our relationship we shared traditional gender roles – I do the laundry, he does the dishes, I fix things around the house, he maintains the car – but other aspects of my relationship I chose to keep private, and I made clear that I expected her to honor those wishes, just as I would do with her and her husband. She did go away from our conversation with new insights into my relationship, but also understood where the boundaries of workplace conversation had been drawn.

Lastly, I would like to stress the importance of locating resources when questions arise for which you have no answer from personal experience or local knowledge. A few years back an employee asked me the difference between transgender, transsexual, and transvestite persons. I did my best to answer from personal experience and provide some basic information, but felt unequipped to fully answer the question since I am not part of that community. I did, however, offer to find some resources for the employee, and even offered to put him in contact with a transgender friend of mine who has lectured on this subject in the past. The employee was grateful for my help, and I later found out that he had a transgender nephew and was looking for information. My openness to his question, and the fact that he knew he could come to me with it, allowed him to receive the information that he needed.

Agreeing to Disagree

One of the most challenging issues facing an openly GLBT administrator is employing a staff member who takes issue with his or her sexual orientation, gender identity, or any "non-work" aspect of life that may be incompatible with the staff member's religious, moral, or political beliefs.

It can be difficult to maintain a cohesive and productive work team in this environment, and can be one of the most complex personnel issues that any manager may face. One method that I have found that works quite well in these situations is to "agree to disagree," or putting aside personal differences for the good of the work environment. Achieving this balance can take a long time to accomplish, but ultimately is worth the time and effort to maintain a harmonious workplace.

Throughout my career I have supervised and worked alongside many people with different religious, moral, and political ideas than myself. In most cases, these issues never entered the workplace, and my being an openly gay man was a non-issue, at least publicly, to everyone involved. I did have one employee who had very deep religious convictions, and who was a very expressive "born-again Christian" at work, who became troubled when she learned that I was gay, and actively sought to help "save me" and see her point of view. I reminded her that the institution in which we worked saw the value of a diverse set of ideologies and beliefs, that I had great respect for her beliefs, and I would never try and make her believe as I do. Through a lot of positive reinforcement of these ideals, and working with the employee on what was acceptable work behavior, we finally agreed that she could never change my mind – and I hers – so we would mutually agree to disagree on this issue.

Openly GLBT library administrators face a number of challenges at work. Coming out to staff and subordinates can be a difficult process, but ultimately leads to a more open and honest workplace. Additionally, having a significant other, and treating him or her as coworkers and staff treat their own spouses or partners increases understanding of your relationship. Being open to questions, and setting boundaries for discussion of your personal life allows you to educate and enlighten your staff, and create a more collegial work environment. Openly GLBT library administrators should also seek support from colleagues, friends, and those they supervise, and work on "agreeing to disagree" when issues arise over matters of sexual orientation or gender identity. I do not guarantee that all or any of the advice that I have given in this article will create a workplace panacea, but I know that coming out of the closet at work has been an excellent choice in my own life, and has created much more opportunity for me than the alternative. Being openly gay truly means being open and honest in everything that I do, and this has helped me in immeasurable ways as a library administrator.

Works Cited

Day, Nancy E. and Patricia Schoenrade. "The relationship among reported disclosure of sexual orientation, anti-discrimination policies, top management support and work attitudes of gay and lesbian employees." *Personnel Review* 29.3 (2000): 346-363. Print.

-----. "Staying in the closet versus coming out: Relationships between communication about sexual orientation and work attitudes." *Personnel Psychology* 50.1 (1997): 147-163. Print.

Griffith, Kristin H. and Michelle R. Hebl. "The Disclosure Dilemma for Gay Men and Lesbians: "Coming Out" at Work." *Journal of Applied Psychology* 87.6 (2002): 1191-1199. Print.

Homophobia in San Antonio

David Allen White

In order to understand how this all came about, you need to know that I'm a major geek. Who else would put call number labels on the books in his personal collection? I started labeling my books when I was in library school at Our Lady of the Lake College in San Antonio around 1970. I was taking a course in Library of Congress classification. I had always worked in libraries that used Dewey and I needed *something* to practice on. That's how it started, and I have continued labeling to this day. Now I'm a compulsive LibraryThing user.

I worked for the San Antonio Public Library twice: once from 1969 to 1972, and again from 1976 to 1985. During the first period, I attended library school at night, and when I finished my MLS in 1972, it was time to move on. It was about this time that, after years of denial, I admitted to myself that I was gay, and I wanted to be in a more accepting environment than San Antonio. To give an example of what I mean, Library Director Mike Sexton transferred me to a different branch as a punishment for growing a beard. At the same time, he fired several young men because their hair was longer than his dress code specified, and they refused to cut it. This didn't seem like a good place to explore my gay identity.

I got a job at the Queens Borough Public Library in New York City in November 1972. Living in New York allowed me to be a part of an open gay and lesbian community. These were years of personal and sexual awakening. They were also the early years of a burgeoning literature of gay liberation, and before long I had new books for my collection, and that meant more labels.

The Library of Congress classification put all gay books in HQ76. That class number was not as sophisticated as it would later become and it didn't suit my expanding collection, so I started tweaking it. After I'd developed some modifications that I felt were more appropriate, I sent a copy to the

Library of Congress, and received a reply from Edward J. Blume, Chief of the Subject Cataloging Division. He said: "Frequently such developments are so idiosyncratic that I cannot make meaningful comment. Yours is not." He added a paragraph on some changes he would have suggested, and ended by saying: "But all of this is off the top of my head and with further thought I might end up with the same scheme you already have." He also said he would circulate my scheme to the social science catalogers for information and guidance in expanding the LC schedule.

A librarian friend suggested that I submit my modified HQ76 schedule to the *Hennepin County Library Cataloging Bulletin* to see if they would publish it. They did, but not while I lived in New York.

By 1976, the City of New York was on the verge of bankruptcy, and if the libraries closed – as many of us feared they would – I would be out of a job. I reapplied to San Antonio and was rehired. Was Mike Sexton still Director? Yes, he was. What had changed? I had. Back in 1972, I hadn't accepted myself as a gay man, but by 1976, I was comfortable with it, and having come out definitively in New York, I could handle being out anywhere.

In June of 1977, a year after I moved back to San Antonio, my article was published.[1] It identified me as gay and an employee of the San Antonio Public Library. At first, nothing happened. I showed the article to a few friends; they seemed mildly interested, and that was all.

One afternoon I was on duty at the reference desk when my supervisor, Marie Berry, told me that Library Director Sexton wanted to see me in his office. I went immediately. He ordered me to close the door and take a seat. He had a copy of my article on his desk. I later learned that he'd gotten the article from Selma Nuessle, head of Technical Services. One of the catalogers, Laurie Gruenbeck, had read the article and showed it to Miss Nuessle. After she read it, she felt obligated to show it to Mr. Sexton. What her motive was, I never found out, but Sexton was furious. He told me in very cold, measured tones that he had read my article. He felt that I had placed the library in the position of advocating homosexuality, since the article identified me as a member of his staff.

I said, "Mr. Sexton, I believe the policy is quite clear. The library takes no position on any controversial issue except the freedom to read. And that presupposes the freedom to write. This library, after all, does not use the Library of Congress classification, so it can't be suggested that my article was work-related in any way."

He reminded me that homosexuality was illegal in Texas, and that I had essentially confessed to a crime. I said that I had done no such thing.

---

1. *HCL cataloging bulletin* #28, p. 35-38 (June 1, 1977)

It was not illegal to *be* a homosexual, and beyond that I had confessed to nothing.

He said, "You make a very good point, Mr. White. However, I am obligated to bring this matter before the Board of Trustees at the next meeting. You need not be present unless you wish to."

I answered, "I most certainly intend to be present, and I plan to be represented by counsel."

With that, he sent me back to my department. When I got back, I learned that Mrs. Berry already knew what this was about. She'd heard it from Miss Nuessle, and by now, it was all over the building. Since returning to SAPL in 1976, I had not attempted to conceal the fact that I was gay, so a number of people knew it already. Mrs. Berry knew, but we had never talked about it until now. I don't think she cared one way or the other; it did not seem to affect our working relationship.

I knew a gay lawyer, so I called him and he was able to see me right away. I told him my story, and showed him my article. He said that there was no way Sexton could pursue this. He would have to prove that the article brought disgrace on the San Antonio Public Library, and since it was safe to assume that not ten people in San Antonio had ever seen this publication, that would be very hard to do. Harder still, since there was nothing salacious in the article. The lawyer told me that if Sexton tried to have me fired or harassed me on the job, I would have grounds for a lawsuit against the City of San Antonio, and against Sexton personally as well. But, he advised that a lawsuit should not be my first step. I must first make use of whatever remedies the city already had available.

Every city department in San Antonio had an Equal Opportunity Employment Counselor, and the library's counselor was Rose Blumenthal, a librarian at the Oakwell Branch. I met with her and explained the situation. She had never before processed a complaint that was related to sexual orientation and she didn't know the procedure. She assured me that she would refer the matter to the EEO Director in the City Personnel Department and ask him what to do.

Several days later Rose called me at home. She said that the EEO Director told her not to do anything because he was going to handle it from his end. I pieced this story together later from several sources. The EEO Director went to the Head of Personnel, who called Sexton directly and informed him that he had received a complaint regarding a city employee who was said to be gay, whom Sexton was harassing. He instructed Sexton to drop this issue immediately and to have nothing further to do with it, because the City of San Antonio would not back him up if he persisted.

When this call came through, the door to Sexton's office was open. After he hung up, he said in a voice loud enough to be heard in the outer office, "I gave that faggot a job after he ran off to New York, but I wouldn't take him back again. We'll see if he gets a promotion as long as I'm director of this library." This was reported to me by three people who heard it, but not one of them was willing to repeat it to anyone else.

From then on, Sexton would not speak to me unless he absolutely had to (not that we were ever bosom buddies before that). Over the next several years I applied for various higher positions, but I was never selected, of course. Sexton was keeping his vow.

One day, everything changed. A woman came to the reference desk and complained that a man was following her in the stacks. I asked her to point out the stalker so I could identify him later. I wanted to call the police if the woman wished to make an official complaint. And I needed a security guard, since I couldn't apprehend the stalker myself. But the guards weren't answering the page. What to do? I couldn't go and look for a guard, stay and call the police, and go with the woman to identify the stalker all at the same time. Consequently, the stalker got away, the guard never showed up, and the woman decided not to call the police. The situation was poorly handled because we had no proper procedures in place. So I wrote a report outlining this unacceptable situation, and submitted it to Sexton.

Sexton was pleased with my report, and subsequently made some changes based on my suggestions, and he also wrote me a commendation. Shortly afterward, the position of government documents librarian opened. It was a higher pay grade, and Sexton sent word to me through one of his underlings that I should apply for it. I got the promotion in October 1984, and I was on my new job just a couple of months when I learned of an opening for a Spanish-language cataloger at the Library of Congress. I applied for it and was selected, and so in February 1985 I resigned from the San Antonio Public Library.

Just before I left for Washington, Sexton stopped me in the hall and congratulated me on my new job. He then had the audacity to say, "It's a shame that after waiting so long for a promotion you decide to quit right away."

I answered, "Yes, I should have had a promotion long before this, but we both know who kept me from getting one."

That was the last time I spoke to him. When I moved to Washington, I still had a lot of anger toward him. But I am not a violent person ... so I worked out my anger by writing a murder mystery, making him the victim and myself the prime suspect, who was later proven innocent. But before a year was out, my anger had cooled and I put the murder mystery away. Maybe I'll finish it one day. Even though I'm not angry anymore, who knows? It still might be a good story. I planned to send Sexton an autographed copy, but he passed away a few months ago.

Sexton was never very popular with the staff at San Antonio Public Library. Among colleagues with whom I still kept in touch, I couldn't find anybody that attended his funeral. One of my friends said, "I wasn't all that fond of the old buzzard."

Part Three:
The Rest of the Rainbow

www.chicagoleatherclub.org www.leatherarchives.org

READ

SEXUAL REVOLUTION

Matt Johnson
Librarian, queer cultural historian
and intransigent pervert

Produced by Chicago Leather Club for the Leather Archives & Museum

Leather Librarian

John P. Bradford

The man who seduced me into librarianship, Nick, is gay. We met through Dignity Lafayette – more a social club than a Catholic organization, and no longer in existence – while I was a student at Purdue. As it was not really possible in mid-1980s central Indiana to get much gay and lesbian fiction at the local public libraries, members of Dignity Lafayette –including my partner and I – would from time to time contribute books from their personal collections to the Dignity Lafayette library. I helped Nick get these books into a semblance of order; he suggested I might want to volunteer at the library where he was director. I was one of at least three members of Dignity Lafayette that he convinced to go to library school at Indiana University. We used to joke about Nick being the high priest of the Church of Library Science.

While at Indiana University from 1990-1991, I noted how much more open Bloomington, Indiana was to GLBT life compared to West Lafayette, Indiana. I was amazed that the big gay bar, Bullwinkle's, was pretty much on the main drag and straight people went there because we had the best DJs.

I worked weekday evenings in one of the residence hall libraries at Indiana University. I think I was the only gay worker at that particular library, but I can only think of one time my sexuality impacted my work: A

Opposite: Louis Lang, as his pledge project for the Chicago Leather Club, used the READ Design Studio software from ALA Graphics to produce several READ posters to promote the Teri Rose Memorial Library at the Leather Archives & Museum. In this poster, Matt Johnson (Librarian, queer cultural historian, and intransigent pervert) holds *Sexual Revolution*, a 2003 collection of essays edited by Jeffrey Escoffier.

patron complained that I spent too much time, and made too much noise, joking and flirting with my *gay* friends (emphasis hers).

At my first professional job (1992-1995 at the Indian Prairie Public Library) I was open about my sexuality and my partnership with Louis Lang. I can only think of one time when one of the Indian Prairie staff made a faux pas: I was wearing a flannel shirt and probably looked a little scruffy from a rough weekend, and a new employee innocently commented that I did not look like the stereotypical male librarian. Puzzled, I asked what she meant, and then had to tell her, well, yes, actually, I *am* gay. She apologized and the incident became an anecdote to trot out to demonstrate how "straight-acting" I am. Louis was accepted as my spouse by the entire staff, and if husbands and wives were invited along to events, Louis was, too.

Two students from the local high school were astonished to see Louis and me out shopping as a couple; they were both regular library users so I knew I would see them again. I was pleasantly surprised when, the following week, they came up to the Reference Desk and started asking about whether we had soundtracks to Broadway musicals. It developed that these two were a closeted couple, and the older one was about to graduate and go off to the Army. They were glad to know of other gay people around, and I pointed them to Horizons,[1] a gay and lesbian social group in Chicago.

In 1992, I was very happy that an AIDS display that I designed was well-received by the community. However, I thought the library director overreacted when she received one complaint. I had distributed over 1200 brochures about HIV and AIDS in the first month, and fewer than 100 on abstinence. Still, I was called into her office and had to explain why the display was important enough to stay up a second month. We only distributed about 800 brochures that month.

When I moved to Arizona in 1995 for a job at the Tempe Public Library, I was excited to find that I would be working with other openly gay people – one in charge of the computer system and automation, and another who worked in the Periodicals and Study Center. Others joined the staff while I worked there as well. My coworkers, by and large, accepted Louis, and many of them came to our housewarming when we bought a house just south of Tempe.

---

1. "Center on Halsted Organizational Timeline." *Center on Halsted History— Chicago's Lesbian, Gay, Bisexual and Transgender Community Center.* Center on Halsted. Web. 21 May 2010.

On my very first day at Tempe Public Library, I outed myself. Chatting in the lunchroom, one of my coworkers asked if I was married or had a girlfriend. I replied that Louis and I had been together for eight years. This was overheard and reported around the whole Department of Community Services, and Will Manley – Tempe's Assistant Director of Community Services – ended up with a column out of it (120).

I became a resource for GLBT and GLBT-friendly high school students, after one came up to me looking for a speech by Harry Hay. I not only knew who he was, I had ordered a book containing that speech. The student told his friends how helpful I'd been, and I started getting asked questions about being gay in college, how to find GLBT organizations in other towns, where to get free condoms, etc.

I also became active in the GLBT Round Table of the American Library Association while working at Tempe Public Library. I was appointed to the Stonewall Book Award Committee in 1999. In 2000, after the committee chose the award-winners, I decided to make up a bibliography of GLBT fiction at the Tempe Public Library. As it happened, the mayor of Tempe, who'd come out in 1996 (Yeager), was being increasingly targeted by the religious right ("Neil, We Hardly Knew Ye"); eventually they forced a recall vote, which he handily won, but nevertheless, my supervisors were concerned that letting people know the library had GLBT materials would harm him politically. I disagreed, and complained to Will Manley, who told the library director to let me issue the bibliography. In the end, we did get one complaint: I had left out some favorite titles of one of our regular patrons.

When Louis got a job in Austin, Texas in early 2001, I moved with him, and looked for a job. Finding a good job in Austin was hard – with a library school right there, salaries were much lower for library work than I expected. Then, too, as one of our friends put it, Austin is a liberal oasis in a redneck desert – and we ended up living in Williamson County, just north of the city.

I eventually found a job working at Galaxy.com, a vertical directory and search engine. They never quite got the finances figured out, and Galaxy collapsed in the dot-com crash. Still, I enjoyed working with most of the people there, including my boss who was openly lesbian. One person gave me problems – a Russian *émigré* who adored Dr. Laura and thought my being gay was decadent and selfish.

A few months later, I was named the Texas Documents Librarian at the Texas State Library and Archives. Even though I thought it was pretty clear on my resume that I was gay, my boss missed that. She even made a homophobic comment during the interview – but I figured she was just trying to rattle me. Anyhow, she never really was happy that she had hired me – but may have had more of a problem with my public library, service-oriented background than my homosexuality. She was pretty much gunning for me the entire time I worked there; she sent me home in tears more than once. When 9/11 happened, and Louis and I were so distant from our birth families, we reevaluated living and working in Texas and I began looking for work in the Chicago area.

The Villa Park Public Library, by and large, has been a good fit. I started out as the Assistant Head of Adult Services in December 2001, and was promoted to Head of Automation & Technical Services in May 2005. I have been very open about being gay. Everyone at Villa Park has been supportive during times that Louis has had to go into the hospital, and staff got together to buy Louis and me a wedding present when we married in Toronto in March 2004. On the other hand, while one person in HR in the Village of Villa Park congratulated me on the wedding, her boss called me specifically to tell me that she did not consider the marriage valid and Louis would not be eligible for health care benefits.

I also was annoyed in January 2006, after the Illinois law forbidding employment discrimination on the basis of sexual orientation finally took effect ("IL Human Rights Act"). The library director made a successful push to drop what she called "the laundry list" of protected groups from the library's non-discrimination policy, rather than list sexual orientation. Well, she no doubt thought it might cost the library a few votes in the referendum she was gearing up for in November 2008 – and which failed pretty miserably, anyhow. The board quietly restored the policy, expanded laundry list and all, in 2009.

When Louis and I moved back to the Chicago area, we also got more involved with the BDSM community. Both of us volunteer at the Leather Archives & Museum (LA&M). I do most of my work in the Teri Rose Memorial Library, and members of the staff know this – no one has raised a fuss about it.

As the LA&M is an institution collecting materials "pertaining to Leather, fetishism, sadomasochism, and alternative sexual practices" ("About the LA&M"), there are few places as open to expressions of sexuality as the LA&M. Just about everyone who comes through the doors is kink – and LGBT-accepting. Many of the staff, volunteers, and patrons are LGBT, themselves. About the only folks not welcome are people under the age of 18; as all the collections contain erotica, this remains an adult establishment (Keehnen). Even notorious homophobe Peter LaBarbera,

Louis Lang, as his pledge project for the Chicago Leather Club, used the READ Design Studio software from ALA Graphics to produce several READ posters to promote the Teri Rose Memorial Library at the Leather Archives & Museum. In this poster, Matt Johnson (Librarian, queer cultural historian, and intransigent pervert) shows Allan Gurganus' *Plays Well with Others*.

then of the Illinois Family Institute, now of Americans for Truth about Homosexuality, visited the LA&M in 2006 (LaBarbera). It really is a welcoming space.

As part of a pledge project for a local leather club, Louis created READ posters advertising the Teri Rose Memorial Library (Bradford, "LA&M READ posters debut"); these have been snatched up at events as different as International Mr. Leather (Bradford, "New READ posters available") and the Diversity Fair at the 2007 Annual Conference of the American Library Association (Bradford, "Road Show display wins prize"). I have copies of these posters in my Villa Park Public Library office, but staff and visitors are more likely to comment on the needlework by Louis' mother, which is also on my walls. One staff member, though, took the time to tour the Leather Archives.

I don't talk about my sex life at work, so not many staff members know how promiscuous I am, or even the sorts of activities I enjoy. One person who realizes that I am a member of the Windy City Bondage Club and the Chicago Hellfire Club (after seeing me in my colors) shops for great deals at the Leather Market at International Mister Leather every Memorial Day. If not a kindred soul, she is at the very least quite open-minded. Another woman came out to me as kinky while I was mourning the loss of a dear friend (and incredible bondage bottom); it turns out she is part of a local munch.

One amusing misconception by some staff at my library grew out of an overheard phone call. I go to a big BDSM event every September that participants euphemistically call "summer camp." Since I also try to go to Campit – a gay campground in southwest Michigan – for bear, leather, and cowboy events, people decided that I love camping. Well, camping is OK – but my first love will always be sex! Those who know what I am really up to enjoy playing along.

Works Cited

"About the LA&M." *Leather Archives & Museum.* Leather Archives & Museum, n.d. Web. 20 Dec. 2009.

Bradford, John P. "LA&M READ posters debut at IML, ALA." *GLBTRT Newsletter* 17.3 (2005): 3. *ALA GLBT Round Table.* American Library Association: Gay, Lesbian, Bisexual, and Transgendered Round Table, Fall 2005. Web. 20 Dec. 2009.

-----. "New READ posters available." *GLBTRT Newsletter* 18.2 (2006): 2. *ALA GLBT Round Table.* American Library Association: Gay, Lesbian, Bisexual, and Transgendered Round Table, Summer 2006. Web. 20 Dec. 2009.

-----. "Road Show display wins prize." *Leather Times* 3 (2007): 13. *Leather Archives & Museum.* Leather Archives & Museum, Oct. 2007. Web. 20 Dec. 2009.

"IL Human Rights Act Protections Regarding Sexual Orientation." *Illinois Gender Advocates.* Illinois Gender Advocates, n.d. Web. 15 Mar. 2010.

Keehnen, Owen. "The Leather Archives and Museum: To protect and serve." *Windy City Times* Windy City Media Group, 21 May 2008. Web. 20 Dec. 2009.

LaBarbera, Peter. "Sodom-by-the-Lake; Chicago's Palmer House Hilton Hosts Perverse 'International Mr. Leather'". Web log post. *Americans for Truth about Homosexuality.* Americans for Truth about Homosexuality, 31 May 2007. Web. 20 Dec. 2009.

Manley, Will. "Will's World—'First-Day Decorum.'" *American Libraries.* 28.3 (1997): 120. Print.

"Neil, We Hardly Knew Ye: Neil Giuliano Bids Adieu to Tempe Mayordom." *Phoenix New Times,* 1 Jul. 2004. Phoenix New Times. Web. 15 Mar. 2010.

Yeager, Kenneth S. "The Outing of a Gay Republican Mayor: Mayor Neil Giuliano, Tempe, Arizona." *Trailblazers: Profiles of America's Gay and Lesbian Elected Officials.* New York: Hayworth, 1999. 147-164. Print.

Gender Changer

Jim Van Buskirk

I was the proverbial "pre-homosexual" boy. I liked playing with the girls – hopscotch, jacks, jump rope, Barbie dolls, and "house" – and had crushes on the boys. Did I want the boys to like me or was it that I wanted to be more like them? I couldn't quite figure it out. I often envied the boys' physical prowess, their artistic ability, or their ease in moving through the world. I knew enough not to confess that I found them handsome and wished I knew how to be more comfortable with them, with myself. I was slow to understand my physical attraction to men. Recently a friend I've known since the first grade, out of the blue, told me she'd always known I was gay. Really? I didn't actually come out to myself until I was nearly twenty.

When I first came out in the early 1970s, it felt weird dancing with another man or holding hands in public or kissing. Of course once I moved to San Francisco everything was much easier. Here, being a member of a sexual minority was increasingly acceptable, if not downright chic. Since then I have been out with friends, family, coworkers, in school. I don't think I ever attempted to "pass" as straight. It seemed much too challenging for this somewhat effeminate boy with a sibilant "s." On the rare occasion when someone assumed I was straight, I was flummoxed.

I attended Bellevue Community College and the University of Washington, but then dropped out, moved to San Francisco and came out as a gay man. When I returned to college at Berkeley in the mid '70s, I plunged into sociology courses on women and the family. These courses, and the powerful women who taught them, revolutionized my thinking. Feminism made so much sense to me; its political framework seemed incontrovertibly necessary. I wholeheartedly embraced feminism's message about the "evils of patriarchy." Was I allowed, as a man, to call myself a feminist? I wanted to be part of this movement, but was afraid of inadvertently being insensitive to the sisterhood. From whom could I solicit permission to join this club? I finally found an uneasy foothold as a male feminist, someone many women still viewed with understandable skepticism.

I had no intention of becoming a librarian when I decided to apply to Berkeley's Library School. While working as a paraprofessional in the library at the San Francisco Art Institute, I learned that I was entitled to receive reimbursement for half my expenses if they were directly related to my job duties. I managed to obtain a grant for the other half. I figured having good research skills would stand me in good stead whatever I decided to do. I thought I knew a lot about libraries having used them since I was a kid, including eagerly searching each installment of *Reader's Guide to Periodical Literature* for new articles about movies.

Library school was a good fit for me: I was surrounded by books and intellectually curious people. With students nearly as nerdy as myself, I debated the choice of main entry, Library of Congress Subject Heading, or Dewey Decimal Classification.

After a somewhat circuitous path, I ended up at the San Francisco Public Library, where I was eventually named head of the James C. Hormel Gay & Lesbian Center. While I like to say I was in the right place at the right time, I also believe my skill set was well suited to the demands of the job. During my tenure I learned a lot. In fact, I think I learned more in that period than in the 38 years preceding it. And much of it turned out to be things I've had to *unlearn*.

At Hormel Center, I learned about the complicated intersections of sex and gender, including sexual orientation, transgender and intersex issues, bisexuality, and more. When the Center opened as part of the new main San Francisco Public Library in April 1996, it represented the first permanent research center in a public library devoted to the documentation of lesbian, gay, bisexual and transgender history and culture. In addition to books, magazines, videos, photographs, posters, pulp paperbacks, recordings, ephemera, and memorabilia, the Center holds archival collections of personal papers and organizational records.

To all outward appearances, I stand at the apex of the world's pyramid of race and gender. Due to inhabiting this 6' 3" tall, white, male body, I have the luxury of being able to play with labels. Inside, I feel powerful, but in a different way, hidden from most people's view. I had a childhood fantasy in which I imagined that underneath the façade of a bookish, nerdy, overweight kid was actually a superpower, someone who hadn't yet come into his own, and whose abilities would one day amaze everyone else. Today I may not feel superhuman but I do know that I am privileged: I pass as a man. No one hassles me on my choice of public bathrooms or confuses their pronouns in referring to me.

I enjoyed my exalted position at Hormel Center. When I was named one of San Francisco's fifty most influential gays and lesbians by the local gay weekly newspaper, the *Bay Area Reporter*, I tried not to let it go to my head. I met many fascinating people, many of them celebrities in the queer world whose faces I'd seen in the news, whose books I had read, and whose films I had viewed. I collaborated on several programs with the *New York Times*' "Times Talks," with the GLBT Historical Society, and other prestigious local and national organizations. I made many mistakes in the course of my time at the Hormel Center. I was publicly accused of plagiarism and censorship; I lost friends and made enemies.

At work, I was responsible for meeting the informational needs of an unpredictable constituency of users. As I worked to develop the Hormel Center's collection scope statement I tried to imagine who might be using the Center and in what ways. Novels, non-fiction, periodicals, films were all obvious collection development areas. And I learned that my understanding of sexual orientation, and even of gender identity and sexuality were relatively narrow.

In 1994 I met Susan Stryker and we began collaborating on *Gay by the Bay: A History of Queer Culture in the San Francisco Bay Area* (Chronicle Books, 2006). As we became friends I realized I was receiving a crash course in Transgender 101. Susan is a brilliant writer, historian, filmmaker, and influential transgender activist. Originally a biological male who loved women, Susan's object choice didn't change when she transitioned to female, and thus, her identity transformed into that of a lesbian. As we researched and wrote our survey of the Bay Area's queer history, Susan patiently explained the dynamics of gender dysphoria. She answered all of my probing questions, often using her own experience as an example. I remain impressed by her knowledge, patience, and ability to guide me to a deeper understanding of transgender issues. As proud as I am to have co-authored my first book with Susan, I am prouder still of our enduring friendship. Her lessons have served me well; I am now better able to understand others' prejudices and misconceptions on transgender issues, as I patiently attempt to dispel them.

Similarly with bisexual issues, I was educated by people I knew. I learned from several female friends who had lived for many years as lesbians before marrying men and having children. Had they been gay and were now straight? Were they always bi? Is female sexuality more fluid than male? It was confusing, but my friends answered all of my increasingly personal questions, and I read probably the single most helpful anthology of voices, *Bi Any Other Name: Bisexual People Speak Out*, edited by Loraine Hutchins and Lani Kaahumanu (Alyson, 1994). I came to understand the frequent feeling of bisexual invisibility, the challenge of being "seen," and the difficulty bisexuals have being accepted in either straight or gay communities. This is often compounded by those who come out as "bi" when they are really afraid to identify as homosexual. No wonder there was so much biphobia. I took all of these issues as a personal challenge to try to help dispel this lack of understanding.

In 1998 the Hormel Center and the Harvey Milk Institute, a now-defunct San Francisco-based LGBTQ educational organization, co-sponsored a Butch/FTM [Female-to-Male] Conference. The library's Koret auditorium was filled with people on the spectrum between male and female, young and old, black and white, straight and gay. The pain and passion in the room were palpable. Butch lesbians raged as they described the betrayal they felt by their sisters who had deserted them by becoming men. FTMs wept as they described the alienating journey to realize their long hidden dreams of living as men. It was only a beginning in an ongoing and often uneasy dialogue, but it awakened me to an even wider range of experience. My ongoing struggle with homosexuality seemed almost inconsequential compared to what these brave people were experiencing. I admired all of them for being brave enough to participate in this intense clash between the personal and the political.

Others who have helped inform my attempts to understand what it means to transcend the gender binary include James Green, Loren Cameron, Jordy Jones, Kate Bornstein, Leslie Feinberg's *Stone Butch Blues*, and Martine Rothblatt's *Apartheid of Sex*. These courageous people have helped open my heart and my mind. When I saw "TransForming Community," the powerful evening of transgender and genderqueer spoken word presentations curated by Michelle Tea at the LGBT Community Center, I sponsored a repeat performance some months later in the library's auditorium. I was pleased and proud to hear the audience's positive reaction to these provocative pieces.

One afternoon on a coffee break at the Ramada Inn across the street from the library, I noticed the lobby was filled with large, hairy men. I had inadvertently happened on the International Bear Rendezvous, the annual gathering of gay men who take pride in their heavy set, hairy bodies. As I looked at the young chubby-cheeked faces with sparse facial hair, I suddenly flashed on the fact that many of these guys looked to me more like Female-to-Male transsexuals than the butch representations of masculinity they aspired to be. Perhaps it was the testosterone, a hormone that must course naturally through my own body, but about which I know little. A friend and I still jokingly quote another friend's offhanded comment, "He could pass for FTM," as code for someone's ambiguous gender identification.

That friend was David Cameron. When David approached me about doing a program on intersex issues, I worried about betraying my ignorance yet again, but agreed to host it. David quickly educated me about what I had previously known as "hermaphrodites," lent me several rare VHS documentaries, then directed me to the website of the Intersex Society of North America. Soon I was ordering books and videos for the Hormel Center's collection, meeting with intersex activists and helping to dispel the misinformation that seemed pervasive and prevalent. In fact, David and I are currently coauthoring a chapter on intersex resources for librarians in the new edition of the classic *Gay and Lesbian Library Service* (McFarland, 1990), now being edited by Ellen Greenblatt, titled *Serving LGBTIQ Library and Archives Users: Essays on Outreach, Service, Collections and Access* (McFarland, 2010).

During the current national struggle for and against the recognition of "gay marriage," I realized that the determination to maintain marriage as between a man and a woman is extremely problematic. Who is defining the terms? What about my intersex, transgender, and genderfluid friends? Is gender dependent on the number of one's chromosomes, genitalia, public presentation, personal identification, or what? While I certainly understand the struggle for equal rights, I personally do not want to embrace such a patriarchal institution.

I am simultaneously thrilled and saddened by the ongoing dialogue between articulate members of the queer and trans communities. The issues are complicated and confusing, genderbending, and mind-boggling. The anguish and anger are inspiring. It's hard to change deep-seated beliefs, but I know from my own evolution that it can happen. Just when I think I comprehend something, I realize I don't understand at all. And the more I fail to understand, the more I realize the need to screen another documentary, moderate another panel, or host another presentation to elucidate the dilemma. I feel as if this struggle, painful as it can be, is creating a new world, one richer and more hospitable.

My eyes were opened again when I attended a sensitivity training workshop for library staff led by Marcus Arana, from the San Francisco Human Rights Commission. I had known Marcus for years when I witnessed the reaction of some of my colleagues who absolutely could not and would not believe him when he revealed that he had been born female. Their minds were blown and I watched their beliefs about sex be slowly reassembled in that drab conference room.

I delight in recalling an instance years ago when the Chief of the Main Library introduced me as "the gay and lesbian librarian." She, of course, meant that I was the librarian in charge of collection development for gay and lesbian subject areas, but I heard it a different way. She was right, I felt like both a gay and a lesbian librarian.

My friend Kim Klausner recounted a long-ago conversation in which her partner, Susan Stryker, had made reference to "male lesbians."

"Do you mean like you," Kim asked Susan, "or like Jim Van Buskirk?" While I laughed, I also felt I had been seen.

Andrew Ramer contributed a personal essay titled "Tales of a Male Lesbian" for an anthology I co-edited.[1] When I read his piece, I realized I was not alone. His identification with lesbians in Park Slope, Brooklyn, was almost interchangeable with my experience in Berkeley, California.

My boyfriend also teases me: one year at the GLBT Pride parade, he made himself a button that read, "I'm not a lesbian, but my boyfriend is." I admire him as he walks through the city daily wearing a pink Tinker Bell backpack.

I have tried to remember the adage: sex is what is between my legs; gender is what is between my ears. I'm still confused about my identity. I still don't feel that I fit into the mold of a gay man. For ten years a small empty container marked "Gender Changer" was pinned above my desk into the wall of my cubicle. When my department head jokingly gave me the package, with its label reading "9 pin female-to-male gender changer wired straight through," I had no idea it once contained a piece of common computer hardware. From time to time I glanced up to ponder the package, priced at $2.99, wondering about the magical gadget it once held. Despite my fantasy of a Gender Changer that would make transitioning from male to female as easy as plugging in a piece of hardware, perhaps what I actually envision is much bigger. I dream of a world in which all of us can safely be who we really are. The fluidity of gender-changing people makes more room for all of us.

The courage and commitment I see around me each day reminds me that the world itself is changing, and for that I am profoundly grateful. And that change is coming about largely because of dedicated people willing to challenge the status quo and come out as who they are: librarians working from within and activists working from the streets, authors writing books, filmmakers making films, and people all over the world making sure that libraries are a source of information for absolutely everyone, no matter who they are.

---

1. *Identity Envy: Wanting To Be Who We're Not: Creative Nonfiction by Queer Writers,* Harrington Park Press, 2007.

The Secret Life of Bis:
On Not Quite Being Out and Not Quite Fitting In

BWS Johnson

Have thy will, I am the love that dare not speak its name.

~Lord Alfred Douglas

I'm at it again. I do it zealously every time the opportunity presents itself. This time, I'm at Sin é, the Irish pub not far from my house, and it's harder than it usually is, 'cause not only am I rusty, I've had three ciders. There are jarheads congregating in the corner, smoke snaking through the crowd to their right. It's an exercise that goes straight to the core of my being. I obsessively engage in it, clinging desperately to one of the last threads of my sexuality. I fantasize about a pop quiz; wouldn't want to be rusty for that! It's one of the few public declarations I make. So after a couple of minutes of tongue wrestling, I pop the knotted cherry stem out of my mouth and stick it on my plate, beaming to the cheers of an old friend and the mild jeers of my husband.

Thankfully, there are very few unbreakable tenets to my marriage. I don't bring the little mister round Librarians, so I can number those in the field that have actually seen us together on one hand with fingers still remaining. We don't suffer the other at the cinema if the film is something not mutually agreeable. This means I get to watch *Milk* on my own, while he has quality time with his space aliens. Much of my reflection on my sexuality has taken place in the cool glow of the silver screen. I have a closet desire to be a film Librarian.

~~~

I'm afraid I present a cataloguing dilemma. I'm reluctant to toe the company line, even when that line is lavender. So, if a patron or colleague is smart enough to ask after my sexuality bluntly, I'll tell them that their hunches are correct and indeed I'm omnivorous. Sometimes if I'm feeling particularly mischievous, or if the petitioner is fiendishly attractive, I'll bare a wicked grin and a little air bite. I've toyed with hinters no end, hinting all manner of incorrect assumption back their way until they ask bluntly or piss off. Why beat around the bush? I suppose this high wall of separation between romantic life and work life makes me hopelessly old fashioned, as well as a hopeless romantic.

A bit after high school, it took an aisling of a redhead from a renaissance faire to bring me to the inevitable and terribly obvious conclusion that I wasn't as straight as I thought I was. She had been seeing a hated member of a small circle of friends. Every other friend present lounging on pillows on the floor of that suburban basement was jealously trying to seduce her away from that rough tongued one, myself included. We all pleaded with her in our teenage awkwardness, assuring her that with her fair form and sharp wit she could do so much better. She relented so suddenly. "Like who?" There it was. She dared us. Provide an alternative. "Well, like me."

To this day I do not know how the Fates silenced every other pair of lips in that room. I'm still not sure how those words made it past the filter between my pea-sized brain and my mouth. Also to this day, when it comes to women, not only am I wrapped tightly about their little finger, but I also best be dragged back to the cave by the hair in order to have it understood that a lady wishes to have her way with me. I inevitably lost my aisling for my lack of confidence in what I was doing.

Later on, in college, it wasn't unusual for me to be the object of attraction for someone who was questioning her sexuality. My tight leather jacket and full array of flannels generated a lot of talk. My piggy comments masked my absolute uncertainty of what I would, in fact, do if multiple women followed me home. For all of my machismo, I wasn't one to kiss and tell, which only cemented my popularity. One of my past loves was a Library Science student with a terrible temper and an incurable addiction to books. When that bold redhead was accused of being a homophobe in a sociology class, I teased that we could always show up to class hand-in-hand to refute the claim. She blushed a furious red and forbade me from doing any such thing.

~~~

The Secret Life of Bis

Like Linus, I cling to my security blanket, in that in most day-to-day business, my sexual identity has naught to do with anything. I seldom venture into uncharted territory and inform an audience of the fact if I feel that it's relevant, as I'm doing now. The results are almost always disastrous, so if you need me, I'll be minding my business behind my clunky desk, thank you ever so much for taking an interest. I suppose this is the tack my high school teachers took. Some of them clearly knew that I wasn't straight, None of them went out on the precipice to discuss that with me.

If you're a clever reader, that "most" I used a few sentences back will leap out at you. Like it or no, compartmentalists, things spill from container to container from time to time. I remember a particularly nasty time when a loud and proud colleague was threatened quite bodily by a patron at one of the branches of the Albany Public Library. Little did he anticipate this "fairy" traipsing about the desk that separated them so that he might face his attacker. I stuck by my coworker that night as the police took their sweet time getting to the scene, and I tried to hold back his temper as he pursued his would be assailant into the night. It all happened so quickly, I tried to get him to come back into the Library – anything might happen beyond that door in the pitch. Again I tried to help him check his tongue as he was interviewed by callous cops. I wonder what might have happened had the coward had a bit more spine. If it had come to the threatened blows, would onlookers help or hinder? No one asked for us to drag our sexualities into the workplace, but there it was. It was natural for me to swoop about the library after him, so that if the bully wanted a piece of him, he'd have a piece of me as well. I wasn't quick enough mentally to throw back abuses as my coworker was.

The whole incident with the bigoted patron was enough to give me a flashback to a time when I'd come into contact with those cowards in sheets: the KKK. This time it was in Washington's Crossing. I suppose they assumed that being in the Southern part of New Jersey would help them drum up support. How very wrong they were. Overall, there were more of us representing the opposition, lining the roads in our lavender sheets. I can still picture a male couple that humoured me by kissing each other upon demand. I must have stared for hours at the beauty of that gesture. I suspect the rally didn't last quite as long as the Klan organisers had hoped, nor did it end with the sort of bullying they might have had in mind. Once again, when the time arrived for the opposition to take up the good fight and cross the line from peaceful resistance to violent protest, they shied. It is our side of the fence that holds Stonewall.

It was even easier to stick by my coworker against management scrutiny for ordering *The Advocate*. Like it or no, if one walked a few steps down the street, one came across a number of Pride flags. This was the proper neighbourhood for *The Advocate*. Would this level of scrutiny be raised across the board? Were librarians hotly questioned over ordering boating magazines in landlocked Albany, too? Arguably, the Main Library ought to have had copies of *The Advocate* on the shelves, as the other large concentration of family was right across the way on Lark Street. But here we had black marks being doled out for questioning authority. If it is in the spirit of multiculturalism for us to collect for African Americans, Latinos, Irish Americans, and many other groups, why is there a double standard when it comes to collecting high quality gay materials? Queerness is in us every bit as much as skin tone, with an equal chance of it changing.

It wasn't all bad. There was always great puffery and sighing from the circulation desk managers when folks complained about our lack of gay literature. If one took the time to try and sort out this patron complaint, which was somewhat frequent, in general it was satisfied by a short tour of the library. The villain here was classification gone awry more than it was homophobia. But the latter kept informational inquiries from being properly addressed more often than not. There was something in the air that signaled to patrons that they were not welcome. It was strong enough that I can scarcely forget a coworker deciding to introduce her partner as her "lunch friend." When pressed gently about the terminology, she didn't yield much, so I often found myself smiling and winking at her "lunch friend." I've often wondered if that introduction led to a private upbraiding. Is that all we are to one another? Lunch friends?

~~~

At my next library, a tiny place it was, nestled in the Berkshires (by all means go in the fall if you've never been; the eruption of colour made the hour commute worth it when the snow was up to the edge of the wheel wells on my Toyota), it seemed like my sexuality was much less of a daily issue than it had been in the city. There were far fewer patrons to accommodate, the tiniest segment of which were gay. A couple of smart folks knew my leanings, but discussion was very limited. Ever polite. As much of a bad rap as rural folks get, I felt more welcome in the Berkshires than I have anywhere else barring Dublin. If one decided to discriminate, one would quickly find oneself with no one to talk to. There were a few people that decided to stick to their own bitterness and dated attitudes (there always are) but by no means were they in the majority.

Initially, the most I did at that tiny library was ensure that gay titles were pulled off of the bookmobile in case any of the locals had a problem with me ordering them directly with town funds. As it became evident that no one had a beef, I grew a little spine and ordered a few permanent additions of interest to the gay community. Many patrons of all stripes commented positively on how open I was to ordering whatever materials they wished to study. I ordered books on Eva Braun, the Marquis de Sade, the unexpurgated diary of Anne Frank. Doing what a Patron tells you to, even if it sends a shiver up the spine in a commingled collection, is the bottom line of librarianship. Do it with a smile and no hint of judgment and not only are your funding problems solved, but you'll also enjoy the deepest conversations humans share with one another.

The closest shave I had to being outed in that rural castle was during a discussion some teens were having. One of my clerks had come out a few weeks prior. A couple of the teens had been in lively electronic competition, frantically gaming with each other, and 'ere long, one was calling the other "gay" for lack of skill. A hush fell over the boisterous crowd of teens, and I was just about to get up and give them a talking to when they policed themselves. "Someone that works here is gay." I was clicking through my mental abacus, trying to figure out how they had figured me out, when I realised from further breathy gossip that they meant my brave clerk.

Even though I felt more welcome in a rural setting than an urban one, I felt my teens had zero support in coming to grips with their sexualities. Help was literally miles away. Rugged individualism isn't any comfort to a lost teen, though that copy of *Brokeback Mountain* or *Boys Don't Cry* may have been. How much are we keeping off of our shelves for pre-censorship's sake, anticipating the complaint that never surfaces? Does the cost in hassle-free collection development equal the cost of teen alienation? Is there a bookmobile sort of solution out there for all of us to explore? One grand, gay moveable collection?

~~~

Grants are the lifeblood of a small library. Every year we're called upon to lie to a funder about new revenue streams that are just round the corner if only we'd show initiative. So I found myself – an Indian stranded in a colonial setting overnight that gave me the creeps – having a discussion about my least favourite topic, me, in order to secure the almighty dollar. Should likeability factor into awarding a grant? No. Knowing that it did kept this discussion rolling, and I suspect that the consumption of alcohol didn't hurt in terms of the direction the conversation took. Among the clink of the glassware and the chatter of 40 or 50 librarians, the query was barely audible.

"Have you always been a woman?" Unless you're transgendered, I don't believe anyone ever really anticipates this question. I was so taken aback by it, that I believe I muttered a "Beg your pardon?" with a fervent prayer that the petitioner wouldn't have the guts to repeat herself. Alas, she did. I cast my eyes over to her superior, pleading for rescue, only to sink to the realisation that our side conversation wasn't heard over the noise of the dinner. My beloved second had gone home to her family, or she surely would have saved me from this. She was perfect for her ability to always say the right thing in any given situation, and I cursed her absence. I gulped, fumbling for the best choice of words to extricate myself, casting about for something, anything, to bring me back to *terra firma*. I settled on the mildly flirty: "I assure you that I have always been quite female." The goddess was clearly with me in giving me the ability to get those words out of my head and into the air without a stammer. I have ever been plagued by stuttering brought on by the sheer beauty of clever women.

I felt like it was a good compromise between the harsh, "None of your damn business," and the far – too-cute-for-my-own-good: "I don't usually consider blondes with your pedigree to be in my league, madame." And it was most certainly superior to naughtier comments about more solid ways to verify one's findings.

When I got back to my library, I ran this whole scenario by my second to see if she found it odd, and I had to spend the next half hour talking her down from a tree amidst allegations of sexual harassment. In retrospect, I suppose it's a fair question: I do have a deeper voice; I do dress like a man; most people never actually meet my husband; when I write, I use my initials instead of my full name. (Even if I did use my full name, it's still gender neutral. My Board never knew if they were going to be interviewing a male or female, and they wisely decided in the end that it didn't matter.)

I didn't feel like she meant to make me feel that awkward; it was raw curiosity. Yet the event made me feel compassion for transgendered people. Is it really of substance that they are what they are if that's not what they were in the past? Does their personal story really have an impact on anything in public? Should they have to stomach someone prying into their identity? In terms of application, would it really be that difficult to have unisex bathrooms when we design a new building?

~~~

The Secret Life of Bis

In the larger frame of bi rights, is this how it will always be? Are we forever relegated to the backwater? That lonely alley between straight and gay? We have our feet in two canoes. There's no way straight people get us. Conversely, I often comment that one of the reasons I don't feel terribly at home in the gay community is that it seems like every year we add a letter to our LGBTQ acronym, and yet I'm just three letters in and still don't feel particularly welcome. May the 40 little gods help the trans folks and the questioners and queers.

Maybe "real" gays don't marry their best friend who happens to be a straight guy, but there was a time before him, that I held my fiancée early in the morning after our testosterone filled male neighbours heaved a chair through the glass panel of our front door. The police left the matter with a knock on their door and a warning. I'm not sure they would have filed a report in the event of injury. Add to that raw night the Army hazing I endured, when my fellows must have spotted her and me hand-in-hand elsewhere on campus, and I've lived my share of prejudice. It's paralysing to not be afforded the same liberties a straight person enjoys in terms of public displays of affection. Would you know what to do as a loyal bowman when the world's most gorgeous blonde leans back into your lap in the boat, looks up at you with gorgeous blue eyes, and smiles an incapacitating smile? I might be too young to have been around for Stonewall, but I'm old enough to know that we're here, we're queer, and folks still ain't used to it.

Not to say that I've never felt pride. There were nights at the George in Dublin that were heady. Oh the good discussions there over cider! Oh the scandalously straight dirty dancing with that skinny redheaded bloke. I'm certain we were nearly tossed out on a few occasions. Further in time, there was the moment I couldn't speak for an attractive young lady placing me at the local Pride parade. I made a mental note right then and there that I'd better well not miss a pride parade ever again if it meant being able to receive divine inspiration.

~~~

Getting down to business, as open as the Library and Information Science community is, do our shelves reflect ourselves? I had an enchanting conversation with a colleague about my perception that the field was disproportionately populated by family, as well as a juicier conversation about flirting with the same sex versus flirting with the opposite. When I donned a chef's jacket, I felt like the restaurant community was one big rainbow. Folks well know the likelihood of one of their favourite Hollywood actors not batting for the straight team. Yet you won't catch too many homophobes steering clear of the cinema or eating out. In appealing to the mainstream, are we burying too much of our values? In doing so, are we missing a service opportunity? Do we have to add the *Lambda* to our out of scope of the collection "See Also" list? Is this sinister, or innocent? I believe it to be the latter, and the evidence I would present on that would be a glance at your library's professional collection. We, like other care providers, tend to ourselves last. So will the HQ7xs perpetually be the last box on our collection development checklists?

While I'm on that, does anyone else feel that sinking stomach when we come to the realisation that our place on the shelves is between the deviates and the masochists? There's something great in all of us in having to quest by all of that paraphilia to find a book.

What about reference? How do we tread the line between "approachable to the gay community" and "palatable to mainstream patrons"? I'm not saying that all of the straight population would be turned off if we wore beads or another visual clue for our petitioners, but I'm not living in a fantasy land where all strokes work for all folks. Do we have enough data yet on queer questions asked electronically versus in person?

What about recognition? We have the GLBT Round Table Stonewall Book Awards; we have the *New York Times* Librarian of the Year; but do we have an amalgamation for folks brave enough to be out in the field?

I suppose the inevitable anti-conclusion I'm coming to is this: the further I get from my own narrative, the closer I come to saying that there is much work to be done collectively. The harder the writing gets, I find myself able to make fewer statements. As the sands of our history shift with rulings like *Lawrence v. Texas* and actions like the Vermont Legislature's, and we're deluged by pictures of gay couples getting hitched, what are we doing in parallel within the field? How are we building our house? How is it that we can best continue, including those on the down low, as well as those that are out and proud? Where do we go from here?

Passing Tips and Pronoun Police: A Guide to Transitioning at Your Local Library

K.R. Roberto

When I began my career as a librarian, I was a queer female cataloger. Now I'm a queer male cataloger, and removing that one syllable has been quite a trip.

~~*~~

I was raised Catholic by a couple of depressive fatalists, so it never occurred to me that I could change anything about myself; even if it had, my childhood was traumatic enough that I quickly learned to live in my head in order to avoid anything resembling reality. As a kid, I didn't really feel all that much like a girl, but I took that as just another one of my immutable and frustrating qualities, much like my predilections for misbehavior and sloth. I didn't particularly feel like a boy, either, so I just didn't think about it and continued to sass my elders and avoid my chores. I visited the public library every Saturday to check out the maximum number of books I was allowed, did reasonably well in school considering my love of procrastination, and got labeled as the smart one in the family; if forced to do so, I would describe my prepubescent gender as "androgynous bookworm."

Despite multiple readings of *Are You There God? It's Me, Margaret*, I was genuinely appalled when puberty came around. While I recognized what was involved during that very special time in a girl's life, it never occurred to me that this meant I was going to have my own special time. To be fair, I should note that I wasn't all that worried about the salient physical characteristics I was getting, I just didn't want to deal with all the care that this would require. Shaving my underarms and legs? Dealing with pads and tampons once a month? To hell with all of that. I wanted to stay in the low-maintenance body I'd had in fifth grade, but I knew that was impossible.

Fortunately, peer pressure kicked in about a millisecond after this realization, so I quickly become a boy-crazy fashion plate. This was in the late 80s and involved many horrible appearance decisions; luckily, I can now pretend that my gender identity disorder was obviously to blame for my innumerable bad accessorizing and hairstyling choices. Transsexuality works as a better excuse for ridiculous teenage actions than it really should, but you do have to have a sex change to get away with using it, so it probably isn't for everyone. This Awesome Beloved Teen Girl archetype also involved pretending to be less intelligent than I actually was, so I started deliberately misspelling words and avoiding the library. Since my urge to check out twelve books a week hadn't actually dissipated, though, I tried to visit the library in secret. "Oh, I'm just here to do my homework! It's not like I *like* to read or anything! What are *you* doing here?" (My speech was heavily italicized from ages 12 to 14.) Was this insipid behavior caused by my desperate wish to successfully present as female, or by the patriarchal, biologically essentialist power structure that bombards young women with messages on what successful womanhood should entail? Pick two. By the time high school rolled around, I had become a sullen alternateen who wore a lot of black and was perpetually growing her bangs out. This identity made it okay to visit the library, but you had to read Anne Rice. My gender dysphoria popped up in odd ways, like when I told a friend of mine I wished I were male so I could treat her right, and the six months or so I spent trolling gay chat lines pretending to be a twink named Sean.

College found me interested in punk and hardcore, and reading Noam Chomsky instead of melodramatic vampire novels. This was when Riot Grrrl was first becoming popular, and angry punk feminism fit nicely into the self-righteous radical left punk persona I'd formed by then. During my junior year of college, I realized that a bachelor's degree in anthropology was not going to magically make me employable, so in the time-honored tradition of liberal arts students everywhere, I decided to get a master's degree. I was tired of anthropology and was searching for a new field to explore. A friend of mine from South Carolina had just started a graduate program in library and information science, mostly because an ex of his had talked him into it. Continuing in another time-honored tradition of liberal arts students everywhere, I told myself that I would make a great librarian because I loved books and wanted to bring information to the people. I spent that summer investigating LIS programs and my sexual orientation, two topics that resulted in my spending a lot of time in the wonderfully air-conditioned university library. When I wasn't using the library computer lab to find LGBTQ information, I was browsing the stacks to find out where they kept all the homo books. I am one of the people who identified their sexuality by looking at materials classed in HQ76. Talk about time-honored traditions, right?

After numerous library trips, I finally came out as queer, and it felt so *right*. It still does. Sexual orientation and gender expression have been socially linked for decades, so it was very easy to rewrite any gender ambiguity on my part as a physical manifestation of my queerness, especially since I considered myself an equal opportunity dater who didn't take gender into consideration. It wasn't that I was unsuccessfully female at all; there were multiple ways to be female, and my gender was just one of these ways. I was delighted to have discovered a theoretical framework that allowed me to stop worrying about gender. I figured I could stop worrying about that and get down to the business of becoming a radical reference librarian.

I spent the first semester of library school in a state of abject terror, convinced that I'd made the worst mistake of my life; on the first day of classes, I went to my cataloging class, and was handed a printout of a text string that was supposed to be a MARC record, whatever that was. I went home in tears and dropped the class shortly thereafter. I didn't know what any of the acronyms meant, I couldn't understand the jargon, and none of my classmates seemed to have any problems. (Obviously, this was before I realized that everyone in grad school fakes it till they make it.) I somehow fell in with a couple of Hennepin County Library catalogers who introduced me to the delightful Sandy Berman and his incessant work towards user-centered cataloging. I greatly admired his achievements, and still do, but I was terrified of cataloging and vowed to never do any if I could help it. Naturally, I was then offered a graduate assistantship that required me to catalog materials, and taking a cataloging course was a prerequisite. The HCL Sandynistas must have been a terrible influence upon me, because I enjoyed the job and decided I wanted to become a cataloger who never worked with the public. I graduated from library school and started on the career path that made me the world-famous millionaire cataloger I am today.

My first professional positions mostly involved improving my cataloging skills and participating in library melodrama. Over the years, acute gender dysphoria slowly made its presence known. I realized that I didn't fit into the binary gender system all that well, and the internet helped me discover the word "genderqueer," which is a term used to describe exactly that. This led to a good number of years where I obsessed over my gender identity and compartmentalized the entire process. I was female-identified at work, and some flavor of transgender almost everywhere else; as I've never really been able to completely separate my personal and professional lives, this was incredibly difficult to do. After a few years, it was pretty clear that I was of the female-to-male (FTM) persuasion, and that made the juggling act far more precarious. Eventually, I was out as male to queer colleagues I knew through the American Library Association, and living as female among my actual coworkers; since I hadn't yet taken any steps towards physical transition, such as surgeries and hormone treatments, I was able to keep faking them out. I spent a lot of time at conferences worrying that the two groups would collide and that my secret gender would be a secret no more. In some ways, I was reminded of my undercover teenage library visits. "Oh, I was just having people call me 'he' for a social experiment! What are *you* doing here?"

Basically, that's what happened. The situation at my job had become very stressful for a number of reasons, including the fact that I had started presenting as male at work and felt as if I was walking around with a target painted on my back. I decided to look for jobs in areas where I might feel comfortable at least *thinking* about living full-time as male. I applied for a position in an area where I already knew a few queer librarians, one of whom suggested I use her as a reference. Since she was a good colleague – and, better yet, friends with librarians on the search committee – I took her up on it. The search committee checked my references via phone interviews, and whoever talked to her used male pronouns to refer to me. Since my friend knew I was FTM, she didn't correct the person; unfortunately, my friend didn't know that I wasn't out to any of my other references. The members of the search committee, possibly being more perceptive than the people who actually employed me at the time, noticed the incongruity, but invited me to interview regardless. About a week before the interview, the library's human resources person called and alerted me to the issue. She said they wanted me to be comfortable during my interview, and wanted to know what my preferred pronouns were. After pausing for several milliseconds to have a panic attack while appreciating their thoughtfulness, I mumbled my wish for male pronouns. Then I hung up the phone and promptly lost consciousness.

Okay, that last part is a lie. While they did really call me, I didn't really pass out afterward. My reaction was more along the lines of "oh-my-god-how-did-they-find-out-oh-my-god-this-is-totally-scary-oh-my-god-DOES

THIS MEAN I COULD TRANSITION AT WORK?!" Surprisingly enough, my interview went very well; they were impressed with my depth and breadth of experience and won over by the charm I somehow managed to ooze. They offered me the position. I accepted and promptly outed myself to a good sixty or so librarians I knew professionally, including former coworkers, most of whom reacted incredibly well. I scheduled a transition-related surgery. I started this new job, where I was going to be immediately accepted as male and have the happy ending I richly deserved. Right?

Well, not quite. Starting a new job is like falling in love; you start taking everything at face value, promptly forgetting that you are both selling yourselves as better specimens than you actually are. I'm pretty sure I sounded wildly enthusiastic about cataloging serials on microfiche, which is not exactly true. My new employer sounded as if they dealt with transgender staff all the time, which is also not exactly true. I figured this out pretty quickly, though I'm still not sure how many of them know that I am not wildly in love with microfiche. (To keep this secret safe, I may have to carefully vet my library's copy of this book before it gets cataloged. Not that I would ever advocate deliberately defacing library materials. Ahem.) My coworkers didn't have much experience with a trans colleague, but I didn't have much experience *being* a trans colleague, so ultimately we were well matched. Things were very awkward at first, and there was some initial confusion about how best to classify me as male (weak pun fully intended) when my legal documentation clearly said female. As much as my gender-nonconforming self wishes this hadn't been the case, the fact that I hadn't started any physical transitioning before starting this job did make things difficult; I had hoped that my gender expression and magical ability to grow the facial hair of a twelve-year-old boy would automatically lead to people calling me "he," but this didn't always happen. In their defense, my coworkers would look utterly mortified after mixing up my pronouns, which I took as evidence of their good intentions. Once we clarified the response I wanted to see in this situation – which, for the record, was for the errant pronouner to look utterly mortified and then use "he" – things got much better. It seemed that people meant well but were clueless about what to do, so removing the cluelessness was a real help.

My gender long ago ceased to be any sort of novelty in the library. I'd like to think it's because I've been working there for nearly three years and everyone's used to it, but my starting hormone therapy is the more likely cause. Once my voice dropped to a baritone and I grew the facial hair of a *fifteen*-year-old boy, most people I encountered didn't think of me as anything but male, albeit a flaming one. The idea that I now "pass," that people usually consider me unequivocally male, is surprising to me, though not exactly in a bad way. I wish that I'd been able to command the respect I needed considerably earlier in this process, but I'm relieved to receive it at all. That said, it is pretty ludicrous that I should feel grateful and lucky to have coworkers who respect my identity and administrators who didn't fire me for transitioning. It hasn't always been easy, but things have mostly worked themselves out. This isn't to say that everything is perfect and my coworkers are now knowledgeable enough to facilitate Trans 101 workshops, but we've all survived. There is so much work that still needs to be done everywhere, not just where I work.

And now, as promised by this piece's title, here is a guide to transitioning at your local library. These are guidelines that have been useful for numerous transgender library workers, including me (that's right, we walk among you; why, your workplace bestie might be trans without your even knowing it!). Of course, your own experiences may differ wildly from what is listed below.

1. Contrary to traditional advice, you need not move to another part of the country and start a new life before transitioning, though you will probably wish you had at several points during the process. It is a very good idea to have some idea of what level of stealthness and/or outness you're willing to have; it is an even better idea to realize that this will probably be situational and may very well change over time. If you were already professionally active before transitioning, don't expect that knowledge to magically disappear; thanks to co-editing a book before transition, I have the Library of Congress authority record to prove it. That said, don't assume that you'll have no choice but to always be out due to running for ALA president in a previous manifestation. After all, I can always change my authority record to eliminate references to my old name if the spirit moves me. (However, I am far too bibliographically noble to do so; at least, that's what I like to say.)

2. While transitioning from one gender to another is very processual in nature, do not expect your colleagues to automatically understand this unless they've had a lot of therapy or frequently use phrases like "tip of the iceberg." Some of them may be unable to grasp the concept until they see changes they consider to be concrete, such as a legal name change and/or changes in your physical appearance. On a bright note, if you have had these changes and they still refuse to accept it, you may now shun them with a clear conscience. At some point, they will look very silly using the incorrect name and pronouns for you while everyone else has it right. When that happens, feel free to smile serenely, not unlike the Mona Lisa.

3. If your library doesn't already have a strong collection of LGBTQ materials, this is a good time to subtly urge your coworkers to start one. Librarians love building diverse collections and using this as evidence to demonstrate that diversity training is unnecessary, so you may as well use this opportunity to acquire all the wildly expensive books and DVDs on this topic that you can. After all, the transgender library users that you undoubtedly have, whether you realize it or not, might not want to shell out money for personal copies of those expensive documentaries either.

4. Accept that you will be That Transgender Library Staffer for a while, just because this may be new and unusual at your work, and because people love to gossip. If you become heavily involved in workplace activism, you may ultimately become That Angry Transsexual Library Staffer Who Ruins Everything. Enjoyable as you may find such an epithet to be (guilty as charged right here), it doesn't look that good on business cards and may prevent you from becoming That Brilliant Transgender Library Staffer or, alternatively, That Angry Library Staffer Who Ruins Everything. Either way, your trans identity will be really intriguing for a while, but something more intriguing will eventually replace it.

5. Resign yourself to the fact that at some point you will have to educate others on how to be a good ally, in spite of the fact that continually forcing oppressed groups to enlighten the dominant group does not disrupt their privilege and only reinforces marginalization. Resist the urge to point out that your coworkers work in a library and should be able to look things up themselves, since this may be viewed as uncollegial and, worse yet, not very librarianly. No good library worker would refuse to answer a reference question, after all. If possible, get bonus points by using this as a teachable moment that demonstrates the need for a stronger collection. See #3.

6. Identify potential allies and put them to work. This will help with any feelings of isolation you may encounter. Also, correcting people's pronoun slips gets exhausting if you're the only one who will do it. The odds are very high that you have at least one coworker who desperately wants to Get It, so use this to your advantage. It's win-win.

7. Most importantly, just remember that no matter how frustrating your colleagues can be, *you can get through this*. Realizing you're transgender, let alone making tangible decisions about it, is genuinely difficult. Compared to that, cataloging, handling problem patrons, negotiating license agreements, and even finding a new job or filing discrimination charges, if need be, are relatively easy. Don't give in to the haters.

Part Four:
Coming Out in Time

Out Lines:
An LGBT Career in Perspective

Robert Ridinger

In the early years of the gay liberation movement, there were many slogans that attempted to translate a previously invisible population into the sunlight of visibility and, ideally, acceptance as full citizens. One of the most memorable was the phrase "the personal is political." For gay or lesbian librarians seeking to integrate their reality and culture into their work lives, a better formulation would be "the personal is professional."

Such an approach to being "out" (a concept that has many definitions) has taken me down many fascinating and challenging roads in the nearly three decades that I have served as a member of the library faculty at Northern Illinois University.

The road began with my appointment in 1981 as Subject Specialist for Anthropology, Sociology, and Geography, which also included collection development and bibliographic instruction responsibilities for these disciplines, as well as the fields of Black Studies, Women's Studies, and the emerging Latino/Latin American Studies program. In the process of learning my way around my new campus and reentering the American academic world after serving as a Peace Corps Volunteer Librarian at the National University of Lesotho for three years, I became aware that there were, and had been, faculty members in the social sciences at NIU who had conducted gay-related research as early as 1974, thus making this topic an acceptable part of the local landscape of scholarship and professional involvement.

My primary initial involvement with gay materials at work took the form of asking that the paper copies of *The Advocate* be sent to me when removed from the periodicals collection. The few copies that survived the public's attention raised my awareness that there was an entire genre of publications that was missing from most of the mainstream indexing sources, and research into the availability of such news sources on microfilm indicated that this was an option, but that it would be a major effort to track them down. Thus, in the autumn of 1982, I decided to create an index to the first 15 years of *The Advocate* as my research contribution to qualify for tenure in the University Libraries, an eventually successful project that lasted for three years and gave me an in-depth lesson in the problems at the intersection of gay materials and professional library practice.

Once the project was underway, I contacted Barbara Gittings of the Gay Task Force of the American Library Association to keep her informed of its progress and to ensure that nothing similar was underway elsewhere. Barbara responded with enthusiastic support and invited me to be a speaker on the Task Force's program at the 1985 annual convention in Chicago. The news that I had been asked to appear on an ALA panel as a speaker was received by the Department Head to whom I reported, Dr. Joseph Parot, with approval, as I had kept him informed of my work. His own research and publication on the Polish community in Chicago had made him familiar with the need to explore and retrieve local history sources. My presentation was well received, and marked the expansion of my involvement with LGBT librarianship from the local to the national scene, taking my "workplace" to a new and diverse clientele.

Part of the reason for my success was due to the history of Northern Illinois University in the area of gay rights, a story that began in 1970, with the creation of a campus Gay Liberation Front, which evolved into the Gay and Lesbian Union student group, whose name was later changed to the Lesbian/Gay/Bisexual Coalition. The presence and activity of such a group on campus provided a focus for the discussion of gay rights issues from a civil rights perspective as part of university life, and raised awareness of incidents of verbal harassment, vandalism, and written threats to gay and lesbian individuals.

In 1988, Article IX of the University Constitution was revised to state that all members of the University community should be entitled to "fair, impartial and equal treatment regardless of any factor unrelated to scholarly or professional performance, including sexual orientation" ("Building Community" 10). This action provided all openly gay or lesbian faculty with a level of protection that had not existed when I began my indexing project six years before.

On October 30, 1991, officers of the Gay and Lesbian Union met with then – President John LaTourette and other University administrators to submit a seven-page proposal for the creation of a "Presidential

Commission on Gay, Lesbian, and Bisexual Concerns," citing a range of anti-gay actions on campus. On January 13, 1992, the birth of the Task Force on Discrimination Based on Sexual Orientation was announced. I attended the initial meeting of the Task Force, and was appointed to it (the only member of the University Libraries faculty appointed), eventually serving as its recording secretary for the period of its deliberations. This involved not only keeping detailed minutes of each diverse (and sometimes contentious) meeting, but also spending a good portion of the 1992 Christmas break transcribing the results of the detailed campus survey on LGBT issues that the Task Force had designed and distributed. The frank comments from faculty and students ranged from departments where being closeted was a necessity, to open and accepting work environments with supportive colleagues. During the two years the Task Force was in operation, I also served as its researcher. When I mentioned this to LGBT colleagues from other academic institutions (both public and private) during ALA Midwinter and Annual Conferences, their reactions usually took the form of "I wish my school had something like that."

The Task Force's final report, "Building Community: The Inclusion of Gays, Lesbians and Bisexuals," issued in September 1993, prompted the creation of the Presidential Commission on Sexual Orientation and Gender Identity in 1994. Due to my history of involvement with the Task Force, as well as my ongoing research and publication in the field of LGBT librarianship, I was asked to serve on the Commission (later upgraded to full University Committee status).

With the successful (if turbulent) process of achieving tenure successfully completed in the spring of 1986, I continued to work at researching and writing about the status of gay and lesbian materials in librarianship. This became one of my areas of expertise, and led to an expectation among my colleagues that any topic that had anything to do with being gay was something I would be able to clarify for them (an attractive, if sometimes inaccurate, notion); however, their willingness to ask questions often allowed me to de-mythologize subjects unfamiliar to them.

The fact that I continued to write and publish on gay and lesbian subjects and maintain active involvement with the Anthropology and Sociology section of the Association of College and Research Libraries (ACRL), as well the Gay, Lesbian, Bisexual, and Transgendered Round Table (GLBTRT),[1] placed my work in a context that made it comprehensible to my colleagues. That most of the University Libraries faculty were

---

1. The name taken by the Gay Task Force at its reorganization in 1986 upon the resignation of Barbara Gittings.

engaged in writing and publication in various fields relating to their academic credentials also assisted me in having my work taken seriously by both my immediate colleagues and the Dean of Libraries. The *Index to The Advocate* was succeeded by two in-depth annotated bibliographies: *The Homosexual and Society* and *The Gay and Lesbian Movement: References and Resources*. I was careful not to make gay studies the *only* focus of my library-related writings however, and explored the literature of the archaeology of Africa and India, as well as compiling a research bibliography on the Peace Corps. Engaging in this diverse range of scholarship kept my interest in the field from going stale through sheer exhaustion, and allowed me to investigate subjects of interest to fill other gaps in the reference literature in anthropology.

A second new venue for LGBT writing that fit well with NIU librarianship was the emergence in the early 1990s of several major reference book projects specifically focused on gay and lesbian subjects. The first of these was *Gay and Lesbian Literature,* followed in 1995 by the *Gay and Lesbian Literary Heritage,* and in 1997 by the *St. James Press Gay and Lesbian Biography.* Through writing a number of pieces for each of these works, I gained a greater knowledge of much of the LGBT literature of the twentieth century, which was directly useful in my reference work and collection development duties. My work on assembling a complete back set of the Chicago community newspaper *Gay Life* (with the assistance of the late Joseph Gregg of the Gerber-Hart Library) and arranging for its preservation on microfilm led me both to work on assembling a research collection on microfilm of the gay press of the Midwest at NIU (massively expanding the NIU holdings in this area and creating a new permanent strength for the University Libraries) and to contribute to library literature a piece assessing the status of efforts in this area to date, which I called "We've Been Framed: Microfilm Technology and the Gay and Lesbian Press." This combination of being able to translate personal questions into professional research that filled gaps in the available literature was very stimulating.

In 1997, I learned of a project originating in Ontario to assemble a volume of the reflections of LGBT librarians, the first such compilation, and contacted the editor, Norman Kester, with the idea of telling the history of the *Index to The Advocate* project and its consequences. I felt that this was essential to do both to create a record of exactly how the problems of indexing the gay and lesbian press had been addressed, and also because several of the people I had worked with, such as Joseph Gregg, had died of AIDS since 1986, leaving me as the only surviving member of some of the early projects still able to tell the tale. Kester was enthusiastic about including this piece of the history of LGBT librarianship, and the article that eventually appeared in print as "Playing in the Attic: Indexing and Preserving the Gay Press" began to form.

The late 1990s also brought the opportunity of serving as a member of the Stonewall Book Award Committee of the GLBTRT, a committee that selects the Stonewall Book Awards in fiction and nonfiction. After completion of my term in 1999, I was faced with the question of what to do with the large pile of titles that remained from the previous two years work of review and assessment. Knowing that other awards had been used as the basis of special collections elsewhere (and the absence of any collection of record for the Stonewall Awards in any American library), prompted me to approach Glen Gildemeister, then-head of our rare books area, with the idea that NIU become the home for such a unique body of material. He was very much in favor of the notion, and thus the Stonewall books became the nucleus of what would shortly be renamed the Gender Studies collection. Glen's successor, Lynne Thomas, supported the new collection, accepting the books I carted home from each year's Book Awards breakfast and filling in the gaps from her own budget. A second tour of duty on the Committee from 2008–2010 gave me a chance to see how extensive the changes in LGBT writing had been in the last decade.

In 1992, my partner moved to the Chicago area and brought with him the opportunity to charter a new chapter of the Trident International, a gay men's leather/levi club, which had originated nearly twenty years before in Montreal and then spread to the United States. In the process of obtaining a charter and setting up a home base at one of the Chicago bars to allow for meetings and fundraisers, I became aware that there was no written history of the International, and began gathering information on the other Trident chapters, both current and defunct. Our chapter also affiliated with the Mid America Conference of Clubs (MACC), an organization of similar groups founded in 1974, and with a geographical coverage from Minnesota to Louisiana and Ohio to Nebraska. Wanting to learn more about this community's past, I asked about reading its history – only to learn that there had never been an historian of the group, and that no such printed history existed. The idea that so much history of this part of the gay and lesbian Midwest was in danger of vanishing was one I could not stand to think about, and so I began informally to gather information from senior members of each of the member clubs, gradually piecing together a coherent picture of the past.

In the second year of my work on these histories, an announcement appeared in the national leather community press of the formation of a project on a national scale that paralleled the work I had been doing for the

Tridents and the MACC. Led by Chicago businessman Chuck Renslow, the new organization took the name of the Leather Archives and Museum. Fearing that this group might attempt to duplicate some of the research I had already completed, I contacted one of the Board members, Dr. Anthony De Blasé. He was very interested to hear about my work and invited me to be a member of a panel on the subject of leather community history and its research problems to be held at a national meeting in Portland, Oregon in the autumn of 1996. This was the first time my blending of the personal and professional with regards to the leather community would be highlighted in a national forum, and I looked forward to discussing the issues of finding and preserving primary sources with others who had been working in this field. It was not until I was actually in Portland and discussing my work that I became aware that there was no similar history of a regional leather/levi conference in existence anywhere in the United States. My work was far more cutting-edge than I had imagined, and De Blasé invited me to become a part of the LAM as a staff librarian, as most of the work of collection and organization that had been done thus far had been carried out by a small group of volunteers without library training. From 1993 onward, I worked with the Archives, first at its initial storefront space on Clark Street in Chicago, and later at its building near the campus of Loyola University, fulfilling the requirement of the University Libraries in the category of community service. This unique opportunity to aid in the formation of a major research institution offered professional challenges on a level I had not met with since my time as a Peace Corps volunteer. In 2001, I was asked to stand for election to the Board of Directors of the Archives and have served as one of its two academic members since that time.

In 2000, I decided to tackle an area of primary sources in LGBT studies that had not been previously assembled into book form – or even addressed in such basic works as Katz' *Gay American History* – the speeches given by activists at various events over the years. Haworth Press (then-publisher of the *Journal of Homosexuality*) found the idea interesting, and so began four years of sifting through the past. One notable feature of this project was the degree of networking I was able to do with veterans of the gay rights movement and the lesbian feminist movement through the good offices of Barbara Gittings and especially Barbara Grier of Naiad Press. Being able to contact someone such as author Sally Gearhart and tell her that "Barbara Grier said I should call you," opened doors to me that might well have been impossible to find otherwise. The remarkable thing about seeking these ephemeral pieces of LGBT history was that so many of them were referenced in publications such as *The Advocate,* but so few of the actual texts seemed to have survived, posing a major problem for librarians and later historians. Another surprise was that the gay and lesbian press had, in the main, only occasionally reprinted such speeches in full, usually contenting themselves with striking quotations in the context of a feature article. The work eventually appeared (with a striking wintergreen cover) in 2004, dedicated to the poet John Eric Larsen, who had died of AIDS in 2001. The title was subsequently adopted by the Gay/Lesbian/Bisexual/Transgender Communication Studies Division of the National Communication Association for a panel discussion: *Speaking for Our Lives: Rhetorical Artifacts of the Lesbian and Gay Rights Movement,* held during its ninetieth conference on November 11, 2004, in Chicago. It was chaired by a colleague from Northern Illinois University's Department of Communication, Dr. Robert Brookey, who invited me to serve as a panelist. Presenting my work on the range of LGBT rhetoric to a different academic audience outside librarianship proved to be both challenging and an illustration of how much more research there remained to be done on this aspect of LGBT history.

The field of LGBT studies at NIU had continued to evolve academically, based on a recommendation in the academic affairs section of the 1993 Task Force report that encouraged this area to be developed as a distinct program. Having a somewhat more flexible schedule than the other faculty members who were interested in working on this area, I served as coordinator for an interdisciplinary course in its first three incarnations between 1993 and 1997, whose success established precedent for the later creation of a certificate program in LGBT studies. The new program also sponsored monthly noontime seminars to highlight ongoing LGBT research through monthly public seminars, at one of which I told the tale of creating *Speaking for Our Lives.* The same years also saw the inauguration of an annual award recognizing NIU faculty, staff, alumni, and students who had "made significant contributions for the betterment of the lesbian, gay, bisexual, and transgender community, either locally, regionally, or nationally." Named for local pro-gay and PFLAG activists Howard and Millie Eychaner (who were its first recipients), these awards were inaugurated in 1995, adding a formal mechanism for the NIU LGBT community to honor its own.

In the spring of 2004, I received a phone call from Dr. Diana Swanson, informing me that I was to be the recipient of the 2004 Eychaner Award, the first faculty member to be so recognized. The basis for the nomination had been the variety of my work (both in the classroom and in print) that had begun with the first index card of *The Advocate* project 21 years before.

The sheer variety of workplace experiences (whether at the local level or working nationally) that I have walked through while integrating an LGBT identity into a professional library career has left me with a legacy of impressions. First, there are and will be as many definitions of "out" as there are librarians to claim them, each keyed to an individual's unique institutional situation, clientele, and regional cultural environment. And defining "activism" is equally problematic, because we must allow for flexibility within local contexts. Bringing politics into the workplace can best be done if it is remembered that issues familiar to members of the LGBT community may be totally unknown to workmates at all levels, or imperfectly understood. A low-key approach allows librarians to maintain a stable working relationship with colleagues and administrators, while at the same time opening up the chance for useful dialogue. The question of institutional limitations (whether cultural or legal) is one that should be carefully considered during the hiring process – accepting a job with the idea that "I'm going to change things when I get there" may result in mutual unhappiness, although the increased openness of many libraries to offer information on the status of LGBT people under their roofs (both online and face-to-face in the interview) shows that the overall climate of the profession has altered for the better in this respect. Researching LGBT topics can be worked into one's job description, no matter the type of library, if it is done with an eye toward this population as part of the client pool. Finally, it is up to every librarian who decides to be open in the workplace to choose a definition of that word that best suits his or her own ideas and interests. Your workplace begins at your desk – and how far "out" it extends into the wider electronically-linked universe is a question and challenge that must be answered with courage, determination, a touch of humor, and a sense of the possible.

Works Cited

"Building Community: The Inclusion of Gays, Lesbians and Bisexuals." *President's Task Force on Discrimination Based on Sexual Orientation.* De Kalb, IL:, Northern Illinois U, 1993. Print.

Constitution and By-Laws. Northern Illinois University. DeKalb, IL: University Council, Northern Illinois U, 1976. Print.

Gay and Lesbian Biography. Detroit: Gale, 1990. Print.

GayLife. Chicago: LifeStyle, 1975-1986. Print.

Katz, Jonathan. *Gay American History: Lesbians and Gay Men in the U.S.A.: A Documentary.* New York: Crowell, 1976. Print.

Malinowski, Sharon and Tom Pendergast. *Gay & Lesbian Literature.* Detroit: St. James, 1994–1998. Print.

Ridinger, Robert B. *An Index to The Advocate, The National Gay Newsmagazine, 1967–1982.* Los Angeles: Liberation Publications, 1987. Print.

-----. *The Homosexual and Society: An Annotated Bibliography.* New York: Greenwood, 1990. Print.

-----. *The Gay and Lesbian Movement: References and Resources.* New York: G.K. Hall; London: Prentice Hall International, 1996. Print.

-----. "We've Been Framed: Microfilm Technology and the Gay and Lesbian Press. *Microform and Imaging Review* v.25, n.2 (Spring 1996): 61–64. Print.

-----. "Playing in the Attic: Indexing and Preserving the Gay Press." *Liberating Minds: The Stories and Professional Lives of Gay, Lesbian, and Bisexual Librarians and Their Advocates.* Ed. Norman G. Kester. Jefferson, N.C.: McFarland, 1997. 92–97. Print.

-----. *Speaking for Our Lives: Historic Speeches and Rhetoric for Gay and Lesbian Rights (1892–2000).* New York: Harrington Park, 2004. Print.

Summers, Claude J. *The Gay and Lesbian Literary Heritage: A Reader's Companion to the Writers and Their Works, From Antiquity to the Present.* New York: H. Holt, 1995. Print.

Outness and Social Networks: From Closet to Container Store

Lia Friedman

For many of us, juggling multiple social media personas is becoming a familiar phenomenon. Many librarians balance professional and personal online presences, and grapple with the implications of friending colleagues, students, and bosses in the same digital spaces as friends and high school classmates. This intersection of worlds creates a disconnect between what social networks are supposed to facilitate (openness), and what they afford in reality (negotiation).

This dynamic can be further complicated by non-normative gender expression, sexual orientation, or other socio-politically fraught aspects of one's identity, the expression of which becomes a central aspect of the negotiation. When we friend colleagues, students, and bosses, we engage in strategic decision-making: should we add them to dialed-down profiles, or into our "honest pages," where we might tout our love of queer square-dancing and Drag King shows? Sharing queer identities in personal/professional social networks means negotiating degrees of outness: stages of caution and revealing based on the character of our institutional and personal affiliations.

In examining the ability of social media to separate and compartmentalize our lives, does the traditional process of personal/private queer identity negotiation take on an entirely different character? Or is it simply an example of how coming out is an ongoing process adaptation that follows the wider continuum of our lives? Separate work-specific Flickr, Facebook, or Twitter accounts make it simple to facilitate a work/life division, but what effect does this have on the analog relationships that merge across these spaces, not to mention the work it takes to juggle them?

Online spaces are used to connect, communicate, and share; they also require the user to self-define according to the following social attributes.

- **Identity:** who are you?
- **Reputation:** what do people think you stand for?
- **Presence:** where are you?
- **Relationships:** who are you connected with? who do you trust?
- **Groups:** how do you organize your connections?
- **Conversations:** what do you discuss with others?
- **Sharing:** what content do you make available for others to interact with? (Connolly)

It could be argued that until the most recent generation, gays and lesbians came of age in the "era of the closet," with identity and perception being key to how one moved through both personal and professional worlds, and with appearances closely tied to that identity and perception (Seidman 87). What, then, does it mean to be out in the era of social networks, when "internet use is developing as an important part of the management of an emerging individual gay identity ... [some going] so far as to suggest that internet use may even become an additional stage in the coming-out process" (Henrickson)? To my many friends with queered online identities, I ask: is coming out in the age of the social web somehow easier than when coming out was exclusively negotiated in the "real world"?

Irrespective of queer affiliation, there are degrees of social acceptability in any public expression of sexuality. Think about it: did you avoid sharing those pictures of you and your partner at Pride on a work-connected account out of fear of retribution, or because you both happened to be wearing assless chaps? If we only allow ourselves to "like" the Tom of Finland Foundation Library in an analog sense rather than the Facebook sense, are we perpetuating internalized self-censorship? This dynamic suggests the emergence of a new digital slant to the notion of "passing." Might we now (consciously or unconsciously) create normative, vanilla versions of our digital selves in order to be more palatable to our extended professional communities, however progressive they might be?

By virtue of the pervasive library social web, it is now almost impossible to be digitally circumspect if we are active in our communities of practice. Separation between personal and professional, between "real" and academic life, was simpler to maintain before online networking. The time when lady librarians living together were immediately assumed to be roommates, when bachelors were assumed to be no more than professionally devoted, is long past. So in the short span between *The Children's Hour* and your queer librarians of color conference we now share so much personal information that there is almost no point to workplace speculation. Before the advent of collective online identity formation, it was simply not possible for us to know so much about each other so easily or immediately.

Technical affordances in the array of social networks provide different strategies for managing degrees of outness. Much of this has to do with how closely we are able to define and manage communication with our digital "audience." Consider the difference between Facebook, where your network may be large but you can still control who sees what within a defined orbit, versus Twitter, where a tongue-in-cheek comment that might have been understood by a more defined network could potentially (and probably will) be retweeted into the social stratosphere comprised of individuals who have little-to-no knowledge of your politics, gender, or other affiliations.

Because social media allow us to control the content we share within our networks, they also afford us the ability to shape the conversations we once engaged in outside of those networks, including the interminable dialogues that surround the coming-out process. Some see this open field of social transparency as a backdoor boon: coming out becomes a lot more streamlined if all 400 of your friends see you listed as in a relationship with a same sex partner, which is the homo equivalent of not having to answer the same questions over and over at your high school reunion. Perhaps another affordance of digital media is structured avoidance: online forums can provide the means for mutual escapism from difficult conversations, precluding or substituting conflict that is an inherent part of human relationships. For its part, dealing with a homophobic family member or coworker in person and dealing with them online seems little changed: one can easily unfriend or delete a snide comment, but painful memories are similarly impossible to erase.

This raises a fascinating dichotomy: assumption versus declaration. If online forums can subvert the real-time negotiations that can be so difficult to manage among acquaintances, how "out" do we have to be to assure that we are recognized? Am I seen as closeted or out because I don't denote my relationship status, post frequently on GLBT issues and events, or belong to groups like Transgender Librarians? Should I assume that people believe I am a socialist (which, I'm not) because I post articles from socialist journals? Obviously, my straight colleagues don't have to come out as straight; they are the social default, and need only mention a legal spouse or post a wedding photo to enjoy the safety and privilege of not having to negotiate their identity to quite the same degree of urgency. This, again, addresses the degrees of outness. Is it easier to let the assumption float out there without having to declare? To be the poster boy for good queers?

Those of us lucky enough to be employed at libraries where queerness is accepted, even embraced, face a different reality than those who are employed at private (perhaps religious) institutions, where don't ask don't tell is the norm, and where one would never consider bringing a same sex or queered partner to a work function. It's possible that many of my non-California based colleagues may feel safer keeping their relationships to themselves no matter what the institution size or administration, or gender of their partner. It also must be noted that these same colleagues may be keeping to themselves because they feel that gender identity, sexuality, and relationship status on the whole is personal, and not a manifestation of the "post-closet era ... [where] many individuals no longer feel the need to hide their homosexuality." (Hutson).

Perhaps the most important affordance of queering social/professional networks will be acceptance through osmosis, and the slow subtle degradation of homophobia itself. If sexual orientation is reduced to nothing more than a "status," perhaps it can become as socially trivial as hometown, or favorite TV show. In this sense, maintaining a studied degree of digital/professional outness may therefore become a political act, with the potential to affect the fates of those of us not able to express our identities in more conservative contexts. Examine how you interact with those you work with in person and online, and consider this: how much does your sexual and/or gender identity (and the perception thereof) matter to your professional life? How important is it for us as librarians to occupy and express our queer selves, fully and without guile, in both the online and the analog workplace?

Works Cited

Connolly, Shaun. "7 Key Attributes of Social Web Applications." *Open Thoughts on Software, Business, Life. connollyshaun.blogspot. com.* Google, 24 May 2008. Web. 12 Aug. 2010.

Henrickson, M.. "Reaching out, hooking up: Lavender netlife in a New Zealand study." *Sexuality Research and Social Policy* 4.2 (2007): 38-49. Print.

Hutson, David J. "Standing OUT/Fitting IN: Identity, Appearance, and Authenticity in Gay and Lesbian Communities." *Symbolic Interaction* 33.2 (2010): 213–233. Print.

Seidman, Steven. *Beyond the Closet: The Transformation of Gay and Lesbian Life*. New York: Routledge, 2003. Print.

The Challenges of Coming and Being Out in Historical Perspective

Richard P. Hulser

My experience has ranged from being a librarian in academic and corporate environments when LGBT people could be fired for being gay, to living through the transition of it being more acceptable to be out in the workplace. Being out in the workplace, and in the library profession as well, helps others to realize that living with integrity about who we are will not be detrimental to our careers.

As with all things, deciding to be out at work was a progressive development for me. It started personally, but grew to positively affect others in both the workplace and the library profession in general. While working as a librarian at IBM in the 1980s, the corporate environment was such that GLBT folks had to be careful not to reveal anything about their personal lives. Being gay was something we kept quiet about if we didn't want to risk an unpleasant work environment and even our careers. And the situation in Special Libraries Association (SLA),[1] where I was most active, was very much like my work environment.

When my job duties for IBM transitioned from librarianship to marketing products and services to libraries, I joined the American Library Association (ALA).[2] As I became a more active member in ALA over time, I started to meet people in what is currently known as the Gay, Lesbian, Bisexual, and Transgendered Round Table of the American Library Association (GLBTRT).[3] It was through interactions with members of the GLBTRT that I was able to better understand how others managed being themselves in a professional association. Even so, things were not

---

1. SLA Website: www.sla.org
2. ALA Website: www.ala.org
3. GLBTRT Website: www.ala.org/ala/mbrps/rts/glbtrt/index.cfm

progressing easily. I was present at a GLBTRT meeting in the late 1980s at which a question arose, asking why there still wasn't a visible GLBT group within SLA. A member who was also on the SLA board of directors was present during that meeting. As I recall, after a bit of discussion, he made it clear to the GLBT folks that while it was an idea to consider, neither SLA nor he for that matter was ready for such a group to exist in SLA, and he was not willing to pursue it at that point. So, it would take a number of years and initiative from brave individuals from the SLA general membership to revisit the idea and move it to fruition, but I'll get to that shortly.

The mid-1990s turned out to be a watershed time period for more openness in professional environments for many people, and I experienced it as well. During that time, while attending meetings of the Art Libraries Society of North America (ARLIS/NA),[4] I noticed how their Special Interest Group for LGBTQ[5] demonstrated that a gay and lesbian group can also be an integral and positive part of a professional association's activities. This group had members not only serving in various ARLIS/NA leadership capacities, but also ensured conference programs and related conference formal and social events included LGBTQ-related elements. These activities helped create a more open and welcoming meeting environment for all attendees that translated further for me back in the work environment.

The experiences at ALA and ARLIS/NA made me more comfortable in those organizations, but they also made me realize what was sorely needed at SLA. A particular spark of action happened at a social gathering during the SLA annual conference in Atlanta in June 1994. It turned out that as I was considering how my experiences at other library associations could benefit SLA, my library colleague David Jank, a researcher at FIND/SVP at the time, was thinking the same thing. According to David, the genesis of the idea for creating a GLBT caucus at SLA came from talking with other out colleagues he knew in other associations, who would occasionally bemoan there not being a more visible GLBT presence within SLA.

So how did our idea come to fruition? David points out that he was on the SLA advisory council at the time (1993/4), and having formed a baseball caucus the year before, he knew the procedures for moving forward on creating another one, this time for GLBT interests. In a basic grassroots effort, he put up a sign on the conference message board during the SLA 1994 conference in Atlanta that had his contact information and a date and time to meet. He also included the option for people to leave a note on the

---

4. ARLIS Website: www.arlisna.org
5. ARLIS Special Interest Groups Web page: www.arlisna.org/organization/sigs.html

board. The result was that he had a LINE of people at his hotel room door at the appointed time, me included, plus dozens of messages on the board. Conversations that night centered on the need for a more formal group that focused on bringing gay and lesbian issues to the attention of the general SLA membership. We were not, however, interested in the group taking any political or social stance at that point, since the ALA group was already doing that, and doing so in SLA would not be acceptable anyway. After a lot of discussion, we got down to the logistics of what needed to be done to make it happen.

David volunteered to create the required petition with a draft scope note about the purpose of the caucus, as well as rationale for its establishment, including the caucus's objective and how it would be a service to the profession in the areas of human resources, special collections, and other resources. He spent much of the night putting this information together to ensure it met the deadline needed for presentation to the SLA Board at their meeting later in the week. In his recent correspondence with me recalling the events of the time, David reminded me that he took great pains to make it NOT sound politically motivated, though some people would later inevitably make accusations that the group was for just that purpose. While canvassing people throughout the conference that week to sign the petition, he received very warm and enthusiastic responses. It was particularly thrilling to see the number of *non*-GLBT folks who were willing to sign. A sad counterpoint of the times was the number of so-called "out" people at the conference who would *not* sign the petition for fear of being "found out" and losing their jobs. Even so, 20 people signed the set of documents that were submitted to the SLA Board for approval (a minimum of 15 were needed to form the caucus). The group would initially be known as the SLA Gay and Lesbian Issues Caucus (GLIC).

David submitted the paperwork and appeared before the SLA Board meeting at the end of the conference to answer their questions and concerns. He was greeted with some questions and skepticism at first, but ultimately the caucus petition was approved by unanimous vote in June 1994, with it formally in place January 1995. But the work was not done. The caucus could not officially be approved without the $6.00 caucus membership fee from those who signed the petition, but most had gone home, so David fronted the money and was reimbursed by each of us afterward. Only one convener was required for the group to exist, but both David and I agreed to be the first co-conveners; we weren't sure how much work and effort would be needed to support the activities, and our regular jobs kept us plenty busy.

A key outcome in forming the SLA GLIC was the strong support from many "first-year members" who were straight allies, and did not care that their SLA membership renewals for the next year were going to show up with the GLBT caucus on it. They did not "fear" their employers anywhere near as much as some of the out or closeted GLBT members. As has happened with other GLBT organizations, much appreciation goes to the many straight people who did their utmost to help in the creation of the caucus. David notes that these people were very supportive "dating way back to *before* 1994, to when this was just a dream." He also points out, and I agree, that if it were not for them, it might not have happened when it did. If it were left up to only the GLBT membership of SLA at that point in time, we are skeptical whether it would ever have even happened.

In January 1995, the GLIC was set to be officially in place, but during the SLA Winter meeting, which I attended, there were further questions from the Board. David was not able to attend that meeting, but since I was there as co-convener, I was asked to represent the caucus and address the Board's concerns. As much as there was strong support in forming the caucus the previous June, there were still concerns by some members of the Board that the group had a political agenda and that it would be more "social" than anything else. I reminded them that there were no political aspirations, as they could see from the initial petition David submitted, and that GLBT issues existed across many areas, including management, resources, and special collections. They further pressed (half jokingly) that it would be nothing more than a way for us to meet each other – a social group. I said yes, that was true, but I also countered that should not really be a big concern, since there was already a baseball caucus in existence that was mainly social; and indeed, libraries have baseball collections, including the Baseball Hall of Fame. I also had to point out the many GLBT collections that existed on their own throughout the world, in addition to materials that were part of broader collections in all types of libraries. That appeared to satisfy any lingering concerns and the caucus was allowed to remain in existence as originally approved.

A concern that still exists for some members of the caucus today is privacy, lest they be "found out" by their employers. A significant number of people were very interested and supportive of the caucus, but due to their work situations in particular, did not want their names as official members.[6] They were very concerned that the annual SLA membership

---

6. "In 30 states across America, it is still legal to fire someone based on his or her sexual orientation, and in 38 states, it is still legal to fire someone for being transgender" (Human Rights Campaign). http://www.hrc.org/12973.htm

renewal would include the caucus name on it, and someone in HR or Purchasing would cause problems for them because of it. For this reason I worked closely with the SLA headquarters staff to work out a way to keep the broader membership informed of caucus activities, while only formally listing those people who did not have concerns. Yes, in the mid – to late-1990s, this was a serious concern, but sad to say, it is more of a concern now in some work situations than it was even back then.

The first formal meeting of the caucus was in Montreal in June 1995. Though David Jank and I worked closely on plans for the meeting, he was unable to attend the conference that year and I represented both of us as convener. An amazing surprise was having over 100 attendees from the SLA membership, as well as a number of people who were vendors at the first meeting. It was clear that the time was right for the caucus to exist. Among the many topics of the meeting, a concern was brought up about the group's official name. This prompted a lot of discussion. After all comments and ideas were heard, including proposed name alternatives, it was determined that given the SLA political climate at the time, and the work it took to get the caucus started, it was best to keep the name as Gay and Lesbian Issues Caucus for now. This was done with the idea that an expanded or alternative name could be considered in the future. The discussion about the name continued on and off over the next few years, with the name of the caucus eventually changed to be more inclusive in 2006 to the SLA Gay, Lesbian, Bisexual and Transgendered Issues Caucus (GLBTIC).[7] Further background on the creation of SLA GLIC can be found in Howard Fuller's article in *Information Outlook* (April 2001).[8]

Things did not go smoothly even after formation of the caucus. In fact, there were a number of uneasy and unhappy SLA members and a few political complaints about the process. There were "in passing" hallway comments David heard about "the gays trying to take over SLA like they did at ALA." He even received a very harsh letter in the mail from a librarian who was extremely upset that the new GLBT caucus was going to "destroy SLA as we know it." David was also accused of trying to make SLA into a public librarian's organization, and this person said that because of him, she was going to drop her SLA membership and her chapter was going to break its ties from SLA and form their own independent group. I had heard similar comments about the caucus as well. I know there were

---

7. SLA GLBTIC Web page: www.sla.org/content/community/units/caucuses/index.cfm
8. "SLA Caucuses: Creation, Purpose and the GLIC" *Information Outlook* vol. 5, no.4 (April 2001): 47–52.

several times over the years when SLA members and units threatened to secede for reasons not associated with the GLBTIC at all. Perhaps some people have discontinued membership as a result of the caucus (there is no direct evidence of this), but no unit has ever separated from SLA for any reason.

While progress with the GLBTIC caucus was taking place within SLA, a major diversity initiative was put in place around the same time period by IBM executive management. The IBM diversity initiative had a focus on eliminating barriers and understanding regional constituencies and differences between the constituencies.[9] This included having a safe and open working environment for all employees, regardless of sexual orientation ("gender identity or gender expression" was added to the IBM non-discrimination policy in 2002). A part of that initiative was the formal recognition of the first GLBT group in the company, known as "EAGLE at IBM".[10] The group was allowed to call itself EAGLE at IBM, but not IBM EAGLE as it was not, and is not, an official part of IBM. I was part of the first group of members that were already in existence "underground" as it were, so it was great to finally be publicly acknowledged and accepted. It was uplifting to be able to get to know others "like me," and to be able to openly discuss workplace issues, as well as enjoy social gatherings with company colleagues. In addition, company events that were strictly for IBM employees and their spouses now enable a "partner" to attend.

Forming SLA GLIC enabled issues of concern to the GLBT membership to be brought out in open discussion to SLA leadership, so having the support of GLBT people at work made that even more comfortable to do. When I was elected to the SLA Board of Directors in 1996, I was able to participate in policy discussions, including those on behalf of our GLBT members. This further strengthened a welcoming environment for members of the GLBT library community to participate in professional association activities, with the intent to also bring that experience and confidence back to their workplace.

One of my hopes when the SLA GLIC was formed was to have a formal mentor program in place for GLBT members. One was initiated in 2001, and I volunteered to be the first mentor. However, it soon became clear through discussions and trial and error experience that our best route would be to utilize a mentor program already in place, and to have a GLBT member be eligible for it. SLA has the Diversity Leadership Development Program (DLDP) Award, which provides a formal mentorship

---

9. IBM Diversity Website: www-03.ibm.com/employment/us/diverse/
10. EAGLE at IBM Website: http://home.earthlink.net/~eagleibm/index.htm

with another SLA member for the year, along with a small cash stipend. When I broached my idea to members of the DLDP award committee, they greeted this idea with strong objection. Their feeling was that the DLDP did not include the broad definition of diversity in its scope. It therefore required a lot of discussions by many people over time to reevaluate what is meant by "diversity" and adjust the guidelines for the award to accommodate a broader spectrum of potential recipients. Diligent work resulted in a GLBT member receiving the award for the first time in 2008. It was an exciting moment, as it provided another visible way for GLBT members to be recognized for their current and future contributions to the profession. This is important not only for the recipients, but for the general audience and the rest of the GLBT community to see and understand how GLBT librarians contribute to SLA and to the profession at large.

In 2000 when I joined Infotrieve, a document delivery company, I wanted to feel confident that being gay would not be an issue, and fortunately it was not a concern, as the senior management wanted to have a productive and welcoming environment for *all* employees. Having an inclusive, diverse environment made a huge difference in how everyone at Infotrieve worked together.

My subsequent responsibilities as a member of the library management team at Amgen provided an opportunity to ensure appreciation of diverse opinions and backgrounds in the working environment. This enabled me to also become involved with the Amgen GLBT diversity group known as ANGLE, for which I served as president for one year. During that time, we were able to strengthen awareness of the group to the entire company in a variety of ways, including having Betty DeGeneres provide a keynote speech and participate afterward in a social gathering during June Pride. These major advances in professional organizations and the workplace have provided a platform of confidence and an ability to apply the experiences to future workplace endeavors for GLBT information professionals.

As I think about these experiences, the question comes to mind whether or not this affected my career. I would have to say more than likely yes, both directly and indirectly. As we know, today the GLBT community still faces challenges in the workplace and yes, even in our professional associations. That is why it is important to not be complacent and think that everything is just fine. We need to work with each other to ensure that there is an accepting and comfortable work and professional environment for all. Being an out librarian in the workplace reminds me to be open-minded in how I treat others of diverse backgrounds and ideologies. In a managerial role, it has been invaluable in providing a welcoming environment, and it ensures more open discussions during staff performance assessments and career growth guidance. Being out at work also helps me to think more broadly as I assess content for access or additions to a collection. There continue to be many challenges, of course, but it is important to be confident in who we are and to bring that diversity as an asset to our work experience and our personal lives.

Curating William Inge

Marcel LaFlamme

> **curator.** One who has the care or charge of a person or thing. In modern usage, the officer in charge of a museum, gallery of art, library, or the like; a keeper, custodian.
>
> ~The Oxford English Dictionary

I.

To name a person as gay, to classify him or her (as we librarians are wont to do), is to risk reducing a complex human being to a generalized category of identity, as though, in the words of D.A. Miller, "there were nothing else to say about them, or nothing else to hear them say" (24). In his brief, evocative album of moments, *Bringing Out Roland Barthes*, Miller wrestles with the question of how to understand French writer Roland Barthes as a gay writer, without doing violence to his memory or trivializing Barthes's own rejection of such labels. "In a culture," Miller writes, "that without ever ceasing to proliferate homosexual meaning knows how to confine it to a kind of false unconscious, as well in collectivities as in individuals, there is hardly a procedure for bringing out this meaning that doesn't itself look or feel like just more police entrapment" (18).

The fragmentary structure and the deeply personal tone of *Bringing Out Roland Barthes* represent Miller's attempt to navigate this ethical and epistemological quandary. "Any knowledge I was able to produce of a 'gay' Roland Barthes," Miller decides, "couldn't help being a knowledge *between us* and *of us both,* fashioned within the practices and relations, real and phantasmatic, of gay community, and across the various inflections given to such community by, for example, nation and generation" (6). Indeed, he goes on, "what I most sought, or what I most seek now, in the evidence of Roland Barthes's gayness is the opportunity it affords for staging this imaginary relation between us, between those lines on which we each in writing them may be thought to have put our bodies" (7). By implicating himself in the text that he produces about Barthes, Miller approaches his subject not as an ensnaring policeman, but as an equally compromised fellow traveler. And, by drawing attention to the intimately corporeal act of writing, Miller daringly imagines not only his words brushing up against Barthes's, but also his yearning, amorous body.

This essay is a meditation on what, following Miller, I will call my "homosexual encounter" with the Pulitzer Prize-winning playwright William Inge. Inge died, by his own hand, almost a decade before I was born, and yet I have been brought into a relationship with him as the librarian entrusted with the largest existing collection of his writings. Like Miller, I am interested in tracing the faint, flickering lines of kinship that would connect my life to that of a writer who walked where I am now walking, who desired and made love to other men, as I do. Yet Miller's notion of "bringing out," in the double sense of revealing a person's sexuality and teasing out meaning from a text, is not as resonant for me. Others have already "brought out" William Inge, from Stanley Kauffmann's 1966 screed about homosexual drama and its disguises to Albert Wertheim's more recent and more sensitive account of the gay sensibility in Inge's plays. For me, as a librarian, it is instead the notion of curatorship that ties me to Inge. I serve, of course, in a professional capacity as the curator of Inge's manuscripts, his correspondence, the sketches of movie stars that he did as a boy. Yet, as a young, openly gay man who grew up in a world that the closeted Inge would have scarcely recognized, I think I also understand something about the older, ecclesiastical meaning of the word *curate*: one who is charged with the heavy burden of another's soul.

II.

William Motter Inge was born on May 3, 1913, in the prosperous oil town of Independence, Kansas. The youngest of four children, William ("Billy") was much fussed over by his mother, Maude, and by the unmarried female schoolteachers who boarded with his family. Inge showed an early talent for acting and recitation, and Maude proudly trotted him out to ladies' club luncheons to deliver pieces, dolled up in a Norfolk jacket and knickerbockers. His father Luther, a traveling salesman, was distant, and Inge later recalled that he considered his son's acting "a little unmanly"

Curating William Inge

(qtd. in Voss 19). Indeed, the label of "sissy" was one that stuck with Inge throughout his high school years, a label from which his mother tried to shield him. In one of Inge's earliest plays, *Farther Off from Heaven,* a mother who bears more than a passing resemblance to Maude tells her son: "You're just ... not like the other boys. You're a speckled egg, and the old hen that laid you can't help wonderin' what you're going to hatch into.... You'll find people somewhere you'll get along with. You'll find other speckled eggs. But somehow I just can't see you spending your life in this little burg" (Inge, *Farther* 3.9-10).

Inge graduated from Independence High School in 1930, and enrolled at the University of Kansas that fall. He returned to Independence for a year at the junior college when family finances got tight, but otherwise he would never live in his hometown again. After college, Inge earned a teaching degree in Tennessee, taught for several years in Kansas and Missouri, and eventually landed in St. Louis as an arts critic for one of the city's daily newspapers. It was here that Inge met Tennessee Williams, and the friendship that the two men formed would point Inge's life in an entirely new direction. Inge traveled to Chicago to see Williams' new play, *The Glass Menagerie*, on New Year's Eve, 1944. He was stunned by the play, calling it "the most beautiful play I had seen in years" (qtd. in Voss 83). After the performance, the two men wove their way through several bars, and on their way back to Williams' hotel (how I love to picture the two of them lying there, together), Inge confessed to Williams that he wanted to be a playwright.

After a few false starts, Inge wrote what would become the first of his major plays, *Come Back, Little Sheba,* in the summer of 1948. He sent it to Williams' agent, Audrey Wood, and by the spring of 1949 the play had been optioned by the Theatre Guild. A few months later, Inge moved to New York, where *Sheba* opened, to strong reviews, on February 15, 1950. The show would run for 190 performances, and the New York Drama Critics Circle voted Inge the most promising playwright of the 1949–1950 season. Three more hits followed *Sheba*, with movie versions close on their heels: *Picnic* (1953), for which Inge won the Pulitzer Prize; *Bus Stop* (1955); and *The Dark at the Top of the Stairs* (1957). By drawing upon the speech patterns and social conventions of his small-town Kansas upbringing, William Inge had established himself as the preeminent American playwright of the 1950s.

After this, however, the story turns tragic. A bruising piece of criticism in *Harper's* shook Inge deeply toward the end of 1958; Inge's biographer, Ralph Voss, records that Inge wept on the phone when he called the critic to protest (182). Inge's next play, *A Loss of Roses,* was panned by critics upon its opening in 1959, and the play closed after just 25 performances. He briefly returned to the spotlight in 1962, winning an Academy Award for his screenplay for the movie *Splendor in the Grass.* But, by the early 1960s, the alcoholism and depression that had plagued him throughout his adult life were beginning to take their toll. He sold his apartment in New York, fled to California, and worked intermittently on a series of shorter works that dealt (clumsily) with contemporary social issues like race and urban anomie. "I can't write like I used to," he told an interviewer, a few weeks before his death. "It's a terrible feeling to feel used up" (Steele 21). On June 10, 1973, he flooded his garage with exhaust fumes and took his own life.

III.

Some five years earlier, the president of Independence Community College, Neil Edds, had addressed a letter to Inge at his home in California. The college was planning the construction of a new campus, south of Independence, and Edds wanted Inge's permission to name the college's new theater after him. Inge's reply, written at a time when his popularity was near its lowest ebb, suggests how touched he must have been by the request: "You have bestowed an honor upon me I never could have expected" (Inge, Letter). The letter goes on to explain that, while Inge's finances would not permit him to make a contribution toward the construction of the theater, he would consider presenting the college with a gift of some books, magazines, and memorabilia. The following year, Inge sent the college library five of his typewritten manuscripts, which he said in an accompanying letter that he hoped would be used by scholars conducting research. These five manuscripts, which arrived in Independence in November 1969, would form the cornerstone of the William Inge Collection.

On April 13, 1975, at the dedication ceremony for the William Inge Theater, Inge's sister, Helene Inge Connell, announced her deceased brother's intention to donate his entire personal library to Independence Community College. Connell's announcement set off a firestorm of activity in Independence. Staff members, including librarian Del Singleton, drama instructor Margaret Goheen, and assistant dean Tom Snyder, recognized the magnitude of the gift and scrambled to allocate space and resources to house the collection properly. At the same time, a grant proposal from this time period indicated that "the [college's] board of trustees, in addition to not having surplus funds for the project, has a political problem in allocating money to the collection. Inge's personal life style remains a very controversial issue with some taxpayers of the district" ("History" 2). Neil Edds underscored these concerns in a 1977 letter to the president of the Alumni Association, Harold Baden, in which he explained that "not all Board members are too excited about anything regarding William Inge. At one time a certain Board member vowed to do most anything to keep even one of the books from being in our library" (Edds).

In the end, thankfully, cooler heads prevailed. A $21,000 grant from the ARCO Foundation paid for the renovation of a seminar room adjoining the library into a dedicated space for housing the collection, while support from the National Endowment for the Humanities allowed the college to engage the services of project consultant Jackson Bryer, a noted scholar from the University of Maryland, and cataloger Bill Pfannenstiel. On August 27, 1981, Helene Inge Connell designated Independence Community College as the archival depository for research materials relating to William Inge, and three months later, on October 25, the William Inge Collection officially opened to the public. In the years that followed, subsequent donations from International Creative Management, Inge's literary agency, and from other members of the Inge family positioned the Collection as the most extensive of its kind.

I am embarrassed to admit that I did not even know who William Inge was when I applied for a job at Independence Community College in December 2007. I had only been to Kansas once, a few months before, and I had no particular background or interest in theater. But I was within a few weeks of finishing my library degree at Simmons College in Boston, and I had gotten the idea that I wanted to take a job in a rural community on the Great Plains. Growing up in small-town western Massachusetts, I knew how important my hometown public library had been to me, as a bookish little boy perhaps not so different from Billy Inge. I can remember spending the summer before my senior year of high school in that library, reading every book I could find about homosexuality and tucking each title behind the cover of a *Time* magazine so that no one could see what I was reading. Like Billy, I knew about being a "speckled egg," and I saw taking a job in a rural community as an opportunity to let others like us know that they weren't alone.

I didn't know, when I took the job in Independence, that a homophobic Board of Trustees had once considered rejecting the gift of Inge's personal library because they objected to his "personal life style." But neither was I under any illusions about small-town Kansas as some sort of haven for sexual diversity. "Move to the nearest city," Harvey Milk had advised queer young people back in the 1970s, and here I was, going in the opposite direction. I've always felt politically committed to the idea that I shouldn't have to live in New York or San Francisco just because I'm gay, that it isn't fair to ask queer kids from rural communities to choose between their sexual identities and their homes. So I packed up my car and I drove west, through New York, Ohio, and Indiana, watching the snowy landscape flatten out into the plains of Inge's childhood. I wonder what he would think if he knew that his life's work had passed into my care.

IV.

In more ways than one, I feel like I've failed William Inge. When Independence Community College hired me in 2007, they decided to consolidate two professional library positions into one: mine. While I sometimes joke that this move must have reflected the college's overwhelming confidence in me, the reality is that providing for the day-to-day information needs of the college's student body often means giving the Inge Collection short shrift. I spend my days cataloging books, evaluating databases, and delivering research instruction, and I generally feel like it's been a good week if I've spent a single afternoon on Inge. Mostly, I answer reference questions concerning the Collection as they come in, and I give the occasional visitor a guided tour, pointing out the rude sculptures that Inge fashioned during a stay at a psychiatric clinic, the dusty sample cases that once belonged to his father.

That's not to say that I've shirked my curatorial duties altogether. During the summer of 2008, I worked with Peter Ellenstein, Artistic Director of the William Inge Center for the Arts, to reproduce some of the unpublished manuscripts in the Collection and make them available to Inge's literary agency. The agency, in turn, has worked on placing the scripts with professional theaters around the country. Our work, so far, has resulted in a staged reading of a three-act play entitled *Off the Main Road,* with actors including Sigourney Weaver and Frances Sternhagen, as well as a full production of a one-act play called *The Killing* at a festival of short plays in New York. Back in Independence, we've had much of the framed artwork in the Collection re-matted and re-framed to arrest the processes of U/V damage and paper acidification. And, just a few weeks before this writing, the library received a small grant to purchase equipment that will monitor the temperature and relative humidity in the Collection with a high degree of precision. In time, we hope to use the data that we collect to land a larger grant that will pay for a dedicated, archival quality climate control system.

Still, I have the sense that there is so much more to be done, and that I owe it to William Inge to do it. There is a backlog of materials to be processed that will take months to work through, and there are basic decisions to be made about how to provide researchers with access to information about the Collection's holdings. Through a detailed finding aid, which would need to be created from scratch? Through individual MARC records, interspersed with the library's circulating materials in our online catalog? Clearly, the aging, print-based annotated bibliography upon which we currently rely is not serving anyone well. And that's to say nothing of the conference papers that have been delivered for years at the annual William Inge Theatre Festival and deposited in the Collection. I dream of a fully searchable institutional repository that would make this body of scholarship available to researchers with a few clicks of the mouse.

When I say that I feel like I've failed William Inge, though, I'm not only referring to my professional responsibilities as curator of the Inge Collection. I can't help wishing that there was more I could have done for William Inge the man, the self-loathing homosexual who spent years in psychoanalysis, the aging suitor whom the young composer Ned Rorem remembers jumping into his lap "like a Saint Bernard imagining himself a Pomeranian" (145). Perhaps I can explain it best by reference to the work of another gay writer, French journalist and novelist Hervé Guibert. When Guibert's novel *To the Friend Who Did Not Save My Life* was published in 1990, it stirred up considerable controversy because of its lightly fictionalized account of philosopher Michel Foucault's previously private battle with AIDS. The second half of the novel chronicles the wasting effects of AIDS on Guibert's own body, and the book's apostrophic title – accusatory as an arrow – is apparently directed at Guibert's friend Bill, the manager of a pharmaceutical laboratory who promised to inoculate Guibert with an experimental AIDS vaccine and then failed to keep his promise. Yet *To the Friend Who Did Not Save My Life* simmers with a rage that is not only reserved for Bill, and to read it, knowing that Guibert died the year after the book's publication, is to feel the heat of that rage even now.

I wish that I could have saved Guibert's life, or Foucault's, or any of that first generation of gay men whom we lost to AIDS. I am haunted by them, even though I was a child when the lesions started forming on their lungs, the cysts ravaging their brains. In a very real way, I feel guilty about being alive when they are not, about the historical accident of being born when I was and thereby having the knowledge that they did not have about how to protect myself from infection. So, too, I am torn between feeling blessed to live in a time where I, as a gay man, don't expect to live my life as a persecuted minority, and feeling alienated from those who came before me and who did. In the end, I can't fully understand the guilt and shame that William Inge felt about his sexuality, the deep unhappiness that drove him to the point of suicide. Nor can I personally relate to it. I have sat in the back row of the William Inge Theater, holding hands with a boy who had come up for the evening from Tulsa, even as on the other side of me sat the chairman of the college's Board of Trustees and his wife. This experience would have been inconceivable to the man whose name the theater bears. And I'd like to think that he would smile, to see it. But, as his curator, his curate, I am still the friend who did not save his life, and I do not know if I can forgive myself for it.

So curating William Inge, for me, has become more than just tending to his manuscripts. It has become a vow, a kind of obligation that I feel, to live my life in Independence more openly and honestly than William Inge ever felt that he could. It has meant placing a "safe space" sticker in my office window on my first day of work, despite a college nondiscrimination policy that pointedly excluded sexual orientation as a protected category. It has meant starting a subscription to *The Advocate* and ordering books like Susan Stryker's *Transgender History,* so that there is at least one place in Montgomery County, Kansas where these materials are available. And it has meant reaching out to other queer librarians, like Tami Albin at the University of Kansas, who is conducting a large-scale oral history project aimed at documenting the experiences of gay, lesbian, bisexual, transgender, and intersex Kansans. Now, do I go out of my way to discuss my sexuality with some of my more conservative coworkers at the college? No. But I do try to be honest about who I am, and in doing so, to honor William Inge's memory.

As a literary critic, D.A. Miller wrote about an imagined liaison between himself and Roland Barthes, "between those lines on which we each in writing them may be thought to have put our bodies." As a curator, my relationship with William Inge is different, but no less tactile, no less embodied. I run my finger along the spines of the books that he left behind, looking for names of authors whom I also love, as I would on my first visit to a boyfriend's childhood home. I rehouse the folders, heavy with his writings, in new, powder-gray archival boxes, as though I were helping my companion to replace a shabby, ill-fitting overcoat. I caress the delicate typing paper to which he committed the inner landscape of his mind, as though it were the translucent, purple parchment of a lover's foreskin. I have cared for him, as best as I know how.

Works Cited

Edds, Neil. Letter to Harold Baden. 17 May 1977. TS. William Inge Collection, Independence, Kansas.

Guibert, Hervé. *To the Friend Who Did Not Save My Life.* Trans. Linda Cloverdale. New York: High Risk Books, 1994. Print.

"History and Duration." 1980? TS. William Inge Collection, Independence, Kansas.

Inge, William. *Farther Off from Heaven.* 1947? TS. Margo Jones Collection, Texas/Dallas History & Archives, Dallas, Texas.

-----. Letter to Neil Edds and Margaret Goheen. 8 Oct. 1968. TS. William Inge Collection, Independence, Kansas. Print.

Kauffmann, Stanley. "Homosexual Drama and Its Disguises." *New York Times* 23 Jan. 1966, natl. ed., sec. 2: 1. Print.

Miller, D.A. *Bringing Out Roland Barthes.* Berkeley: U of CA, 1992. Print.

Rorem, Ned. *The New York Diary of Ned Rorem.* New York: Braziller, 1967. Print.

Steele, Lloyd. "William Inge: The Last Interview." *Los Angeles Free Press* 22 June 1973: 18+. Print.

Voss, Ralph F. *A Life of William Inge: The Strains of Triumph.* Lawrence: UP of KS, 1989. Print.

Wertheim, Albert. "Dorothy's Friends in Kansas: The Gay Inflections of William Inge." *Staging Desire: Queer Readings of American Theater History.* Ann Arbor: U of MI, 2002. 194-217. Print.

Part Five: Coming Out in Place

Activism in Colorado: How Life and Librarianship Bloomed in the Desert West

Chris Hartman

In the summer of 2007, I moved to Durango, Colorado for my first professional academic library position. Located in the Four Corners area, where Colorado, Utah, Arizona, and New Mexico meet, Durango is surrounded by desert, mountains, Indian reservations, and a few even smaller towns. Having lived in the Midwest and on the East coast my whole life, the landscape was completely foreign to me. At first, all I could see was barren earth – hardscrabble, spindly, and seemingly always brown.

Though it's not lush, I now recognize that this land supports all kinds of life, despite the lack of water. The LGBT community here is similar: it is easy to miss, but upon closer inspection, you see robust life, thriving in spite of a lack of resources. In my time here, I have also learned about the importance of setting. It impacts not only how I relate to my own sexuality, but also to how I do my job as a librarian.

Durango has a reputation for breathtaking beauty that provides an arena for a number of outdoor sports. It is also known as a very progressive town, and much of its reputation is well deserved. In comparison to the rest of southwest Colorado, Durango could be fairly described as a hotbed of liberalism. It has a surprisingly large queer community for a town of its size (population roughly 16,000). Durango High School and one of its middle schools participate in the Anti Defamation League's No Place for Hate program.[1]

But the mythology of Durango as a haven of progressive inclusiveness is an oversimplification of a more complex reality. Admittedly, my experi-

---

1. http://regions.adl.org/mountain-states/programs/no-place-for-hate-2009-2010.html

ences tend toward the other end of the spectrum; since coming out, I have lived in Pittsburgh, New York, Chicago, and Madison. Even so, it struck me as unpromising that there aren't even the most basic resources and services for queer people in Durango. Anecdotally speaking, the safety that the community enjoys often seems to depend as much upon the discretion of its members as anything else.

This is a town that espouses the stereotypical "live and let live" attitude that the West is known for. But allowing others to live their lives is not the same as celebrating them, or even accepting them. Leaving people alone is not the same as actively supporting them. This attitude of rugged individualism can provide a measure of protection in the form of privacy, but it does not accommodate a high level of nurturing or support.

Shortly after I moved here, there was a combative series of editorials in the local paper about homosexuality. While the content of the anti-gay editorials was predictable, the vindictiveness and vitriol with which they were written was horrifying. People I spoke to were quick to point out that the editorial writer (who lives outside of town) is infamous for her hate-mongering, and that her voice is not representative. Many also defended our town by drawing a distinction between it and the less enlightened populations of the surrounding areas.

There have been several high-profile incidents of bigotry and hate crimes against LGBT individuals in nearby towns. Farmington, New Mexico's Piedra Vista High School has repeatedly been the site of controversy. In 2005, the ACLU protested an anti-gay essay contest sponsored by the school ("Civil Rights Groups"), and in 2007, the proposed creation of a student Gay-Straight Alliance had the town up in arms (McCoy). More recently, a gay man was beaten by three men while being called a faggot (Monteleone). The most tragic event, however, was undoubtedly the 2001 murder of Fred Martinez, a Two Spirit Navajo teenager.[2]

As far as I know, there have been no similar incidents in Durango, which tends to be more liberal than the surrounding communities. But the notion that ignorance lies only beyond our borders is problematic at best. Even if that were true, the underlying issues remain, and we must contend

---

2. Two Spirit refers to a Native American from any tribe that identifies as what might be called LGBT. Although traditionally revered, Two Spirit individuals have often faced discrimination, since the imposition of European culture. A documentary about Fred's life and the Two Spirit community has been screened at several film festivals (http://www.twospirits.org/). For national coverage of Fred's murder, see: Barrett, Jon. "Getting Along In Cortez." *Advocate* 848 (2001): 26; Quittner, Jeremy. "Death of a Two Spirit." *Advocate* 845 (2001): 24-6.

with them. Our neighbors and much of the student body at the town's college – my patrons at the library – come from those places.

In some ways, I think that Durango's reputation as a liberal enclave does the town a disservice. That perceived status permits a nonchalance about providing true support to minority communities. In fact, this oversimplifying mythology can complicate, and even erase, queer lives, much as the claim to color blindness dismisses the realities of people of color. A comparatively large town in a mostly rural area, Durango is a symbol and destination for many in the surrounding communities. The lack of visible support for its LGBT people speaks unintended volumes.

Because I have previously lived in places that are largely gay friendly, I have had the luxury of living a private, quietly out life. I made no attempt to hide anything, but I never felt compelled to be active politically or in the community. But in this new setting, I find it extremely important to be visibly out – in particular because of my role as a librarian at Durango's small, public, liberal arts college (FTE 3,685).

Living in a place without gay bookstores, bars, and coffeehouses made me unsure of how to engage with the community. Reflecting on the issues surrounding coming out and visibility lead me to think about our students at the college. As an information professional who has been out for 15 years, I had trouble finding the community and understanding how to engage with it. How do students just beginning to question their identities fare? Coming out in a small town can be a complicated affair, even in a resource-rich environment with access to public queer spaces. What could I do to offer support to these individuals, many of whom came from places where the predominant images of queer people are harmful stereotypes?

As a faculty member, I have felt completely accepted by my peers. The college employs openly gay individuals in high-level positions, and there is a truly welcoming atmosphere on the level of faculty and administration. But most college employees are transplants from other places. By contrast, most of our students come from the surrounding rural areas. Moreover, there is also a difference between tolerating individuals who have come to terms with their identities, and providing a safe environment for young adults to confront these issues for the first time. While I appreciate the tacit acceptance I feel in the workplace, it is not the same as overt support. I believe that we have an institutional responsibility to provide a nurturing and safe environment for our students, and this includes offering services and resources that they need, but may not be capable of articulating for themselves.

I am fortunate enough to work in an environment where participation in the campus community is strongly encouraged, and I have a great deal of freedom to direct my participation. One of the things that I love about my job is that I not only get to do the standard librarian duties of reference, instruction, acquisitions, etc., but I also am able to be a part of a larger thriving campus community. Having actual examples of out individuals can make an enormous impact on students who are grappling with their identities. Just being out feels tremendously important in this climate. But even more important than being out is finding ways to visibly and actively support the students in their own process of discovery. I devote as much of my time as I can to activities and endeavors that will hopefully ensure a safe and happy environment for queer students, both in the library and in the larger community.

My job directly relates to LGBT issues in a few ways. Librarians at my school are assigned as liaisons to different departments, and as much as possible, we try to utilize librarians' experiences and interests. Happily, I was able to add the Gender and Women's Studies major to my liaison areas. That allows me the opportunity to direct funds toward purchasing informative, up-to-date, and relevant titles related to the lives of LGBT people. Perhaps more importantly, it has given me the authority to weed the collection. Historically, we have not had a lot of time to devote to weeding, and the collection contains many outdated and offensive titles. In a large research institution, a title such as "Sex Perversions and Sex Crimes," published in 1957, might be helpful for someone conducting primary research on historical attitudes toward homosexuality. But the level of research that occurs at our institution does not, for the most part, require use of this type of text, and its presence on our shelves is troubling.

Another way I work with LGBT issues in my described job duties is by working with the faculty and majors of the Gender and Women's Studies program. I attend the GWS faculty meetings, so I know what issues they are grappling with, and I am afforded an opportunity to present the library's position on issues. We also offer individual reference appointments with students. Because of my association with the GWS program, I frequently assist students who are working on research papers about LGBT issues.

I have also directed my optional activities, as much as possible, at LGBT and diversity initiatives on campus. Our campus has a chapter of the Anti-Defamation League's Campus of Difference program called Code Red.[3] This group provides anti-bias training and workshops for the school.

---

3. http://www.adl.org/education/edu_awod/awod_campus.asp

These workshops take place in freshman orientation, in RA training, and in classrooms upon request. While Code Red's stated goal is to provide a safe campus for all individuals by increasing awareness, the conversations often center around the diversity represented in the room at any given time. I joined Code Red because I wanted to be an active member of the community, and believe that the group can have a positive impact on our campus. Through my involvement, I have realized that it is also a wonderful opportunity to include the LGBT perspective in these dialogues with students.

Currently, the only resource available to LGBT students is a club called PRISM. The group has been around since 1991, and like most student organizations, has waxed and waned over time. I started attending meetings my second year at the college, and though they are open to anyone, the only other non-students who attended were faculty advisors. When the current advisor expressed an interest in stepping down, I jumped at the chance to take her place. That experience has enriched my professional life immensely.

Until my involvement with PRISM, my interactions with students were limited. Although librarians at my school have faculty status, we do not teach our own classes; our instruction is integrated within other professors' classes. Our reference desk is not extremely busy, and due to my classification I do not advise students. Therefore, my personal relationships with students did not extend beyond interactions with library student workers. As faculty advisor for PRISM, however, I have had a wonderful opportunity to interact with a number of students and develop relationships with several of them.

My role as PRISM advisor has also expanded my understanding of the spectrum of realities embodied by people who defy the norms of heterosexuality and gender binaries. Interacting with Native American students (who make up nearly 20% of our student body), has introduced me to the Two Spirit community, of which I was previously unaware. Although frequently thought of as Native LGBT individuals, the identity of Two Spirit is much richer and more complex than that; it frequently invokes a reality we have no term for in English – identification as both male and female. The more I learn about this community, the better I am able to work with students in class, on the reference desk, and in person.

This position also allows me the opportunity to shed light on LGBT issues in different ways. When I introduce myself to a class that I am teaching, for instance, I can include my role as PRISM advisor as a fact about myself. Students are frequently unaware of the club. Coming out to groups of people can be terrifying, and it is nothing that I ever would have considered before moving to Durango, but I believe it is a good way to spread the word about the group and plant seeds about the existence of LGBT individuals on campus.

It is a shame that there are not more resources for LGBT students on campus, but that absence is compounded because nothing exists in town, either. The fact that Durango is the largest town in the area means that far too many LGBT people lack access to possibly life-saving resources. The Four Corners Lesbian Network is an online forum for women to connect,[4] and there is also a local chapter of GLAD, called 4CGLAD (Four Corners Gay and Lesbian Alliance for Diversity).[5] Both groups are primarily social organizations. They serve an important function, and regular Friday happy hours are a staple of many people's social lives, but neither group is politically influential. They do not have a physical presence in town, nor do they have the resources to provide other types of services and support. Our Sister's Keeper, a Native American domestic and sexual violence prevention organization, recently created a support and educational group for the Two Spirit community, and hopefully they will have the resources to make a difference.[6]

The absence of a resource center both in town and on campus is problematic for our students because PRISM alone is incapable of meeting all their needs. Many of our students are just beginning to question their sexual identities, while others have been out for years. This leads to an incredible range of services and resources required. As a student-run organization, PRISM is not able to provide the support that our queer and questioning students require. Nor should it; such needs exceed the scope and capabilities of a student-run organization.

For several years, a group of faculty members have been working to get an LGBT resource center established on campus, and I have joined them. As our proposal for the resource center discusses, silence is a voice in any discourse, and it speaks volumes. We have seen the power of communal spaces on our campus with the creation of a Native American Center and El Centro for Hispanic students, both of which are active, thriving environments. These centers also stand as a symbol to the entire community that our school welcomes and supports those students. Their popularity and success speak to the need students feel for such safe spaces. Visible institutional support for LGBT individuals is essential for all of our stu-

---

4. http://groups.yahoo.com/group/fourcornersln/
5. http://www.4cglad.org/
6. http://oursisterskeeper.org/

dents, straight or otherwise. I hope to be at the college long enough to see this become a reality.

When I first moved to Durango, all I could see was barren, dry land. I wasn't even able to recognize the changing seasons for what they were. To my eyes, seasons seemed like nothing more than brown or more brown. But over time, the subtleties have become more apparent to me. There are different kinds of seasons here than I am used to, the seasons of the river, the seasons of the desert southwest. I have learned to appreciate the life that thrives here, despite all odds. And I wonder what else could grow here, given enough water.

Works Cited

American Civil Liberties Union. "Civil Rights Groups in New Mexico Denounce High School Contest Soliciting Anti-Gay, Anti-Choice Student Essays." *ACLU.org.* ALCU Foundation. 22 November 2005. Web. 11 August 2010.

Micah McCoy. "ACLU: School Must Allow Gay-Straight Club." *ACLU.org.* ALCU Foundation. 26 September 2007. Web. 11 August 2010.

Monteleone, James. "Men face hate crime charges: First local charges involving sexual orientation." *The Farmington Daily Times* 17 Dec 2007. Print.

In and Out Behind the Desk—In and Out of the Country

Kimberli Morris

In the fifteen-plus years I've been a law librarian, I've been in and out of the closet. Or, more accurately, I've been out, back in, and back out again. That status could change at any time.

NOT Out In Front of the Desk—life as a library patron

I didn't really start coming out until I was in law school. Because I was raised in a fairly conservative household, I very consciously did not allow myself to think too much about my orientation. From middle school on, my pat answer to teasing and/or pointed questions about when I was going to get a boyfriend was "I'm very serious about school – I don't have time to be distracted by that." Amazingly enough, the pat answer pretty much worked. I didn't get near the pressure about dating and marriage that my two older sisters got. And, I actually was serious about school. Wanting to be a lawyer meant I had to prepare now in order to do well in high school, to get into a good college, to get into law school. But, being "serious about my studies" meant that I was in libraries a lot, which gave me the opportunity to "research" issues of sexual orientation. Back in the early 70s, a joking comment from a friend's mom that it was fine to be such a tomboy, as long as I didn't go so far as to get a sex change, started some clandestine research at the public library. I think the library staffer who came to shoo me back into the children's section was totally flustered to find me looking up "hermaphroditism" in the encyclopedia. Turning to books for answers became a lifelong pattern for me.

Years later in high school, on a freshmen year field trip to a major university library, using the venerable *Off Our Backs* as a resource for the politics surrounding the new "gay cancer" (later to be termed AIDS) was eye opening enough – accidentally getting a copy of the new magazine

On Our Backs was a whole other ball game. Another memorable read was Gloria Anzaldúa's *Borderlands: the New Mestiza = La Frontera* for a political science class in college.

By law school I was ready to let myself think about my orientation. I'm not sure if it was law school itself that allowed me to see my coming out as a justice issue as opposed to a religious issue, or whether distance from my family's version of religion led me to other, more accepting theologies, or if it was simply that, since I would soon be finished with school, my personal excuse for avoiding the issue was about to run out. As always, research led the way for me: feminist jurisprudence texts and general human rights / civil rights texts for the justice implications and John McNeill's *The Church and the Homosexual* for more inclusive theologies. . . . I had no role models, and obviously totally missed the context early on (really, hermaphroditism?), but just having access to the books pointed me toward answers and perhaps other ways to frame the questions. Later, in library school, when we talked about biblio-therapy I realized that that's exactly what I had been doing for years. That experience as a questioning LGBTQ library patron has thoroughly convinced me as a librarian that building our collections – at every type and level of the library – is in itself an important act of leadership and advocacy.

Out Behind the Desk as a library employee

It may have taken me a while to come out personally, but in 1994 I started life as a library employee completely out of the closet. It wasn't so much a political or social statement, but more a function of naiveté and good luck. By the time I was finishing up with library school, I'd already been lucky enough to meet my life partner. I was at the job search stage and she was at a point in her education where she could move fairly easily – we evaluated job prospects and possible locations together. For law librarians, especially entry level academic law librarians, the annual conference of the American Association of Law Libraries is where the majority of initial interviews take place. California Western School of Law (CWSL) in San Diego was one of the law school libraries that offered me a second interview. In addition to the official invitation, a few of the librarians contacted me individually, one of whom let me know that CWSL offered domestic partnership benefits. The topic was not broached at the initial interview of course, but occasionally it does pay to look a tad stereotypical.

Knowing that, without knowing how rare it was, and just assuming that all partnered folks – whether straight or gay – made relocation decisions collaboratively, I asked for my partner to be brought out to the second interview with me. I just assumed that employers knew that both parties in a couple had to be able to evaluate a new location, especially one across the country. I think they were a little shocked at my audacity in asking, but with a "Friends-Fly-Free" flight they agreed to my request. While I interviewed, my partner checked out the city, housing options, and opportunities for her to finish her education. Together we decided that if we got the offer we would accept. And we did.

The fact that my partner would be able to be on my health insurance at CWLS was appealing, but wasn't central to our decision in that first round of job searching. However, when she was diagnosed with cancer it became critical to our lives. CWSL was absolutely amazing in their support of both my partner and me. It was, of course, a good business practice. With my partner having chemotherapy and radiation treatment, I was a distracted employee for a while. But that distraction was nowhere near the level it would have been had we been trying to find affordable health coverage for her. With attitude being such a big component in fighting cancer, I'm certain that the support of my employer and coworkers was a major factor in my partner becoming a cancer survivor, instead of a cancer victim.

At CWSL, the commitment to the policy was more than just good business; it was also viewed as a justice issue. The CFO at the time was relentless in making sure that employees with domestic partners were given the same benefits as employees with spouses. At most places that offer DP benefits the employee is responsible for paying the extra tax that the government imposes on those benefits (ie the employer's contribution for the partner's insurance is attributable as income, and is therefore taxed by both the federal and local governments). But at CWSL, they adjusted our income so that our final take home pay was the same, whether married or partnered.

During that same time period (I called it the year of the bad bodies), when I needed to have a routine surgery, CWSL worked with me and the relevant insurance companies to assure that, in the unlikely event that something did happen to me, my partner would still be covered for as long as she was having cancer treatments. Finally, when I left CWSL to accept a fellowship overseas, they went above and beyond to make sure that all the COBRA benefits were given to her. Since COBRA is a federal law, the insurance company was not legally obligated by the legislation to provide those benefits to domestic partners. The law school administration made it clear to the insurance company that when they negotiated insurance coverage for domestic partners it included COBRA post-employment benefits. This is still an issue at many companies today, so CWSL was definitely ahead of the curve in treating LGBT employees fairly.

I have been mostly out in my library career so far, and most of the time the response has ranged from okay to actively supportive. CWSL was definitely the most supportive and the most thoroughly fair. Domestic partnership benefits have become more and more important to me. Initially, either the position had to offer DP benefits, *or* the location had to be in a city large enough for my partner to be reasonably confident that she would be able to quickly get a graphic design position that offered insurance benefits. She is very good, but a city needs to be a certain size before there is much of a market for graphic designers. There was a law school in Florida where I very much wanted to work, and they very much wanted to hire me. But, the school didn't offer DP benefits at that time, and the small college town didn't have many graphic design positions at all. We were all frustrated, but the library administration was very understanding about my decision to decline their offer.

The offer that I did accept was in Maryland, and in a city that was large enough to provide good job prospects for my partner. While the law school and library administration were certain that the university offered DP benefits, a call to the university human resources department revealed that the university did *not* offer such benefits. At that point in time, the administration didn't understand the importance of this issue to me. Because they hadn't discriminated in hiring me, they didn't think that the unavailability of a "perk" was such a big deal. Their conception of support and non-discrimination was very narrow. But, the city was large, so we did go ahead and move there. At both the Florida and the Maryland schools, the campus organizations that were fighting for domestic partnership benefits asked me to write a letter indicating that the DP issue was critical in my decision to either reject the offer or to move on to other employment. Both universities now offer DP benefits – many kudos to the organizations that painstakingly collect the evidence of impact and keep bringing home the importance of the issue.

On the flip side, one place I interviewed responded to the DP benefits question with a frustrated, "that would be nice, but no we don't." But, when I asked at the main HR department, they said, "of course, and we have for years." Somehow that information hadn't gotten out to the library rank and file. Somebody had fought hard to earn these rights, but then dropped the ball in letting folks know they had, in fact, been won.

Out Behind the Desk and in front of law students

Just as it affects my ideas about collection development, my own coming out process shapes the way I interact as a law librarian with law students, faculty, and the public. In law school, before I had finished coming out even to myself, there was a straight faculty member that was a very vocal ally to gay folk and LGBTQ issues. Her support was appreciated, but a tad overwhelming – especially when she complained in a seminar class about students not coming out while looking pointedly at a few LGBTQ students in the class. This was during the ACT UP/Queer Nation era and lots of outing was going on. I do think that she had the best intentions, but it felt pretty close to outing, and instead of being supportive it felt threatening. Like many in my generational cohort of female students, I resented the frequent assumption that as a woman I would be primarily interested in women's law issues. I did not want my gender to define my career. Similarly, I did not want my orientation to define my career. While I respected the work of Urvashi Vaid, Lambda Legal, and the Human Rights Campaign, I did not want to be a "professional lesbian." Regarding both my gender and my orientation, I probably took it too far to the other extreme. To keep from being typecast, so to speak, for a while I ignored issues in which I was actually interested. Everybody has to decide for themselves where to draw the line between who they are and what they do. And that is probably never a *finished* process. I don't draw that line at the same place now as I did then. But, initially at least, I wanted to tightly focus on access to legal information, international law, and international legal development.

Given that, despite my brazenness at my first interview, I did not typically bring up the fact that I am gay. I never hid it if the topic came up – and I was more assertive when it came to healthcare for my partner – but I didn't stray anywhere near territory that could be considered activism. Law libraries tend to be small shops, so I was out to all of my coworkers, but not to the law school at large. One of my coworkers said that she liked that I would talk about my partner, but wasn't "all-in-your-face" about it. That one set off a small twinge that perhaps I wasn't doing enough, but for the most part I liked the comment.

It was a conversation with a student that really started the shift in my thinking. He had overhead a water cooler conversation where a colleague and I were discussing some of the universal pitfalls of coupled life. Something along the lines of one partner squeezing the toothpaste from the middle while the other one wants the tube rolled up neatly, one wanting to watch TV in bed while the other just wants to sleep. . . . Afterwards, the student asked if he could ask a personal question. He couldn't understand why, as such a private person, I would talk about having a partner. He, of course, had no problems with homosexuals, but didn't think I would want people to know that about me. From his perspective, just mentioning the fact that I had a same-sex partner was sharing some deep dark bedroom secret, and totally non-analogous to him mentioning the fact that he had a girlfriend. That's when I started to better understand how being too quiet lets people keep their notions that homosexuality is some shameful secret that "otherwise nice" people should keep hidden.

I still won't just assume that a student is gay, and I won't denigrate any student or coworker's decision not to be out. But, I display a rainbow sticker in my office; I serve on a diversity committee; and I participated in a student organized protest of a speaker associated with the Prop 8 case in California. Just from those steps, tiny really, a number of students have come to talk to me – straight and gay – about personal LGBTQ issues, about career implications of being LGBTQ, and about researching LGBTQ issues. It still hasn't been "in-your-face," but it has started a great number of conversations both with people that needed to hear me and with even more people that I needed to hear.

NOT Out Behind the Desk

Despite my general and growing inclination toward being out at work (and my general inability to keep from talking about my partner), there have been three distinct situations when I have chosen *not* to be out, or to be only selectively out. Two of the times were when I was working outside of the United States, and one when I was working in a prison. All three of those positions were ones that let me contribute to providing access to legal information and to international legal development at a very fundamental level. As such, they were important opportunities for me to further the causes that had actually brought me to law school and then to library school. Each instance carried very different short – and long-term implications.

The time I ran a prison general library and law library service was probably the most neutral – both long-term and short-term. Being out could have *possibly* become a safety issue. Mostly, it was just easier not to mention anything and avoid possible hassles, whether from inmates or officers. As usual for me, civilians and officers with whom I worked closely quickly figured out that my partner was more than just a roommate. But none of the other officers knew, and you just don't give out any kind of personal information to inmates. I'm not sure I ever even mentioned my dog's name. Any concrete impact on the library from my being a lesbian was limited to some of the books I added to the collection. Perhaps a few astute correctional officers noticed some LGBTQ themes in some of the fiction we purchased – but I don't think so. At first I worried that perhaps an inmate would be targeted if he or she were seen with such a book. That never materialized though. I think in that particular situation, not being out saved me a bit of harassment, and being out might not have hurt, but really wouldn't have served much purpose either.

My first international job – in 1997 – was the first time I decided not to be out. Initially, it seemed that staying in the closet wouldn't have much impact. It was a chance to work with the Parliament of Uganda under the auspices of an eight month American Libraries Association / United States Information Agency Fellows Program award. (Sadly this program has been discontinued as part of the USIA being folded into the State Department). The Fellows program did not cover spouses or significant others (no matter the orientation), so while being away from my partner for eight months was incredibly difficult, I didn't feel like I was being treated any differently than the Fellows who were married. Because of cultural differences, and because my partner wasn't with me, I didn't plan on being out. The opportunity to work with the Parliament as they set up their library and information service was nothing short of amazing. On the personal side, it *did* seem that the second or third question was always whether or not I was married. I treated this question pretty much like I had in my youth: I'd smile, say no, and then deflect the conversation back to work topics. Obviously, I was very serious about my career, which they considered typical of western women. For the most part my sexual orientation was a non-issue while I worked there. There were a few close friends (other ex-pats) with whom I would commiserate over missing our partners / spouses. But, I never talked about it with my Ugandan colleagues. As an outsider, I didn't think being out would really make much of an impact. And I did think it could possibly have a negative impact on my ability to do the work I came to do. At that point, in that job, I decided silence was the best option. But given what is going on now with the anti-gay legislation proposed in the Ugandan Parliament, I think my silence was a huge opportunity missed. Perhaps I should've dealt with it the same way I dealt with the issue of trousers.

In Uganda at the time, a woman wearing pants was considered immodest at best and most likely promiscuous. Just a cultural difference – a skirt above the knees was fine but trousers were not. Skirts, dresses, and I do not mix. So even before I left, I decided that I would still wear nice trousers and deal with any misperceptions as to my sexual availability. Truthfully, I don't think I got any more propositions at the taxi park than skirted western women. Of more concern to me were any ramifications to my effectiveness at Parliament – but since I was moving books, crawling under desks to set up computers – I decided I would just have to let my actions over time reverse initial assumptions.

And they did. Initially, every morning I would be let into the Parliament building by the senior officer, who always gave me a fierce scowl. I'd say good morning and go about my work. Gradually, he started to return my greetings and smile a bit, which would then be followed by a puzzled frown. Finally, one morning he asked me: "Ms. Morris, you seem like a nice person and a respectable lady, WHY do you wear pants?" So I explained to him that I'm more comfortable in pants, that I'm often moving books and crawling under desks to set up computers, just sitting on the floor in front of the shelf I'm working on, and that I didn't want to have to deal with the restrictions of skirts or risk having it fly up, or ... He thought a minute, agreed that I did seem to be very active, and then said, "So you wear pants because you ARE modest."

Partially it was accepted of me because I was a foreigner, but still, by sticking to my decision and explaining it, I convinced a number of people that a woman in pants isn't necessarily promiscuous. After a couple of months, even at the taxi park the bus driver for my regular route would shout down anyone he heard heckling me. If I had used the same strategy about being a lesbian, perhaps there would be a few more people in Uganda who would see through the growing propaganda claiming that all LGBTQ people are immoral, pedophilic prostitutes bent on destroying the country.

The legislation as proposed at this writing would potentially subject me to the death penalty if I were to return to Uganda. As a lesbian whose "victim" (my partner) is disabled, my offense would be that of aggravated homosexuality – for which the death penalty is declared. The legislation claims jurisdiction over extra-territorial acts – the offense does not even have to occur inside Uganda. The legislation also imposes jail time for those who fail to report. I have a colleague and friend here at Penn State who is from Uganda, and we used to discuss ideas for programs that would be both useful to Ugandans and attractive to funding organizations. Now we discuss how harmful this legislation could be if enacted, and in fact already is. If we decided to go ahead with such a program, and if she were the director of the program and, thus, a "person in authority" she would have 24 hours to report me as a homosexual or be herself subject to a fine and imprisonment of up to three years. Any business or organization that "promotes" homosexuality – say, by recognizing same-sex marriages or providing domestic partner benefits – is subject to having its license revoked and its director imprisoned for up to seven years.

Obviously that has significant ramifications for NGOs and donor organizations operating in Uganda. There has been an international outcry against the bill, with statements that NGOs would no longer be able to work in Uganda. Partially because of that, President Museveni is talking about softening the bill, and, as of this writing, it has been tabled for now. In truth, NGOs that continued to operate would probably be overlooked, with foreigners probably just made to leave the country. But the damage to Ugandans is already occurring – gay people are being outed in newspaper articles, straight people in the political opposition are being outed falsely for political purposes. There has been a fair amount of press about the role that Americans have played in stirring this up.[1] In hindsight, I regret the missed opportunity – as an American – to have shown, even to just a few Ugandan colleagues that, just as a woman in trousers can still be respectable, LGBTQ people can be respectable as well. I'm not sure it would even have amounted to a drop in the ocean, but I regret my silence in this case.

The third instance in which I made the decision to stay closeted was during another chance to work internationally. In February 2004, I was able to work with the International Human Rights Law Institute (IHRLI) of the DePaul University College of Law, as they assisted three law schools in Iraq. Beyond the obvious difficulties from the wars that Iraq had been in, the legal profession and access to legal information had been severely restricted during the entire Ba'ath era. Of the three law schools with which we worked, none had had a book budget since the 1980s. The chance to work with them as they reestablished their libraries and collections was, again, nothing short of amazing.

Very early 2004 was also the time when the Human Rights Campaign, the ACLU, and Equality Maryland were seeking couples to be part of a lawsuit seeking the right to marry. By this point, my partner and I had been together for 10 years. We'd gone through her cancer together; we'd moved across the country together, twice; we'd purchased a car together; and we'd bought a house together. We'd seen, firsthand, how incredibly difficult any of these events are for those who are not married. We'd rejected and accepted jobs that we would not have had to, had we been able to be married. We'd spent at least $2,000 getting all the legal documentation

---

1. See Gettleman, Jeffrey. "Americans' Role Seen in Uganda Anti-Gay Push." New York Times 4 Jan 2010, New York edition: A1. http://www.nytimes.com/2010/01/04/world/africa/04uganda.html, and Kaoma, Kapya. "Globalizing the Culture Wars: US Conservatives, African Churches, & Homophobia." PublicEye.org. Political Research Associates, 2009. Web. 31 Mar 2010. http://www.publiceye.org/publications/globalizing-the-culture-wars/.

needed to assure that our finances and medical wishes would be as secure as possible. And *still* our protections were not as good or as secure as those that straight couples enjoy just by the virtue of being married. We were incredibly interested in being part of that litigation.

We were selected as one of the finalist couples, but by that time I was already in Iraq. It may even be that my being in Iraq was part of why we made it to the final selection stages. Engaging back stories about the litigants are always sought, and, admittedly, a lesbian couple with one partner in Baghdad helping rebuild libraries makes a pretty interesting back story. All the required publicity that the case would engender however, would have serious implications for the work I and my colleagues were doing in Iraq. Although half a world away, my Iraqi colleagues would surely have read the news stories. (The day after I arrived in Baghdad, one of my colleagues showed me the ALA report from my work in Uganda. Once they had the name of who would be coming, they found virtually every scrap of information about me that existed on the Internet.) Convincing law school deans, university presidents, and fathers and husbands to let their female librarians travel for training was going to be difficult enough as it was – if the accompanying sponsor was known to be a lesbian, it would become impossible. My being out would not only affect the library part of IHRLI's work, but all components. And realistically, it could easily have trickle-down effects on all academic US-funded initiatives in Iraq. It would undoubtedly raise the personal risk involved in being in Iraq. And again, not just for me, but for all of my colleagues as well.

This was an incredibly difficult decision for me and my partner. The marriage equality issue was important to us, both as an intensely personal issue and as an issue of fundamental justice. But the work in Iraq was equally as important to both of us. Such a very small part of the rebuilding efforts were going toward education at all. And if we wanted to help the nation to establish the "rule of law," surely we had to start with getting access to the law for at least the attorneys. After much discussion and consideration, we decided to withdraw from the litigation process. I'm still not sure how to weigh one social justice effort against another one. But the US litigation actually emphasized the importance of the work with law libraries in Iraq. Without access to the law, lawyers in Iraq were ill-equipped to take action on human rights violations like lawyers for the ACLU and Equality Maryland were doing at home. Lawyers without access to even their own law, and to international standards on human rights, can't begin to explain those rights to the populace, or hold accountable those who violate those rights. That being said, in the end, for me it came down to the fact that while there were many couples ready and willing to press the issue of marriage equality, there just weren't many law librarians waiting in the wings to head off to Iraq.

Looking back, I would not change that decision if I had to make it again. My contribution in Iraq was miniscule in the grand scheme of things. But it was still an important contribution that I am glad I was able to make. As with most such projects, we end up getting more than we give and learning more than we teach. Ironically, it was my time in Iraq that has finally turned me into at least a moderate activist – it put the final touches on a process for me that started with the discussion with the law student at the water cooler many years before. My experience in Iraq demonstrated clearly that librarians, just by doing the routine (and maybe even mundane) task of deciding what materials to acquire, cataloging, or otherwise processing that material to make it accessible, and just by answering reference questions that lead patrons to that material, *are* activists. And by being an out, lesbian librarian, I can provide needed information and at least one context for that information. As I said earlier, the decision of whether to be in or out is probably never totally static, and while I'm completely out right now, that could well change in the future. But now, hopefully, I make that decision by considering the full spectrum of long – and short-term implications for myself, my law students, my colleagues, and for the anonymous library patron that I may never even see.

"Do They Know?"
A Gay Librarian at a Catholic University

Martin Garnar

Before I became a librarian, I worked for a trucking company in upstate New York. It was in the mid-1990s and I was out to my office mate and boss, but otherwise was very careful when discussing my private life with other employees, as I assumed that my sexual orientation would not be well received. After I tendered my resignation to move to Colorado, my coworkers threw a party for me after my last day of work. Arriving at the party, I was immediately asked where my partner was. My first response was, "You know his name?" My second response was, "You know I'm gay?" They all said, "Of course we know!" and they were disappointed that they didn't get to meet my partner. Chagrined by my lack of trust in my coworkers, I vowed to never again be closeted in my work life.

Fast-forward six months to Denver, Colorado. Amendment 2, the statewide measure approved by Colorado voters to forbid discrimination protection for LGBT people, had been struck down by the U.S. Supreme Court a month before I moved to the state, so Denver's municipal ordinance providing job protection for LGBT workers within the city limits was back in force (Joslin). I had been working two part-time library jobs while looking for a full time clerical position, as I was still a year away from entering the library science graduate program at the University of Denver. I had kept my promise about being out at both jobs, though it wasn't something I announced on my first day. Instead, I waited for opportunities when it was natural to discuss my private life. When asked what my wife did for work, I'd reply matter-of-factly that my husband worked at a bank. No drama, no problems, and I felt secure enough to put a rainbow sticker on my car.

My eventual career goal was to be an academic reference librarian and bibliographer for history and women's studies, so that I could work in a campus environment and still make use of my first master's in European women's history. When a full-time circulation supervisor position opened up at nearby Regis University, I was excited at the possibility of working in an academic library that also happened to be a bike ride away from home. I didn't know much about Regis, but learned it was a Catholic school after I was scheduled for an interview. I was concerned that being openly gay would be a problem, and talked about my fears with one of my current supervisors. As it turned out, she had worked for Regis earlier in her career, and said that I had nothing to fear, as Regis was a Jesuit school. I didn't know what Jesuit meant, but was assured that they were "pretty progressive" for Catholics, and being gay shouldn't be an issue. For those readers not familiar with the Jesuits (formally known as the Society of Jesus), they are the largest male religious order in the Catholic Church (Jesuits). Other examples of orders include the Franciscans, Dominicans, and Benedictines. Still somewhat skeptical of my chances, I went to the interview and was hired for the position. Within a month, I felt comfortable enough with my colleagues that I came out when the right opportunity came along, and was soon bringing my partner to functions like the university's Christmas party and the library's summer picnic.

Within a year of working at Regis, I enrolled in the library science program at the University of Denver. A frequent topic of my student research was library services to LGBT library populations, and I was thrilled to do my practicum under the supervision of Ellen Greenblatt, whose research in this area set the standards for service. Knowing that my research focus would eventually be documented in my curriculum vitae was another step towards being permanently out in my professional life. I always told myself I wouldn't want to work for a library that had a problem with my sexual orientation, so any lost opportunities based on their assumptions weren't truly a loss for me.

When I was near the end of my MLIS program, Regis had an opening for an entry-level reference librarian. I applied for the position and was selected to be one of the finalists for a campus interview. As part of the process, I met with the university's vice president for mission. One of the standard questions in the "mission" interview for all candidates asks what each person will bring to the Jesuit & Catholic mission of the university. My answer began, "Well, as a gay Unitarian Universalist—" and I had to pause as the vice president (already a friend) burst out laughing. Once we regained the serious tone of the interview, I finished my answer by saying that I'd bring an outside perspective on some issues, but also a shared concern for social justice and a focus on service that's congruent with the university's motto: Men and Women in Service of Others. In the end, I was the successful candidate and was hired six months before I completed my MLIS.

Within the first months of joining the library faculty, I also joined the faculty union that represented the librarians and liberal arts faculty for contract negotiations and resolving concerns with the administration. In a conversation with a teaching colleague who happened to be on the union's board, I noted my annoyance at not being able to list my partner in the internal staff directory, which had long provided the names of spouses as a convenience. To my surprise, the issue was brought up at the next union meeting (without mentioning me) and was proposed as an item for debate with the administration. Some of my colleagues opposed the idea by stating that anyone who wanted to have a spouse's name listed should just get married. That's when I spoke up and said that though I couldn't get a legal marriage, I was married in the eyes of my church and would be happy to bring in my wedding album as proof. No further opposition was raised, and the union voted to ask for partners to be listed in the staff directory. The administration's response was to remove the names of all spouses from the directory, thereby removing any appearance of discrimination, though consequently making the directory less useful.

Within the same time period, I was summoned to the administration building to meet with the provost and help diffuse a tense situation. A student living on campus came back to his room to find "Die, fag, DIE!" written on his message board. The student was openly gay and a recipient of a prestigious science scholarship that he accepted only after being assured that there was an LGBT student group on campus. Though there had been such a group in the past, it wasn't active at the time. The student and his parents were furious about the incident, which was eventually explained by the perpetrators as a joke directed at the student's roommate (since everyone knows that "fag" is a general term of abuse and shouldn't be taken the wrong way. Right ...) In the meeting at the provost's office, I found myself being presented as an example of diversity in the Regis community and was encouraged to revive the student group as its advisor, which I did. The student and his parents were somewhat mollified, and I began the task of (re)forming the group.

At the time (1999), our group was affiliated with Campus Ministry, which meant we didn't need to have an official student roster requiring six students to publicly affirm their membership. The former incarnation of the group had been called the Regis Alliance of Gay Students (or RAGS). Not caring for the acronym, we chose the shortened form of the Regis Alliance and began a poster campaign (with a tendency to invoke Star Wars

regis alliance: episode 3

1. Is this when Luke's father goes bad?
2. Or, is it when Leia discovers that nasty hairstyle?
3. Perhaps it's that group of gay, lesbian, bisexual, and straight students that get together to hang out & talk?
4. Does this mean that there's another year of silly Star Wars references that no one quite understands? (Oh, the humanity!)

If you answered #3, you're a WINNER!!!!

If you're gay, lesbian, bisexual, or straight AND you want to hang out with us, come to our first meeting of the year:

When? 4:00 p.m. on Wednesday, September 5th, 2001

Where? Main Hall Rm. 130 (near the cashier's office)

(Yeah, I know – it's not the Aspen Room – we'll try again for the next meeting...)

Questions about the meeting or the group?
Call **x5459** and start humming the theme to Star Wars.
If you're good, we'll answer your questions.
Otherwise, we'll blast your home planet with the Death Star.

⟵ are we allowed to post this? sure - we asked real nice!!! ⟶

imagery of the Rebel Alliance) to advertise meetings. Meeting locations and times were not published on the poster, thus requiring any interested parties to call the published phone numbers to get the necessary details. We ended up with a small, but dedicated group of six to eight students and continued on in this fashion for a few years before eventually applying for, and receiving, official recognition as a student club. We now have over 20 members, a regular crowd at our weekly public meetings, and have adopted the more conventional name of the Gay Straight Alliance. One of our annual events is a "coming out panel" every October. Given the cyclical nature of an audience on a college campus (with our student body turning over every four to five years), I've come out three times as the faculty member of the panel, though there are times when I wonder if it's really a surprise to anyone at this point.

The dearth of potential faculty panelists speaks to the general concern about being out before receiving tenure. Some of my LGBT colleagues are out in their departments or to selected students, but are generally quiet about their orientation in the larger campus community. When I first joined the faculty, there was just one tenured professor who was out (a well respected member of the business department), plus another new tenure-track librarian who was also out. Besides appearing on the coming out panel, I did a few other things to raise my profile as an out librarian. When interviewed by the student newspaper as part of a "day in the life of ..." series featuring various faculty members, I made sure they mentioned my partner as part of my home life. For ten years, I've had the same "safe zone" sign on my office door, though every year fewer students recognize the sign's pink triangle as a symbol of the LGBT community. I'm also a regular guest speaker in courses dealing with LGBT issues, talking both about my personal experience and my professional duty to have an inclusive collection. In these situations, I like to ask if any students knew I was gay prior to my appearance in their classroom. Usually more than half will raise their hands and, when prompted, will say that they know because they heard from other students, they've seen me at the coming out panel, they've seen the sign on my door, or (my favorite) because I spend so much time at the campus gym.

At this point, you may be thinking that my experience at Regis doesn't sound very different from what would happen at a university in any of the states without employment protections for LGBT people, or where the campus culture is more conservative, whether or not it's religiously affiliated. Yet the reality is that I do work at a Catholic university. What does that mean for me as an openly gay man?

Before we examine the situation at Regis, let's look at the Catholic position on homosexuality.

The Catechism of the Catholic Church states that men and women with "deep-seated homosexual tendencies [...] must be accepted with respect, compassion, and sensitivity" (United States Catholic Conference 2358). At the same time, the *Catechism* states that "[T]radition has always declared that 'homosexual acts are intrinsically disordered.' [...] Under no circumstances can they be approved" (2357). At face value, these may seem to be contradictory: how can you accept the person if you disapprove of his or her actions? The *Catechism* reveals the answer: "Homosexual persons are called to chastity" (2359). In other words, it's acceptable to be gay, but I'm not supposed to act on it. As a result, my loving and committed relationship with my partner does not conform to church teachings. This would be a problem if Regis were owned and operated by the church and expected all employees to live faithfully according to church teachings, but that's not the case.

The legal entity behind the university's operations is the Regis Educational Corporation, which was established in 1972, in part to make it legal for Regis to continue to receive federal grants for student aid (Brockway 34). This was part of a growing trend among Catholic colleges and universities in the 1960s and beyond to become independent of the church for financial reasons, while still trying to maintain their Catholic heritage (36). A 1978 court case regarding the ability of Regis students to receive state education grants was finally resolved in 1984 with a ruling that Regis was not a "pervasively sectarian" institution and, therefore, eligible to participate in certain state programs (147). Though this settled the legal status of Regis as an independent institution, we still clearly identify as a Jesuit Catholic institution in our mission statement, and are proud to be part of the larger Jesuit educational tradition dating back to 1548 (Farrell 25). Having established the context of being at an independent (that is, not church-controlled) university operating within the Catholic tradition, I now return to the question of what it means to be an openly gay man at a Catholic university.

Employment rights for LGBT people are not an issue at Regis. In addition to the previously mentioned municipal ordinance, the Colorado legislature added coverage for sexual orientation and gender identity to the state anti-discrimination law in 2007 (Colorado Anti-Discrimination Act). Prior to the state law, Regis had already changed its own nondiscrimination clause from a rather bland statement affirming the principles of diversity with no specifics, to a statement that includes a typical list of protected classes, including sexual orientation. For me, what's important is the introductory sentence from this section of the university's human resource policy manual: "In accordance with its Jesuit Catholic mission, Regis University is committed to maintaining a humane atmosphere in which the civil rights of every individual are recognized and respected" (§2.8.4). Rather than state an obligation to observe local or state laws, the university directly ties its policies to its institutional identity. A further statement on diversity is even more expansive on the connection between our Jesuit identity and our concept of community:

> *At Regis University, the term 'diversity' affirms our faith-inspired commitment to build an inclusive community that values the dignity and contributions of all our members. In this community, human differences thrive in a learning environment characterized by the Jesuit traditions of mutual respect and the pursuit of justice. Age, gender, race/ethnicity, class, disability, sexual orientation, religion, and other human differences contribute to the richness and vitality of our living community. (Regis Univ., "Diversity at Regis")*

Though I'm glad to have legal protection at the state and municipal level, the Regis policy statements are still very meaningful on a personal level. I do feel valued and respected as a member of the Regis community, and it was especially gratifying to see my role as the Gay Straight Alliance's advisor singled out as one of the reasons I received the President's Service Award in 2004.

Although my employment rights are protected and even affirmed at Regis, my benefits are not the same as my straight colleagues. The university does not recognize my committed, monogamous relationship as being equivalent to a legal heterosexual marriage. That's why, when my partner proudly graduated with his undergraduate degree from Regis, he did so after attending at our expense – there was one month when I watched as my paycheck was direct-deposited into our bank account, only to go right back to Regis for tuition. My legally married wife (if she existed) would have received her undergraduate degree free of charge. Likewise, when my partner was laid off from his job shortly after graduation, I didn't have the option of adding him to my health plan, so we'll be forced to consider buying private insurance if he cannot find a job before his coverage expires.

This isn't the case at all Jesuit universities. Boston College and the College of the Holy Cross offer benefits to same-sex spouses married under

Massachusetts law (Boston Coll.; Holy Cross). Other Jesuit schools, such as Georgetown University and Loyola University Chicago, offer benefits for "legally domiciled adults" (LDAs) who are defined in such a way to include same-sex partners (Georgetown Univ.; Loyola Univ. Chicago), while Santa Clara University, Loyola Marymount University, and the University of San Francisco recognize registered domestic partners when providing benefits (Santa Clara Univ.; Loyola Marymount Univ.; Univ. of San Francisco). In all cases, tuition benefits are also available for same-sex partners when they are available for heterosexual spouses. It's worth noting that most of these schools are in states with legal recognition of either same-sex marriage or domestic partnership, which is not currently available in Colorado. In the absence of similar legal changes in other states or at the federal level, I don't know when the other Jesuit schools will follow suit with regards to benefits.

My overall experience as an openly gay man at Regis has been largely positive, the lack of partner benefits notwithstanding. Though some friends and coworkers still express disbelief that I choose to work at a Catholic institution, I have found my time at Regis to be both personally and professionally rewarding. Living and working as an openly gay man gives me the opportunity to bring any number of debates about LGBT issues at Regis, from the abstract to the personal, and I have been there long enough to see positive changes in the campus climate. A final story illustrates this point: in 2009, ten years after the message board incident, an art exhibit in the library featuring works by a lesbian alumna and staff member was defaced with homophobic graffiti. My first reaction was one of dismay that something like this could still happen at Regis. However, the change in campus culture ten years later was evident in the aftermath. The general mood on campus was one of outrage. Faculty from across the university issued a public statement denouncing the incident. Students organized a candlelight vigil to protest what happened, and some wore protest symbols at commencement. In the fall, three campus artists mounted another exhibit in the library featuring art inspired by and responding to the incident. Student and staff volunteers monitored the exhibit for an entire month to ensure there would be no repeat of vandalism, and a series of public readings and programs related to LGBT issues were positively received by their large audiences. Seeing the magnitude of change on campus gives me hope that we are truly in the process of "build[ing] an inclusive community that values the dignity and contributions of all our members" (Regis Univ., "Diversity at Regis"), and I am encouraged by being part of that process.

regis gay straight alliance (gsa): answering all your questions

1. Yes, we still exist. Really.
2. No, we haven't met yet this semester, but we're getting together on **Monday, February 18th at 5 p.m.**
3. We'll be meeting across the street at Venice on the Boulevard.
4. Yes, it used to be called Coffee on the Lowell.
5. OK, technically, it's still "coffee" on Lowell, but the owners changed and wanted something new.
6. No, we don't know if they're installing a canal with gondolas. This isn't Vegas, so it's unlikely. Enough about the coffee shop…
7. We'll be talking about activities for this semester: movie nights, service projects, programs, you name it.
8. Everyone's welcome. Again, it's **Monday the 18th at 5 p.m.**
9. We'll be easy to spot -- it will be the group having the most fun.
10. If you have more questions, just drop by on Monday and ask them.
11. Yes, we did get this approved for posting. See the stamp below?
12. Yes, please resist the urge to tear this down. It would be such a waste of paper, and also a little mean-spirited. (OK, not just a little.)
13. One more time: **Monday, February 18th at 5 p.m.**

Works Cited

Boston College. *Benefits. Boston College.* Boston College, 20 Nov. 2009. Web. 30 Dec. 2009.

Brockway, Ronald S. *Regis: Beyond the Crest.* Denver, Regis U, 2003. Print.

Colorado Anti-Discrimination Act. Colo. Rev. Stat. Ann. tit. 24, art. 34 §402. 2009. Print.

Farrell, Allan P. *The Jesuit Code of Liberal Education.* Milwaukee, Bruce, 1938. Print.

Georgetown University. "Medical Insurance." *Office of Faculty and Staff Benefits. Georgetown University.* Georgetown U, n.d. Web. 30 Dec. 2009.

Holy Cross. *Benefits. Holy Cross.* College of the Holy Cross, n.d. Web. 31 Dec. 2009.

Jesuits. *FAQs: The Society of Jesus in the United States. Jesuit.org.* Jesuit Conf., 2010. Web. 31 Dec. 2009.

Joslin, Courtney G. "Equal Protection and Anti-Gay Legislation: Dismantling the Legacy of Bowers v. Hardwick." *Harvard Civil Rights-Civil Liberties Law Review* 32.1 (1997): 225-247. *LexisNexis Academic.* Web. 22 Dec. 2009.

Loyola University Chicago. "Loyola and You: Faculty and Staff Benefits." *Loyola University Chicago.* Rev. ed. Loyola U of Chicago, 2010. Web. 30 Dec. 2009.

Loyola Marymount University. "Benefits." *LMU|LA: Loyola Marymount University.* Loyola Marymount U, 2010. Web. 31 Dec. 2009.

Regis University. "Diversity at Regis University." *About Regis: What it means to be a Jesuit. Regis University.* Regis U, n.d. Web. 30 Dec. 2009.

Regis University Human Resources Policy Manual. Denver, Regis U, 2005. Print.

Santa Clara University. "Benefits." *Department of Human Resources. Santa Clara University.* Santa Clara U, 2010. Web. 31 Dec. 2009.

United States Catholic Conference—Libreria Editrice Vaticana. *Catechism of the Catholic Church.* 2nd ed. Washington: US Catholic Conf., 1997. Print.

University of San Francisco. "Benefits." *Human Resources. University of San Francisco.* U of San Francisco, 15 Dec. 2009. Web. 31 Dec. 2009.

All About My Job Hunt: The Diary of a Wannabe Librarian

Andy Foskey

When I entered library school, I harbored visions of myself as the media specialist at the Harvey Milk School in Manhattan, or archiving priceless gay treasures at some West Coast university. As graduation approached, I was inundated with career advice, most of which revolved around cleaning up my Facebook page and tailoring my personal look to appear as neutral and inoffensive as possible. I began to fret over every little detail on my resume. To make matters worse, the economy began a downward spiral that will likely go down in history books as being the worst since the Great Depression. I started to wonder if I would ever find a job, period, much less my dream job. But I held on tight, and it looks like I made it after all. What follows is a selection of journal entries that document the first year of my post-graduate life.

December 15

Today I am officially a Master of Library and Information Studies! While I am glad to be done with school, I am honestly a little dubious about the future. Where are the jobs? Why haven't I heard from any of the schools I've applied to yet? I am ready to start my career already! But I don't want to get too negative, because today is for celebrating. I have some pretty great memories from the past two years: working on an annotated bibliography about the Mattachine Society, attending the Stonewall Book Awards Brunch at ALA, and conferencing with a group of queer librarians, archivists, and historians in New York City last spring. This afternoon, there is a little departmental graduation for all the LIS graduates. I hope there will be champagne.

Update: On the way home, I got a message from a community college in the eastern part of the state about a job interview. So things are looking up!

January 20th

It's Martin Luther King Day today. If I had a job, maybe I could have had the day off! Things didn't go so well at the interview. I was way too nervous and underprepared. Plus, the library was next to a firing range, and as I sat waiting to go into the conference room, the silence of the library was broken by the sound of AK-47s every few moments. Toward the end of the interview, the topic of professional development came up. My mention of the GLBT conference I had attended was met with blank stares. After deciphering the acronym, the look on one woman's face read, "I am sitting next to a homosexual and that is making me uncomfortable." The look on the man's face said, "Let's move on to a different topic very quickly!" Why did I feel like I had just put my foot in my mouth? Is being gay really all that taboo these days? Are they afraid I would come into the library dressed in drag and "read" the patrons? "No you can't check out this book honey, your roots are showing!" Or maybe I would deck out the reference desk in hot pink or magenta? Whatever the reason, their attitude and reaction made me not want their stupid job anyway!

February 11th

What a strange experience that was! After being officially rejected by the community college, I agreed to help out my friend who works for the local NPR affiliate and let myself be taped while talking to a job coach. This is for a piece she's working on that will be aired later in the month. It was very nerve wracking, because I hate talking about myself, especially in front of an entire listening area. I worked diligently on my resume, in order to show what a well-balanced and eclectic individual I am. So of course she ripped it to shreds. Where I listed my involvement with the GLBT Round Table of the American Library Association , she wrote, "What does this stand for?" When I told her it stands for "gay, lesbian, bisexual, transgender," she asked if I really wanted to put that on my resume. She also asked if I was trying to hide something by using an acronym. Honestly, I was trying to save precious space on my resume! But she still managed to plant a little seed of self-doubt there. Should I remove the mention of GLBT? That would mean hiding my involvement with a professional organization, which is something that might set me apart from other entry level candidates. However, I don't want someone else's feelings on the subject to get in the way of my career goals. Rather than decide right away, I think I will make two resumes: one "straight" and one "queer."

April 25th

After taking some advice from an online job site, I began applying for jobs in towns I'd never heard of before. The theory here is that everyone and their mother will be applying for library jobs in big cities, so in order to put your career on the fast-track, try applying in places where nobody in their right mind would want to move! I couldn't argue with the logic, since librarians from Atlanta to Anchorage had given me the thumbs down. Well, today I got a call from one of the colleges in BFE. One of the places I sent the "straight" resume to. Only time will tell if this was a mistake. I looked up the college online, and it turns out that a professor there has authored a book on the history of homophobia. This should be interesting!

May 8th

I got back from my job interview yesterday. After spending a few days hiding out at a queer artists' community in the middle of the state, I arrived at the tiny college full of anticipation. My potential future boss met me at the guest house and I noticed the Obama sticker on the bumper of her truck. Our tour around the town did not inspire me, but the view of the mountains from the highway overpass lifted my heart a little. The next day, I rocked the presentation and interview. And it turns out the professor who wrote the book on homophobia is on my search committee. I really ought not to have worried so much to begin with. It feels good to be home, but maybe this won't be my home for much longer!

June 12th

I found out earlier this week that I got the job! I have mixed feelings about this. It is validating to finally have a job offer, and I keep telling myself that I am willing to take a chance to jump-start my career. But if I take this job, it will mean moving from a mid-size urban area with a visible and vibrant queer community to a town where I am likely to be invisible. There isn't much going on in the town or surrounding area, unless shopping at Wal-Mart is your absolute favorite pastime. However, the mountains are nearby and several larger cities are less than a half-day's drive away. The college seems to be a bastion of liberality, despite its Christian affiliation.

And after months of rejection, any offer seems too good to pass up. I wish I could just make up my mind.

September 3rd

The past few months have been super busy, and I haven't had time to write. Since my last entry, I have packed up my entire life, moved across state lines, and started my new life as a bona fide Instructional Services Librarian. Today I created a bulletin board display for Banned Books Week. I went to school for this? All kidding aside, I actually enjoyed it because it gave me a chance to get a little creative and spend some time away from the circulation desk. I made sure to include some writers who are family, which isn't too hard since it seems like books by queer authors get banned all the time. I have a feeling that my sexual orientation will be something of a non-issue here. My boss asked me just yesterday to put George Chauncey's book Gay New York on our to-order list.

October 15th

Last week I processed a donation from an eccentric, retired Army general: copies of the United Methodist Church's Book of Discipline and Book of Resolutions. Since the college is affiliated with the United Methodist Church, I decided to take a look at the church's official stance on the gays. As it turns out, "The United Methodist Church does not condone the practice of homosexuality and considers this practice incompatible with Christian teaching." This is unacceptable to me, but it's not like I'm converting or anything. It isn't all bad either, since in another place it talks about how the church ought to fight against heterosexism and homophobia. This feels very murky and confusing to me, but at least it's somewhat hopeful. A little while later, I made a little sign for my door that says "H▲TE FREE ZONE." I think it is pretty clever, if I do say so myself. Yet, I wonder if anyone will even notice. Things are much slower around here than I was led to imagine. Enrollment is down this semester, and I haven't gotten much of a chance to get to know the students here.

November 1st

I am beginning to feel more comfortable in my own skin, I think. I have noticed how much more closely I guard my personal life here, and that has been bothering me. So today I came out to a coworker. It was during an especially slow spell up at the front desk, and we were having one of those discussions where it seems like any and every topic is fair game. We started talking about living in the rural South and how conservative and homophobic this part of the nation can be. I told her that I knew firsthand just how that feels. Part of me still questions why I chose to move to such a secluded and backwards place, but all I can do now is look forward.

December 17th, 2009

What a year it has been! If you had told me last year that I would end up in such a small, conservative town I might have laughed. Yet here I am. Life moves slower here. The people speak slower, drive slower, and it takes awhile to get to know someone. Like all things around here, my coming out process has also been slow. Rather than preemptively making a big deal about it, I am letting it become something that people will more-or-less naturally learn about me as they get to know me. And I have made peace with that. As I get to know this place better, I realize that it isn't so different from anywhere else. Sure, there isn't much to do, and there is no cohesive gay community. But that doesn't make my experience here any less valuable.

Part Six:
Coming Out in the Field

Pride and Paranoia @ Your Library[1]
Maria T. Accardi

In my library, we have a display area on which the collection development librarian exhibits books from our collection. She usually picks a theme of some kind as the organizing principle for the display – local history, for example, or Black history month. This past summer, I told the collection development librarian that I had an idea for a display, and with her go-ahead, I scoured our catalog for books on my chosen topic. I traveled through the stacks with a book cart and removed books from the shelves, and I also ordered some books I thought we should have in our collection but did not. I arranged the books on the display shelves in a manner I found aesthetically pleasing, and I created a colorful sign to announce the display theme to passersby. The book display area is in clear view of the reference desk, and during the month that my display was active, while working my shifts at the reference desk, I watched patrons walk by the display, and I would hold my breath. I would see people stop and look at the books, and read the sign, and pick up the books, and page through them and read the back covers, and my heart would pound. I braced myself for complaints. I rehearsed imaginary conversations in my head, defending the contents of the library display.

So, why was this display so fraught with anxiety for me? It was a display in honor of GLBT Pride Month. And all of my anticipatory breath-holding was for naught, because no one complained, no one protested. But the fact that I had this intense paranoia and anxiety, the complete conviction that someone would complain and protest, is telling and important and warrants some amount of scrutiny. What can my experience tell us? What does it mean that in a library – a place that presents itself as a bastion of intellectual freedom and champions the cause of free speech – I

---

1. An earlier draft of this paper was presented in October 2008 at the National Diversity in Libraries Conference/Kentucky Library Association Conference in Louisville, KY.

was terrified of being silenced, censored, or persecuted? My investment in this particular display was more than just that of a librarian who cares about diversity and providing patrons with materials that reflect a diverse culture. My investment was particularly charged with anxiety because I am a gay librarian. A rejection of a display of GLBT books is not just a rejection of an expression and diversity – it is a rejection of me, as a person, the actual fact of my existence.

And it is this notion of *visibility*, of having a certain form of diversity on a very literal display, that points to the crux of the issues surrounding diversity and GLBT persons. GLBT persons are *often* an invisible minority. Of course, there are some external cues that those who are attuned to such things might reasonably – or unreasonably – interpret as signifiers of queer identity. But as Winfield and Spielman point out, "There are no distinguishing characteristics of gay people that set them apart physically, emotionally, intellectually, or spiritually from straight people" (33). But more often than not, queer difference is not a visible difference, and it is therefore very easily ignored or erased. And not only is it mostly an invisible difference, but it is one fraught with social and political anxiety. Shari Caudron's discussion of issues of sexual orientation in the workplace explicitly identifies why employers are skittish about and reluctant to include GLBT persons in discussions of diversity: "Unlike any other aspect of diversity, this one pushes all sorts of moral and religious hot buttons" (52). Caudron continues, "The typical argument goes something like: 'Gay people are sinners whom God will punish.' Because some people believe individuals choose to be gay, they don't believe employers should take pains to include them in diversity programs, although it's far from clear that sexual orientation is a matter of choice" (52–53). With attitudes like this, my paranoia about, and fear of, protest of the Pride display in the library is not that difficult to understand.

This paranoia and fear is quite logical on a campus like mine – Indiana University Southeast, an IU regional campus located in conservative and religious southern Indiana. My assumptions about the political and social climate of both IU Southeast and the surrounding region led to much personal trepidation and apprehension about being out. I arrived at IU Southeast after a stint as a reference librarian at liberal and queer-friendly Sarah Lawrence College, and I fully expected that the environment at my new institution would be oppressive, unforgiving, and antithetical to my experience at Sarah Lawrence. However, to my relief and pleasure, coming out at IU Southeast has not been the traumatic, disastrous, or catastrophic experiences that my anxiety-driven expectations had envisioned. Indeed, coming out has facilitated positive relationship building and networking around campus.

However, despite this positivity, it is still not uncommon to find religious preachers at IU Southeast, in the "Free Speech Zone" in the center of campus. Walking across campus and encountering these preachers – and the crowd of students arguing with them – feels somewhat like walking into a minefield. I always want to shout back at them, but mostly I walk around and ignore them, inwardly fuming; shouldn't I have some amount of protection from discrimination in the library, at a public university, in my workplace? After all, libraries are places that historically are deeply concerned with diversity. Libraries construct themselves as bastions of free speech and intellectual freedom. But how accurate is this perception, really? All anyone has to do is open *American Libraries* to read about yet another censorship battle at a public or school library. The narrative of such battles follows a predictable pattern: an adult, usually someone who self-identifies as a concerned parent, discovers that there is a book in the library, typically a children's book, that depicts or treats the issue of homosexuality in an accepting and open manner. The concerned parent protests and demands that the book be removed from the collection. The library fights back, arguing that censorship of reading materials is antithetical to the central tenets of librarianship. The battle continues, and, more often than not, the library compromises: not necessarily removing the book from the collection entirely, but rather placing it behind a barrier where someone will have to specifically ask for it. Privacy is also a central tenet of librarianship, but a patron's privacy is wholly violated when library materials are restricted and require permission for retrieval. As Emily Drabinski notes, "The discursive construction of the library as a space of democracy, and its concomitant mapping on social space, should structure social relations such that the library contains everything and everyone, including the ideas and realities represented by the books put on display for Pride month" (34). Indeed, there should be room for everything in the library, including queer persons and queer things.

Defining Diversity

It is important to examine what exactly we mean by this term "diversity" and how it is exemplified in the library. A simplistic definition of diversity could mean welcoming all viewpoints, but this argument falls apart when we consider what diversity actually means. Diversity is concerned with an openness to difference, the inclusion of the nonmainstream, the correction of inequality. If inequality is a characteristic of the dominant culture, then providing space for groups to support and encourage this inequality operates in direct opposition to diversity initiatives. The dominant culture, by definition, supports and perpetuates the societal structures that permit its continued existence. That is, the dominant culture is primarily concerned with replicating itself by suppressing alternative perspectives and dismissing aberrations from the norm. It is precisely this oppression that diversity initiatives seek to combat. And when considering the notion of diversity, it is difficult to pin down precisely what it means when there is a constellation of terms that circulate around the concept: adding difference, introducing difference, open acceptance of difference, inclusive, underrepresented groups, "cultural health," nonmainstream, correcting inequality. But if diversity is concerned with inclusivity of difference, then how is difference defined, and according to whom? And why do these gestures toward adding difference almost entirely concern racial and ethnic minorities? I am not arguing that these groups do not warrant inclusion. But what I'm trying to put pressure on is the assumption that diversity initiatives seem to privilege a certain kind of diversity – visible diversity. Given that diversity purports to be interested in correcting the inequities of the dominant culture, it is curious that its efforts to embrace difference still perpetuates the marginalization of other minority groups.

Lorna Peterson provides a useful and insightful entree into this discussion of the definition of diversity by examining diversity initiatives in libraries. Peterson argues that: "Difference or diversity is not an innocent discovery made by some looking for something to celebrate, but rather it is a construct devised as a form of social control." (18). Furthermore, Peterson usefully distinguishes between diversity and affirmative action by pointing out that diversity is about embracing and celebrating some notion of "difference," while affirmative action is about rectifying the wrongs of discrimination and oppression. Moreover, she contends that librarianship has failed to adequately differentiate between these two very different concepts: "Ten years of diversity talk in librarianship shows that the conversation is not about redressing past discrimination and it has not even significantly altered the look of the profession" (18). Tracing the origin and evolution of the notion of affirmative action and its attendant litigation, Peterson discusses the notion of protected classes, and the extension of this definition beyond African Americans to others who had been discriminated against in EEO laws, such as the disabled, older people, veterans, and women: "The legitimate expansion of group protection of civil rights, but with limited critical discourse to untie the complexities of the discussion, muddled the equity focus. Emphasis was placed on difference and softened on oppression, facilitating the maintenance of the status quo" (20). This diluting of diversity's message is a fatal flaw in diversity movements. Peterson notes: "Critics of the diversity movement commonly point out that the concept of diversity includes so many groups that the terminology is rendered meaningless" (20). Peterson also observes that critics of diversity also criticize its reductive, essentialist perspective that dehumanizes individuals and reduces them to objects of utility for the benefit of government and businesses: "The citizen is an input value who can help the business compete in a diverse world. Individuals are reduced to tools; they don't have entitlements or rights to protection, they only have uses" (20).

This kind of problematic diversity in libraries does not necessarily begin in the library itself, but has its roots in the training of LIS students prior to their first library job. Peterson critiques the ways in which library students are educated about diversity, as well as how diversity is defined in LIS curricula. LIS accreditation criteria, Peterson notes, requires LIS curricula to "educate graduates for a multicultural, multilingual, global society, yet the interpretation of this is left up to the individual library and information science school" (23). A school, Peterson argues, may simply conflate "diversity" with "difference" or "multiculturalism" while failing to address "issues of equity, justice, and the historical difference in treatment of particular groups" (23). Peterson critiques this "trivialization of discrimination," noting that this presentation of "difference as a non-political, ahistorical concept does not serve to educate for work in a multicultural environment" (23).

We can see from Peterson's analysis that it isn't enough to openly accept difference; it is imperative that this difference is properly contextualized in an understanding of how it became a difference in the first place, and the oppression and discrimination that resulted from the othering of non-mainstream groups. Patricia Kreitz's discussion of how academic libraries can employ best practices for diversity management outlines the changing definition of diversity and the trends shaping its evolution. Kreitz, like Peterson, also connects the notion of diversity to affirmative action. Citing R. Roosevelt Thomas Jr.'s research on diversity, Kreitz credits Thomas with being one of the first researchers to use an inclusive definition of diversity. Thomas argues that to manage diversity successfully, organizations must recognize that race and gender are only two of many of the ways in which human beings can be different from each other (xv). A clear understanding of diversity must be extended to other dimensions of difference: "personality traits, internal and external qualities, and formal and informal organizational roles" (Kreitz 103). However, Kreitz's explanation of Thomas' definition fails to take into account the aspect that Peterson regards as critical. Completely absent from the discussion is any notion of equity or righting the wrongs of discrimination.

In Krietz's view, diversity in academic libraries should not just be concerned with the diversity of the people who staff the library. In addition to "actively recruiting and mentoring diverse staff," libraries should also respond to "diverse customer needs through collections that support the study and understanding of nonmainstream populations" (105). Additionally, "academic libraries can contribute externally to broader campus initiatives by providing support and encouragement to diverse student populations" (105). Libraries can achieve this by "actively recruiting minority students for library public service positions" (105). However, this emphasis of achieving diversity through recruitment of diverse employees is what Paula M. Smith points out as one of the primary flaws in library diversity initiatives: "... the emphasis on diversity in librarianship tends to lean toward providing employment opportunities and increased representation without addressing methods for cultural interactions and communications" (143). Privileging recruitment without addressing retention only serves to marginalize minority employees even further. Hu and Patrick speak compellingly about this marginalization in their account as minority resident librarians at Miami University: "It is unfortunate that we seemed mostly thought of when multicultural and diversity programs came up and representation from the library was required. Inevitably, we felt that our existence was more about politics rather than an honest attempt to recruit and retain minorities" (299). They continue: "Although we welcomed the opportunity to participate in some diversity initiatives, we felt that we were often asked to take on tasks not because of our interests or strengths, but merely due to our physical appearances. We believe diversity initiatives are important, but that they should be addressed by all, not just by those who are visible minorities" (299). This gesture toward the embrace of diversity without actually valuing diversity echoes Peterson's critique of diversity initiatives.

Diversity Initiatives and Privileging Visibility

But how can diversity be valued if it isn't visible? DeEtta Jones outlines the Association of Research Library's (ARL) conceptualization of diversity, which is based on two categories – primary and secondary – and this broad definition of diversity attempts to capture both the visible and invisible forms of diversity. Primary characteristics of diversity are "those parts of who we are that we have little or no control over or are biologically determined" (7). Secondary characteristics "include, but are not limited to, economic status, military experience, religious/spiritual affiliation, learning style, personality type, geographic background, level and type of formal education, marital/partnered status, parental/primary caretaker status, and occupation" (7–8). Jones discusses how ARL uses these categories to design educational programs. Yet, for all its emphasis on both primary and secondary characteristics of diversity, it is worth examining the way ARL presents its diversity initiatives. ARL's website highlights its "Initiative to Recruit a Diverse Workforce," which is defined as "a program designed to recruit MLS graduate students from ethnic and racial background[s] into careers in research libraries."[2] The initiative "offers a stipend of up to $10,000 to attract students from underrepresented groups to careers in academic and research libraries." The initiative "is charged with supporting minority recruitment efforts at ARL libraries." And the site claims that "This initiative reflects the commitment of ARL members to create a diverse academic and research library community that will better meet the new challenges of global competition and changing demographics." ARL may aim to educate the profession about the various kinds of difference that constitute diversity, but its own initiative makes it clear that it privileges and rewards visible diversity only: racial and ethnic minorities.

ALA's Spectrum Scholars program similarly seeks to recruit minority librarians to the profession. "Established in 1997, the Spectrum Scholarship Program is ALA's national diversity and recruitment effort designed to address the specific issue of under-representation of critically needed ethnic librarians within the profession while serving as a model for ways to bring attention to larger diversity issues in the future.[3]" Spectrum recruits and awards scholarships to American Indian/Alaska Native, Asian, Black/African American, Hispanic/Latino, or Native Hawaiian/Other Pacific Islander students.

This notion of "underrepresented" is an interesting one. If queerness is an invisible minority, then how do we know if they are adequately represented in the profession?

If ALA or ARL do not wish to include GLBT persons in diversity recruitment initiatives, then there are other ways in which ALA, in particular, might make explicitly known the value of queer persons in the workplace. The kind of visible support ALA currently provides for GLBT

---

2. http://www.arl.org/diversity/init/
3. http://www.ala.org/ala/aboutala/offices/diversity/spectrum/index.cfm

persons and librarians takes multiple forms. For example, there is the Gay, Lesbian, Bisexual, and Transgendered Round Table (GLBTRT), which is a round table for queer librarians and supportive allies.[4] The GLBTRT promotes access to GLBT-related materials in the library and services to queer populations. It presents the Stonewall Award every year for the best books containing GLBT themes, and also sponsors educational and social events for its members at the Annual and Midwinter conferences. The GLBTRT bylaws acknowledge that one of its roles is to: "work toward eliminating job discrimination against gay, lesbian, bisexual, and transgendered employees of libraries, archives, and information centers."[5] And at first glance, when reading ALA's policies on discrimination, it is good to observe that this responsibility is not relegated to the GLBTRT only. However, because ALA is notably silent on the rights of transgender people its appearance of support of queers is seriously undermined. At this writing, the ALA does disavow discrimination against gay librarians – but not transgender librarians – in its policy manual:

> *The American Library Association is committed to equality of opportunity for all library employees or applicants for employment, regardless of race, color, creed, sex, sexual orientation, disability, age, individual life-style, or national origin; and believes that hiring individuals with disabilities in all types of libraries is consistent with good personnel and management practices.* ("54.3 Equal Employment Opportunity")

The ALA policy manual also includes a statement about gay rights (but not the rights of transgender persons):

> *The American Library Association Council reaffirms its support for equal employment opportunity for gay librarians and library workers. The Council recommends that libraries reaffirm their obligation under the Library Bill of Rights to disseminate information representing all points of view on this topic.* ("54.16 Gay Rights")

This equivocation in the final sentence of this policy statement is telling. What could disseminating information on "all points of view on this topic" possibly mean? Acknowledging the right for religious organizations to dispute the presence of queers in the workplace? Allowing so-called "ex-gay" organizations to send its materials to be added to a library's collection? Implicitly permitting dissent on this issue is not supporting

---

4. http://www.ala.org/ala/mgrps/rts/glbtrt/index.cfm
5. http://www.ala.org/ala/mgrps/rts/glbtrt/bylaws/index.cfm

intellectual freedom – it is implicitly permitting hate speech. ALA should eliminate this waffling and be more firm about protecting and supporting queers in the workplace, and it should most definitely include gender identity and expression in its anti-discrimination positions. At this writing, the GLBTRT is working with ALA to include these changes, but it is incredibly hard to believe that it's taken this long for ALA to become aware of this issue. The ALA is an organization with incredible power. An MLIS degree means very little if it is not obtained from an ALA-accredited program. The ALA, thus, equates itself to the legitimacy of a librarian in the workplace. So, if ALA truly supports equal opportunities for queer librarians, then one way it can do that is to refuse to print or post job ads for institutions that do not include sexual orientation or gender expression in their anti-discrimination clauses. In this way, ALA will be regarded as a true advocate for queer librarians in the workplace.

Take, for example, a job ad that appeared on ALA's JobList website in February 2010.[6] This was an ad for a Coordinator of Technical Services and Systems position at Whitworth University, a Presbyterian university in Spokane, Washington. The job ad stated: "Successful candidates must have a personal commitment to the Christian faith." The job ad also indicated that diversity is important to Whitworth – within certain limits: "Whitworth encourages applications from women, persons with disabilities and members of under-represented ethnic groups." Given the blatant homophobia deployed by the religious right and evangelical Christians, this language in the job ad might give a queer job-seeking librarian some reason to be concerned. Upon further examination, the website for Whitworth University makes the following statement regarding diversity: "Our goal is for Whitworth University to be a place where the richness of an education of mind and heart is available to all people. As a Christian university, we take seriously Christ's example of loving across racial, ethnic, gender, socio-economic and religious differences."[7] While its mention of gender as an important part of diversity is promising, there is no explicit provision for sexual orientation or gender identity whatsoever. The university also claims, "We have not reached the point where we feel 'content' regarding ethnic and gender diversity in our staff, faculty, and student body." It is unclear, however, what they mean by "gender diversity." Of course, Whitworth University has the right to align its policies with its mission as a Presbyterian institution, but the ALA isn't Presbyterian. It

---

6. *Editor's note:* Because the application deadline has passed, this ad is no longer accessible on JobList.
7. http://www.whitworth.edu/GeneralInformation/commitmenttodiversity/index.aspx

has no obligations to support religious institutions or beliefs. By posting this job ad – and accepting money from the Whitworth University to post this ad – ALA implicitly supported an institution's right to discriminate against queers and give preferential treatment to Christian candidates. This is one area where the ALA could be considerably more explicit and inclusive of diversity of queer persons. Moreover, ALA should take its cue from the GLBTRT and add trans rights and the endorsement of materials related to trans issues to its policy statements. The GLBTRT's championing of trans rights in the library does not let ALA off the hook.

Let me return for a moment to the story that opened this paper: the gay pride display I put up in my library, and the fear and anxiety I experienced as a result. It was not reassurance enough to remember that the library is supposed to be a safe place. It was not enough to remind myself that I was at a university, a place that supports intellectual freedom. And it wasn't even enough to recall that the organization that dictates and promotes the ethics and policies of my profession claims to endorse the rights of queer presence in the library. If diversity is supposed to make visible nonmainstream culture, and if inequality is a characteristic of the dominant culture, then providing space for groups to support and encourage this inequality operates in direct opposition to diversity initiatives. Even if I received no negative comments or complaints or vandalism, the mere fact that I was explicitly and visibly making known that there was a queer presence in the library – most obviously in our collections, and also, implicitly, me – was a dangerous act, a radical act, one that could very easily result in violence, persecution, and hatred.

Until diversity initiatives take the bold step of embracing invisible difference, and until ALA makes provisions for *all* queers in *all* of its policies, it is hard to see how queer librarians will ever feel totally safe, secure, and welcome in the professional organization that claims to support them. I know from firsthand experience – as a member of the Class of 2009 in the ALA Emerging Leaders program – that the ALA is a massive bureaucracy, full of red tape, bound by multiple incomprehensible layers of administrivia. I don't expect the ALA to change anytime soon. So, in the meantime, I'll take small victories where I find them. One time, while walking across campus with my library director, I sensed him gently steering me away from the center of campus. I looked up and realized that one of those homophobic, misogynist preachers was busy at work in the "Free Speech Zone," and my boss was trying to protect me by redirecting our path. We didn't exchange a single word about it. It was an unspoken gesture that made me feel safe and respected. Allies like my director are critical to my happiness here in my workplace. Would that everyone could be so fortunate.

Coda

So, there I was, sitting at the reference desk, talking to my friend Emily on Google Chat. It was a slow Tuesday afternoon. A student approached the desk, so I quickly shut down the chat window and began to conduct a reference interview. And in the course of doing so, I learned that this student wanted to find scholarly articles about why it is a bad thing that homosexuality is portrayed positively in the media.

I panicked. My first instinct was to ask someone else to deal with him. I told him, "I'm sorry, could you hang on for just a few seconds please?" I quickly ran to two different librarians' offices, hoping to pawn him off on someone else. However, I couldn't find anyone, and I couldn't keep this student waiting forever. I knew I had no choice but to face this head on. I took a deep breath, resumed my position at the desk, apologized profusely for keeping him waiting, and began to help him.

I asked him what kind of searching he had done so far. I asked him where he had looked, and what keywords he used. He told me that he had found some articles online, but his teacher wanted him to find peer-reviewed material. I directed him to the GenderWatch database. I instructed him on keyword selection and search query construction. I showed him how to find the full text of an article and how to check the "scholarly" box to make sure he's getting peer-reviewed sources. I talked to him about reviewing the results list and evaluating the appropriateness of those sources for his topic. I did all of the correct librarianly things.

But I couldn't help but question him a bit further about his point of view. Here is where it devolved from the neutral reference interview to the personal. I asked him in my politest, most gentle, most *I'm just curious* voice: "Do you really think gay people shouldn't be on television?"

"No," he said, "I just don't think homosexuals should be portrayed in such a positive light, like there's nothing wrong with it."

"So you think it's a bad thing for gay people to be portrayed positively?" I asked.

"Yes," he said. "It's treated like it's not even an issue. I just think it's wrong to be a homosexual."

I couldn't believe that there was an actual person saying these words out loud to me. Here is where I knew I had to come out. Here is where I had to make concrete an abstract concept. I told him, "Well, you're talking to a gay librarian."

He looked momentarily stunned, but quickly regained his footing. "I'm not trying to be rude or anything," he said.

"And neither am I," I said.

"I mean, I'm a Christian," he said, as if that explained everything. But it didn't, and it doesn't.

"You know what? So am I," I told him. It almost felt scarier to admit this than to admit being gay, but this was a true fact. I'm an ex-Roman Catholic turned Episcopalian. I am an active member of the Episcopal Church of the Advent, a very GLBT-friendly parish in Louisville, Kentucky.

He looked at me. "Really?" he asked incredulously.

"Yes, really," I said. "Anyway," I said, redirecting our attention to the computer screen. "Do you think that this database will help you?"

The reference exchange continued and concluded without further incident. I showed him once again how to access the database, and he took notes. I reminded him what I told him about keywords, and he took some more notes. And then he walked away.

It took me awhile to stop trembling. I returned to Google Chat, telling Emily what had just happened. My library director walked by and I told him. And I might have cried a little bit.

I've been obsessing over the incident ever since. Did I do the right thing? Professionally, I think I did. I showed him how to find information on his topic. If I ever were to face such a question again, I might have the presence of mind to talk to him about the actual research in this field and how it would more than likely contradict the point he wanted to make. But I was too disturbed, too shaken up to think of this at the time.

But beyond that, beyond the most basic reference transaction level, I think I did the right thing in a critical, moral sense. Coming out is one of the most effective tools to combat homophobia and bigotry. By telling this kid that he was talking to an actual gay person, I think I pretty much blew his mind. And I think that my admission that I was both gay and Christian seriously threatened his worldview even further. I honestly think that this is a good thing, even if it goes far beyond the bounds of the traditional reference interaction. We do students a disservice if we let uninformed or bigoted opinions go unchallenged. A university education should be about broadening your worldview, not clinging to it and rejecting everything that doesn't fit within its narrow confines.

I also believe that information is not neutral, and the objectivity the ALA Code of Ethics espouses is difficult, if not impossible, to carry out in real life. I am a person, first and foremost, before I am a librarian, and in situations like this, I can hope to be professional, but I would also hope there was still room to be human.

Works Cited

American Library Association. "54. Library Personnel Practices: 54.3 Equal Employment Opportunity." *ALA Policy Manual. American Library Association*, n.d. Web. 10 Aug. 2010.

-----. "54.16 Gay Rights." *ALA Policy Manual. American Library Association*, n.d. Web. 10 Aug. 2010.

-----. "Spectrum Scholarship Program." *American Library Association*, n.d. Web. 10 Aug. 2010.

Association of Research Libraries. "Initiative to Recruit a Diverse Workforce." *Diversity Programs. ARL: Association of Research Libraries*, n.d. Web. 10 Aug. 2010.

Caudron, Shari. "Open the corporate closet to sexual orientation issues." *Personnel Journal, 74*(8) (1995): 42-55. Print.

Drabinski, Emily. "Queering library space: Notes towards a new geography of the library." *Thinking critically: Alternative perspectives and methods in information studies, 2008 conference proceedings.* Eds. E. Buchanan and C. Hansen. Milwaukee: U of Wisconsin—Milwaukee, 2008. 30-37. Print.

Gay, Lesbian, Bisexual, and Transgendered Round Table. "Mission Statement." *GLBTRT Bylaws and Mission Statement. American Library Association,* n.d. Web. 10 Aug. 2010.

Hu, S. and D. Patrick. "Our experience as minority residents: Benefits, drawbacks, and suggestions." *College and Research Libraries News, 67*(5) (2006): 299. Print.

Jones, DeEtta. "The definition of diversity: Two Views: A more inclusive definition." *Journal of Library Administration, 27*(1/2) (1999): 5-16. Print.

Kreitz, Patricia A. "Best practices for managing organizational diversity." *Journal of Academic Librarianship, 34*(2) (2008): 101-120. Print.

Peterson, Lorna. "The definition of diversity: Two Views: A more specific definition." *Journal of Library Administration, 27*(1/2) (1999): 17-26. Print.

Smith, Paula M. "Culturally conscious organizations: A conceptual framework." *portal: Libraries and the Academy, 8*(2) (2008): 141-155. Print.

Thomas Jr., R. Roosevelt *Beyond race and gender: Unleashing the power of your total work force by managing diversity.* New York: AMACOM, 1999. Print.

Whitworth University. "Commitment to Diversity at Whitworth." *Whitworth: An Education of Mind and Heart*, n.d. Web. 10 Aug. 2010.

Winfield, Liz and Susan Spielman. *Straight talk about gays in the workplace: Creating an inclusive, productive environment for everyone in your organization.* New York: American Management Assn, 1995. Print.

When is the Personal not Professional? An Exploration

Kellian Clink

> *Homophobes, right wing nuts, global-warming-deniers . . . how can we help you?*

What is the role of the reference librarian? Is our job to monitor and correct the thinking of our patrons? Or is it our role to help them find the information – however much we disagree with it – that they are seeking? Or is it somewhere in between? How do we decide? In this essay, I will explore the professional obligations of the lesbian reference librarian when helping the student who is writing the paper about how gays shouldn't be married, shouldn't be allowed to adopt, shouldn't be priests or pastors. Hold on, this ride may be bumpy! I will visit the tensions that exist between my personal obligation as a lesbian to teach about the real-life impact of homophobia and my professional obligation to provide free access to information. I will share a little of what I understand about the intellectual developmental stage of college students. And I'll share some musings about ethics and reference service as it is seen in the library literature and through my own professional journey.

Those who work in reference surely understand how often essay writing is personal. When I helped the woman considering an abortion find our atlas of the fetus, on the occasion when I helped the woman find articles for her thesis about how the death of a child impacts the marriage, or the very poignant time I helped the young woman doing research on the impact of losing siblings to drunk drivers, I understood that I was helping patrons find the evidence that they wanted to support the conclusions they had already formed. Rarely are students exploring with an open mind something that is a question in their mind ... they want to *prove* global warming means the end of the world or *prove* that abortion is wrong or... *prove* that gays shouldn't be married. In the coursework that I have completed on the developmental stages of college students, this is normal. Many students are still progressing from black-and-white thinking to more subtle and faceted ways of considering the relative merits of arguments, and they're coming to understand just how difficult it is to fully comprehend, much less truly *know,* anything in absolute terms.

I want to offer here this note on language. I personally identify as a dyke, being of a certain generation, perhaps. But, I use the word queer throughout this chapter because it's a tongue twister to say repeatedly LGBT or GLBT; gay is too exclusive and doesn't really encompass the spectrum of queer people; and homosexual for me is out ... too clinical. I like the word queer because it's all-inclusive in my mind; it is a reclaiming of a word that was used in the past to hurt, and I like the sound of it. It rhymes with dear!

Who am I? I am a 51 year old librarian. I have in my 22 years at Minnesota State University Mankato, provided hundreds of presentations on queer panels for classes, taken a group of fifteen students out to the 1993 March on Washington for Lesbian, Gay, and Bi Equal Rights and Liberation in a university van with Queers R US on the windows cut from pink construction-paper letters, and I wrote my thesis for my Specialist Degree in Educational Leadership on the history of the Queer Center at my university. It was gratifying when I studied the history to see all the notes from one Queer Center Graduate Assistant to the next saying if anyone needed anything, they should find me in the library. I have had death threats and a bomb threat on a session I was teaching for queer kids. I've had epithets yelled at me from moving vehicles. I've been an informal support to many queer kids I've encountered. And I've presented a session at the *National Academic Advising Association*'s Conference on the idea of having queer advisors for queer students. During those same 22 years, I've written and presented about the work of library instruction and reference service in many venues, including the most recent item in *Portal*. I have twice received a campus-wide service award, and I possess three awards by different campus organizations for being student-centered. I feel very privileged to work with students who are in that liminal stage of their life journey. In other words, I've been a queer activist on campus while providing library service, usually about a dozen hours at the reference desk every week, as well as providing +/-80 library sessions per year. In addition, I'm an advisor to students who have not yet declared a major. I'm out, but not to everyone all the time, and not under every circumstance.

My most memorable experience providing advocacy for queer students was when the Graduate Assistant for the Queer Center asked me to represent the students in their sit-in outside of the University President's Office, at which they would be demanding full-time staffing in the center. I approached my boss, and explained that, while this was not perhaps the best way to talk to the President about the situation, the students had asked and I could not refuse. I was one of the three people who successfully negotiated for a full-time staff member for the center. I had the luxury of an understanding boss and a comfortable sense that my faculty union would support me. I write "luxury" because I understand that many on my campus don't feel that they can be out and retain their jobs. I have been lucky in the bosses that I've had, particularly my current boss.

Along with being lucky in where I work, I'm also lucky in where I live: Minnesota is relatively liberal. I come from Wyoming and when Matthew Shepard was murdered, that resonated with me. Sure, the atrocity could have happened anywhere, but I remember Wyoming as very conservative and homophobic. I belong to a faculty union. I'm of a certain generation. And I'm relatively brave on a good day. There are a lot of factors that go into being an out lesbian on a college campus, some of them institutional, others personal, and I've had all the breaks.

What is the tension, then, for me, when a student approaches the reference desk needing to find information to defend his position that gays should not be allowed to marry? Let me tease out some of the elements here. Just as the student's information need is personal, so are my immediate responses. I'm a lesbian, so when someone wants this kind of information, it's like a little kick in the stomach – proof (as though I need it) positive that far too many people out there despise/hate/fear gay people. I'm a thinking person and, even if I wasn't a lesbian, I would find something a little ugly about what I would understand to be the covert thinking of this kind of information need: the patron wants to impose his beliefs on an entire group, wants to oppress an entire group of "others." There is the natural part of me, as a lesbian, that wants to educate and to confront. Recently, I was struck while watching *Milk* that the words of Harvey Milk in 1978 have yet to be fulfilled:

> *I cannot prevent anyone from getting angry, or mad, or frustrated. I can only hope that they'll turn that anger and frustration and madness into something positive, so that two, three, four, five hundred will step forward, so the gay doctors will come out, the gay lawyers, the gay judges, gay bankers, gay architects ... I hope that every professional gay will say 'enough,'*

> *come forward and tell everybody, wear a sign, let the world know. Maybe that will help.*

Yes, it is heartening to see the change in the gay pride parades I've attended for more than 20 years, in terms of the increasing contingencies of police and teachers and other professionals that choose – with fear and trepidation, I'm sure – to walk in the parade. Nevertheless, I still know many on my own campus who don't feel safe being out. While writing my thesis, I conducted an informal survey, and respondents, when asked if they were out on campus, wrote things like, "No – fear of losing job," or "Not tolerated in a male dominant office," or "It would be professional suicide," and "Easy scapegoat in economically difficult times." (Clink 17). It is difficult to get a handle on how many gays are out at work. It is a much larger number, certainly, than in Milk's time, but it is certainly not safe for every professional to be out. And I feel guilty every time I *don't* come out – to plumbers or random strangers who make assumptions, or ask about husbands. But is it my duty, as a lesbian, to educate people full time? *Should* I educate students at the desk about the evils of homophobia? Should we be out all the time and in all situations? Wear identifying insignia? Is it my life-work to educate people about being queer?

The other side of the tension is my role as an information provider. I've conducted sensitive reference work in a medical library. Back in the days when patrons needed an intermediate, I did Medline searches on Dialog. I assisted desperate adult children looking for clinical trials for dying parents. I helped find clinical information about venereal diseases and head lice for patrons. I can put on a façade of neutral information provider while resisting the urge to scratch my scalp. I sincerely want patrons to get the information they're looking for without my acting as judge and jury. My heart wants that and the profession demands it. Patrons deserve it. There comes down to us from library literature explorations of reference ethics.

In her important book, *Private Selves, Public Identities,* Susan Hekman writes that identity politics "forces lesbians to choose their sexual orientation as the essence of their identity, denying all other aspects of that identity"(7). Identity politics is defined as "political activity organized on the basis of cultural, racial, gender, ethnic, or other claims that *prioritize* a particular group identity and experience" (Calhoun 222). Usage varies as to whether identities are treated as fixed bases for politics or are themselves products of political struggle or other identity work. For interesting musings on the personal and political impact of identity politics, the reader is directed to anything written by feminist philosopher Linda Martín Alcoff, Professor of Philosophy, Women's Studies and Political Science at

Syracuse University. Her seminal book, *Visible Identities: Race, Gender and Self,* discusses the philosophical trends in essentialism, queer, and especially transgender identity politics. I will discuss this here, however, as lived identity politics from my own personal journey.

When I came out in 1977, there were two competing pressures: the straight world, which felt hostile; and the lesbian world, which felt constrictive. Looking at the history of lesbians from when I was born (more than a half century ago), there has been a sea change in how queers have thought about being queer, and especially *appearing* queer. In the face of McCarthy-era witch hunts for gays both in the military and outside of it, with FBI infiltrators joining the first nascent queer activism groups, lesbians were urged to conform by other lesbians. The Daughters of Bilitis urged lesbians to fit in, taking great pride when a woman who normally wore men's jeans (the only jeans available) was able "to deck herself out in as 'feminine' a manner as she could" (Katz 429). The idea was that lesbians might be acceptable if only they looked appropriately feminine. It was very dangerous to be a lesbian in the 1950s; it was better to look feminine. But then the lesbian world started to change in the 1960s, as everything else did. The civil rights movement of blacks, the start of resistance to the war, and the first distinct generation of teens with separate music, fashions and lifestyles unfolded. And queer culture, too, morphed. *Odd Girls and Twilight Lovers* describes the trend: "To many lesbians, the stringently mandated butch/femme dress and role behaviors that seemed to confirm the early sexologists' descriptions of 'the man trapped in a woman's body' and 'the mate of the invert' were a crucial part of who they were" (Faderman 168). In the late 1950s and early 1960s, a certain look had evolved: short hair, blue jeans – in short, butch! By 1972, the various civil rights movements had empowered queers, too, to explode with centuries of pent-up demands for equal treatment from police at Stonewall, certainly, but broader societal rights, as well:

> *Unlike in the McCarthy era, when the more homosexuals were attacked, the more they felt compelled to hide, young radical gay men and lesbians in the 1970s understood that the temper of the times allowed support for diversity in America, so that rather than hiding they could use attacks on them to further politicize their cause and publicize their just grievances. (Faderman 199)*

So identity politics was born. Conservative opposition would characterize this as gays asking for "special privileges," instead of American citizens, regardless of their affectional preference, demanding the same rights as other American citizens. While there was a shift, felt in different geographical places and sizes differently, there was more comfort in being maybe a little bit out, in maybe demanding a few rights. In some places, although mostly in my mind's eye, after the start of the AIDS epidemic, gays would get more strident in their demands and there would be even more negative response by the religious right. Act Up and similar gay rights activists demanded that the love that dare not speak its name was the love that was loud, even deafening. It was a matter of survival. But in little Moorhead, Minnesota where I came out, at the Lutheran college I attended, we weren't exactly out in the streets in 1977. In some ways, it was more like the 1950s. I came out, as it were, in the lesbian bars in the Twin Cities in Minnesota, places like Foxies, and it felt as though there was pressure to conform to a certain look still in place in the bars. I shouldn't have my (at that time) shoulder length hair or wear lipstick. I should wear boots and jeans and plaid shirts. And play softball. And improve my pool game.

By 1987, when I started work at my present position, the pressure was different. Because an active gay rights campaign in Mankato was being virulently and loudly rejected by many townspeople (including a few of my colleagues), and because I was active in the Queer Center as a presenter and knew the kinds of pressures queer college students were going through, and for a million other reasons, I felt compelled to be out. I didn't come out during the first few months of my new job, but by Christmas I was out to most colleagues. But at the reference desk? I had a little pink cloisonné triangle I wore, but I wouldn't even do that now. I want to weigh my professional obligations, now, more than my personal identity and it comes down to values. I want to be a neutral information provider not because the code says so, but because I want students to trust that they can come to the information desk and get the information they want. I want them to come back to the desk for any information need they may have.

Librarians have always considered their role in an ethical framework. The 1950s saw libraries struggling with the dilemma of what was perceived as a real communist menace. This seems laughable now, but perusing *Newsweek* and *Time* magazines from the 1950s shows a constant media barrage decrying the threat of communism in the American midst. While many librarians fought the labeling of books (or sequestered or deselected) as subversive or un-American, there were those librarians who agreed with Ralph Leveling of the Detroit Public Library, who objected to the Library Bill of Rights as "contrary to his responsibilities as a citizen, since it allowed access to propaganda and 'subversive' materials"

(Robbins 1420). In the south, African Americans were denied access to public libraries, prompting a codicil in 1951 to the Library Bill of Rights for the right of universal access. But did that mean that blacks were allowed access? No. The ALA web site states that, "Throughout the history of the Code of Ethics, there have been debates about whether there should be a means for enforcing it. The inevitable conclusion to these discussions has been that ALA has neither the resources nor the legal authority to do so" (American Library Association, "History").

There were organizations formed, though, to fight political ideologies interfering with patrons' rights to read what they liked. The Office of Intellectual Freedom was formed in 1967. In 1969, the Freedom to Read Foundation was formed "to promote and defend this right; to foster libraries and institutions wherein every individual's First Amendment freedoms are fulfilled; and to support the right of libraries to include in their collections and make available any work which they may legally acquire" ("About the Freedom to Read Foundation").

Sheila Bonnard traced the history of ALA joining forces with the ACLU:

For example, in the 70s, FTRF filed an amicus brief along with the ACLU in a suit defending George Carlin and his 'seven dirty words' radio skit. In the 90s, FTRF filed an amicus brief in support of Ashcroft v. ACLU, the motion by the ACLU that the Child Online Protection Act (COPA) not be enforced. The act would have required individuals seeking access to certain Internet sites deemed "harmful to minors" to provide a credit card or other adult verification number. The brief argued that this blocking of content was not the 'least restrictive means' to affect the government's interest in protecting children from certain material. (45)

By the 1990s, libraries were increasingly under attack for harboring gay materials by such groups as the "Family Friendly Libraries" movement (Robbins 1420). Much of the library literature discusses the importance of offering services and materials for queer youth. The library is one of the most important sources of information and affirmation to young people coming out, and librarians have organized to urge that these patrons' needs be met. The existence and stated goals of the Gay, Lesbian, Bisexual, and Transgendered Round Table of the American Library Association are excellent, and I am proud to be a member of a professional organization that is committed to these goals:

- promote the improved quality, quantity, and accessibility of library materials and service of particular interest or usefulness to lesbian, bisexual, gay, and transgendered people of all ages;
- promote awareness of and develop funding sources outside of ALA for the Gay, Lesbian, Bisexual, and Transgendered Round Table Book Awards, and programs;
- develop, promote and defend unrestricted access of all library users to information by or about gay, lesbian, bisexual, and transgendered people;
- provide bibliographic services to librarians, archivists, other information professionals, and library users;
- work toward eliminating job discrimination against gay, lesbian, bisexual, and transgendered employees of libraries, archives, and information centers;
- advocate revising classification schemes, subject heading lists, indices, etc., in order to remove terms derogatory to the lives, activities, and contributions to culture and society of gay, lesbian, bisexual, and transgendered people; http://www.ala.org/ala/mgrps/rts/glbtrt/index.cfm

These stated goals are crucial, and show the commitment that librarians have, in theory, to provide access to services and materials for the LGBT population. An interesting study where a young lesbian sought out queer information had mostly positive outcomes, in that "in only three of twenty interactions did Angela detect definite censure of her gay – and lesbian-related questions" (Curry 73). Clearly, while there's room for improvement, the profession as a whole is dedicated to free access, even for populations individual librarians consider marginal. But still hotly debated is the tension between free access to all information and the personal and civic responsibility of the individual librarian.

There is an excellent article about ethics and working the reference desk by Gregory Koster, which I heartily recommend to anyone trying to get his or her head around what is permissible, desirable, and ethical at the reference desk. Koster is an administrator at the CUNY School of Law, and discussed the weaknesses of teaching about ethics using codes or case studies, arguing that ethical situations "should be viewed as situations in which two or more sets of positive values are in conflict" (Koster 71). He argues that ALA codes have "sweeping commandments" that don't accommodate real life situations at the reference desk (71). He then reviews a series of arguments and counterarguments offered by Robert Hauptman and John Swan. Hauptman was dismayed when in his experiment, librarians back in 1976 happily gave him instructions on how to make a bomb. Hauptman argued that their professional ethic of information dispensation "demands an amoral stance – a peculiar perversion to be sure" (qtd. in Koster 73). Swan upheld that there is an "ethical value of sharing information" (qtd. in Koster 74), and argued that in a "time rich in quandaries," librarians are the guardians of free access" (Swan, 115). Koster argues that Hauptman and Swan, "even as their descriptions of their ethical approaches increasingly converge, draw opposite conclusions on nearly every case study" (76). He argues that rather than rely on codes, which cannot allow for the complexity of the reference interaction, or teach about ethics using case studies, which, while they create "an invitation to reflection" (76), do not offer any real guidance for real life situations at the reference desk, library schools should teach about ethics in terms of good values in conflict:

> *We start our ethical analysis from a third point: not by relying on codes, not by looking at case studies; but by looking at our values ... professional values ... And since we are not just librarians, but also citizens, persons, neighbors, and employees our ethical choices should reflect a conscious weighing and balancing of all the values in conflict. (76)*

Koster concludes that we must distinguish between "the unsavory, the asocial and even the unethical on the one hand and the blatantly illegal on the other" and "can't rig the scales so that intellectual freedom wins *a priori*, neither can we insist that none of our personal beliefs be countered" (77).

So, the dilemma: a student comes to the desk and asks for information supporting his claim that gays should not be allowed to marry, or enter the ministry, or adopt children. What are some of the elements that come into play? Ultimately, beyond ALA codes or RUSA standards, beyond case scenarios, what are my professional and personal values, and how do I weigh their relative merits?

One of the pertinent elements is the developmental stage of the college student. While every student is an individual, research does reveal patterns, including William Perry's *Scheme of Intellectual and Ethical Development,* a work which has been the touchstone of understanding college freshmen. He helped us conceptualize cognitive growth "occurring through a series of positions, beginning with basic duality and moving through multiplicity, relativism, and commitment" (qtd. in Habley and Gordon 23). Students may start out with the black/white thinking that "gay is bad/straight is good," move into "I understand that other people think that gay is okay," and move finally into "I understand that gay is good and I'll stick with that thinking." Or not. But when they are freshmen, they might be in a place that is really wed to a certain point of view. And it may change. And when it does, I want to be the place to which they will come for more information.

There is an overwhelming amount of research claiming that queer students are closeted because they fear being out. Most colleges are judged homophobic by the students who attend, and most gay students experience homophobia verbally and/or physically in their years on campus. Moreover, their academic progress is impacted by the homophobia on their campus (Longerbeam 215-216). The research is clear: homophobia is real; it is ubiquitous; and it is damaging. So the lesbian librarian should ride to the rescue, right? Teachable moment, right? In Koster's words, weighing and balancing of all the values in conflict means, for me, weighing the damage done by homophobia, my role as a librarian, my identity as a lesbian. Some of the research Larry Lance reviews in his article on campus homophobia talks about misfires, "unfavorable contact can promote prejudices. Social contact can generate negative results when it results in competition, is unpleasant or involuntary, or it takes place during frustration" (411). For this as well as other reasons, I don't want my identity politics to take over and impose upon the student my personal stake in his five page composition paper about the evils of gay marriage. I don't want his expectation of an informational request turning into an involuntary lesson on the evils of homophobia. Why? Because I want the student to return. The value I hold dearest as a librarian is the value that patrons will have the kind of experiences that will make it clear to them that the library is the place to come when they are considering refinancing their mortgage, when they are ill, when they have to deliver a eulogy or a best man speech. I value that kind of interaction with patrons, and I want them to come back. I value their trust in me as a non-judgmental information professional.

An article based on a study done in Norway discusses the role of trust in the reference interview. Ulvik and Salvesen, librarians at Oslo University College, analyzed conversations between librarians and patrons. They concluded that "ethical consciousness among the librarians clearly would have improved the quality of the actual transactions" (351). They discuss the elements of power differential and of trust in the reference transaction from a "microanalysis" of twenty reference interactions captured at two public libraries. There were different issues uncovered in their analysis, including lack of probing questions, starting on the response before the query is adequately explored, and more youthful patrons tended to be directed to specific sources instead of being allowed to choose between different alternatives. The authors were troubled by some of the behaviors and urged librarians to change places with the user to better understand that perspective. They want librarians to think about the intersection of the golden rule, trust, and ethical reference service. They clearly empathize with the tentative library patron:

> *Users of the library are also often in need of help, and show trust by daring to come forth with their information problem. Without trust, it is impossible to care for others or to help other persons. . . . However, trust gives rise to power. . . . The librarian has more power than the user, by virtue of his/her competence. . . . The librarian may misuse the power and make decisions on behalf of the user, sometimes even reducing the user to a powerless onlooker. . . . This is clearly abuse of trust. This kind of behavior may lead to distrust, to the particular librarian and to the library. (348)*

If a librarian who is confronting a homophobic question were to take over, and show the student research available from the National Gay and Lesbian Task Force, this would clearly lead to distrust. While neither databases nor online catalogs have labeling (i.e., pro gay rights, anti gay rights), and librarians are going to demonstrate how to use resources, rather than make choices for the patron, they should make sure that they find the information sources that answer the patron's need. Clearly, the role of the librarian is not that of oracle but of guide. And guides must be trusted to take the patron to their self-selected destination, not to the librarian's destination.

When deliberating how to answer a question that seems to indicate a certain level of homophobia at the reference desk, there are many thoughts that flit through my mind. I react, initially, perhaps, as a human lesbian who is dismayed by the homophobia. I think about the serious ramifications of homophobia. I consider my values as a librarian. I meditate about how much I've seen students change during the four years they attend college. I contemplate my professional obligations. And in the end, I weigh my desire to prevent homophobia and my wish that students will always find at the reference desk a librarian who will respect them and their information needs. And I help them find the resources to write the paper that *they* want to write.

Works Cited

Alcoff, Linda. *Visible Identities: Race, Gender, and the Self.* New York: Oxford UP, 2006. Print.

American Library Association. "History of the ALA Code of Ethics." *American Library Association,* n.d. Web. 26 July 2010.

Bonnard, Sheila. "Partners in Protecting Privacy and Intellectual Freedom: the ACLU and You" *PNLA Quarterly* 74(1): 44-49. Print.

Calhoun, Craig, ed. *Dictionary of the Social Sciences.* New York: Oxford UP, 2002. Print.

Clink, Kellian. *A History of the Center for Gay, Lesbian, Bisexual, A History of the Center for Gay, Lesbian, Bisexual, and Transgender Students on the Campus of Minnesota State University, Mankato.* Unpublished thesis. Minnesota State U Mankato, 2005. Print.

Curry, Ann. "If I Ask, Will they Answer? Evaluating Public Library Reference Service to Gay and Lesbian Youth." *Reference User Services Quarterly.* 45.1 (2005): 65-75. Print.

Faderman, Lillian. *Odd Girls and Twilight Lovers: A History of Lesbian Life in Twentieth-Century America.* New York, Columbia UP, 1991. Print.

Freedom to Read Foundation. "About the Freedom to Read Foundation." *American Library Association,* n.d. Web. 12 August 2010.

Habley, Wesley R., and Virginia N. Gordon. *Academic Advising: A Comprehensive Handbook.* 1st ed. San Francisco: Jossey-Bass, 2000. Print.

Hekman, S. J. Private Selves, Public Identities: Reconsidering Identity Politics. University Park, Pa: Pennsylvania State UP, 2004. Print.

Katz, Jonathan. *Gay American History: Lesbians and Gay Men in the U.S.A.* New York: Harper, 1976. Print.

Koster, Gregory E. "Ethics in Reference Service: Codes, Case Studies, Or Values?" *Reference Services Review* 20.1 (1992): 71-80. Print.

Lance, Larry M. "Heterosexism and Homophobia among College Students." *College Student Journal* 36.3 (2002): 410-415. Print.

Longerbeam, Susan D., et al. "Lesbian, Gay, and Bisexual College Student Experiences: An Exploratory Study." *Journal of College Student Development* 48.2 (2007): 215-230. Print.

Marco, Guya. "Ethics for Librarians: A Narrow View." *Journal of Librarianship and Information Science* 28.1 (1996): 33-38. Print.

Milk, Harvey. San Francisco, CA. 1978. Audiotape.

Robbins, Louise. "The United States Since 1950." *Censorship: A World Encyclopedia.* Ed. Derek Jones. Chicago: Dearborn, 2001. 1419-1421. Print.

Swan, John. "Ethics at the Reference Desk: Comfortable Theories and Trick Practices." *Ethics and Reference Services.* Ed. William Katz. New York: Haworth, 1982. 99-119. Print.

Ulvik, Synnøve, and Gunhild Salvesen. "Ethical Reference Practice." *New Library World* 108.7/8 (2007): 342–353. Print.

Out in the Classroom

Ann L. O'Neill

My first job after coming out in 1995 was as a professor at a school of Library and Information Science at a southern university. I was out on my resume when I interviewed and to all the faculty and staff. I had no problems with them and was involved with the GLBT community on campus and in town. It was in a very comfortable and welcoming environment.

My one "problem" was how to handle being out or coming out to the students. Yes, they were graduate students, so they should be able to understand the issues. But because I was working in a mid-sized southern university, and living in a small town in the Bible-belt, I was concerned about safety issues and respect for my classroom authority. I also could not think of a good reason to just tell the students, as my sexual orientation really had nothing to do with the classes I was teaching. That first semester, I never did come out in class or to any students.

During my second semester there, I taught a required class in technical services. While discussing the section on collection development and censorship, we talked about Family Friendly Libraries, a group that was very active in my area at that time.[1] Some of their concerns were ALA supporting the GLBT "agenda," promoting GLBT materials in libraries, and out GLBT staff in libraries.

I knew then that I had to decide whether or not to come out to my students. I paused and thought for a few seconds, and decided that this was an important teaching moment. I took a deep breath and said, "In fact, they wouldn't want someone like me teaching you. Because I'm a lesbian, they think I'm going to 'corrupt' you and push the GLBT agenda." I was now officially out to my students.

---

1. http://www.fflibraries.org/

There wasn't much immediate reaction. A few students said that was "silly," and others looked a bit shocked. The discussion about censorship continued, but moved on to other topics.

Although nothing much happened that evening, as the semester progressed, I noticed that students who had been reserved during class spoke out more, and that all students were more willing to talk about sensitive issues. More diverging opinions were stated also. We were able to talk about political and religious topics, with students from *all* sides sharing their opinions. And students listened and respected opinions with which they disagreed. I was most surprised at the number of conservative students who now comfortably expressed their opinions.

Changes started happening outside of the classroom as well. GLBT students stopped by my office to talk about how to be out at work, or whether or not to be out on their resume. We talked about possible topics and questions that might come up in job interviews. They asked questions about what types of atmospheres to expect in different libraries and parts of the country.

There was also more discussion between me and another faculty member regarding me being out in the classroom. Another faculty member was supportive and felt comfortable enough to put up a "Straight but not narrow" button on her door. Some of the GLBT students then also started asking her some of the same questions they asked me.

In my end-of-semester reviews, several students commented on how well I had handled coming out. They said that I taught them about GLBT concerns with grace, but didn't push the issue. Others said that my comfort in how I handled coming out allowed them to be more comfortable in stating their own opinions and talking in class. These statements from my students reflected and validated what I was observing in class.

For that group of students, this may have been their first exposure to an openly gay person. I imagine that many of them had met gay people before, but they might have been unaware of the fact, or perhaps the person was closeted. This was a moment when they had to make a decision about how to "deal with" an out lesbian. It may have been surprising to them because I didn't look like what a lesbian should "look" like. But, they learned that a person's sexual orientation doesn't have to be a major factor in his or her interactions with them. I was also able to occasionally joke about the GLBT "agenda," saying that I hoped that someone would tell me what it was when they figured it out.

The most important lesson for those students was the opportunity to experience what it's like to express different or unpopular opinions in an environment that isn't judgmental. They learned respect for different points of view, upbringings, and cultural differences. It made them better librarians.

Since that coming out moment, I have been more open about my sexual orientation in classes when discussions merit my being so: I mention my partner; I freely discuss hardships that GLBT people meet in the work setting and in society; and I encourage my students to express their opinions. Being out adds an element of diversity to classes that often only consist of white students. I know that my being out in class has helped some students come to terms with their own sexual orientation. Other students are learning that members of the GLBT community live everyday lives.

I'm now the advisor to the university's student PRIDE group, and I love working with young people. It is a way to show them what "adult" life is like and that it is possible to have a long-term relationship with one person.

That moment in the classroom was not just a learning opportunity for my students, but also for me. I learned that I could be who I am in the classroom. It helped all of us to be more comfortable discussing sensitive issues, and listening with respect to people from all backgrounds and ways of viewing the world.

Taking the Homosexual Highroad
Nicola Price

Conservatives often speak of the "homosexual agenda" of gay rights activists who are working to normalize queer lives through the expansion of civil rights. This agenda is often characterized as the imposition of the "gay lifestyle" upon the whole of society: being out, being loud, and getting full civil rights. However, as a queer individual I have a different gay agenda, which requires being quietly in the closet and completely disengaged from gay rights advocacy.

As an information professional serving a state legislature, being nonpartisan in my public life is a job requirement, explicitly outlined in a written workplace policy. I cannot be a member of my local queer rights organization or any other organization that lobbies the state legislature. I cannot attend campaign fundraisers for political candidates, or otherwise endorse anyone. I cannot participate in rallies or other public demonstrations for politically charged issues. Also forbidden are smaller displays of political opinion ideologies– lawn signs or bumper stickers. In essence, I must maintain a complete aversion to taking a stance on all things political, particularly "wedge" issues.

Since I wasn't particularly politically active prior to taking a position in a legislative library, going nonpartisan didn't seem like too big a deal. I wasn't a member of organizations that lobbied in my state, I'd never worked in politics before, and I had an abhorrence of bumper stickers.

But once I became a nonpartisan legislative employee, it became clear that upholding the ethical standard of nonpartisanship would be more difficult than I originally thought. For one thing, I am now very informed about what is happening in the political world. Previously, my intake of news could be typified by an occasional viewing of "The Daily Show," but now I skim through hundreds of public policy publications a month. As I've become more educated about the political landscape around me,

I have, inevitably, begun silently caring more about the fate of particular legislative issues. But as an information professional committed to my library's nonpartisanship policy, I've kept these feelings inside.

However, the greater difficulty has been navigating my legislative workplace as a queer person. One can understandably check one's Democrat or Republican self at the door when entering the library. But how do I "check" my queerness? In America's current climate, who I am is inherently political and usually a partisan issue. I am the wedge.

I strongly believe that nonpartisan research and information offices, including libraries, are necessary in government, particularly in the United States' politically polarized environment. Patrons must be able to rely on the information provided by librarians and researchers without worrying about the possible political agendas of these information professionals. The knowledge that the services rendered at the library are as unbiased and fair-minded as possible allows for a foundation of trust between librarians and legislators (and legislative staff) that is the entire basis of the reference-desk relationship. Without this assurance of the ethics of legislative librarianship, patrons' use of the library would be chilled; that is, the fear of receiving biased information services would lead to patrons choosing not to use the library. If these information needs were not met elsewhere (and, for the most part, they are not), the general quality of legislation would suffer due to the patrons' inability to make information-based decisions, indirectly impacting all state residents.

As a queer person, it is a true psychic challenge to provide library services in a nonpartisan environment. I find that the only way to survive is to dedicate myself full-force to library ethics, at the expense of my expression of my personal identity. Those close to me have affectionately dubbed this the "homosexual highroad."

Taking the homosexual highroad means putting my queer identity aside to serve the information needs of legislators and legislative staff, regardless of party affiliation or the subject matter of the inquiry. I alert legislators and their staff to timely articles on a variety of topics, and I include both pro – and anti-gay rights articles (as any librarian adhering to the professional ethics of our field would). But I know that doing so may inspire the introduction of legislation from members that may seek to limit my rights as a queer person. I warmly greet the president of the local right-wing religious advocacy group that lobbies against my right to equal representation under the law, just as I would any other patron. I do not mention my partner in casual exchanges about how I spent my weekend. I let references to my presumed singlehood pass unchallenged. I hide my queer identity from my patrons for fear that who I am, with all of its political and social ramifications, may be enough to cause them to mistrust my information services or the library's nonpartisan stance.

In a lawmaking setting, a nonpartisan library is a necessity. Again, without such restrictive rules on the political expressions of library workers, the chilling effect on patrons would render the library useless.

Providing information resources to patrons that don't necessarily jibe with the personal or professional principles of librarians themselves is nothing new. For example, librarians regularly routinely answer reference questions about topics for which they struggle to find "authoritative" information – conspiracy theories, UFOs – and select materials covering ideas with which they may disagree with – abortion, the occult. This is all part of the tradition of professional ethics that is at the foundation of librarianship.

But applying these same ethics in a legislative library requires more extreme dedication and personal sacrifice. It means staying in the closet; it means providing information even if that information might be used to craft legislation that aims to limit my civil rights and the civil rights of others in the queer community.

It is not that my professional ethics have bested my personal ethics in a battle of wills. Rather, my professional ethics are my personal ethics. While I would like to be granted the full legal benefits and responsibilities of federally recognized marriage, for example, I believe in the larger principle of unfettered access to all information without judgment (including judgment about what one might do with the information). It was the application of this principle that allowed many of us to get our first validation of our queer selves in the pages of a library book.

My choice to take the highroad hasn't been a popular one in my group of friends or my relationship. Any friends that I describe my situation to immediately protest that they could not do such a thing. Sometimes they jokingly suggest that I'm "aiding the enemy." My partner disagrees with my decision, but respects my right to make it. Ironically, my partner works in a gay-owned, politically progressive organization – a place where employees are expected to be unapologetically out about their sexualities and political opinions. After several attempts at discussing my decision to place my professional beliefs above my personal welfare ended in stubborn silence, we now avoid delving too far into the subject.

Despite the positive effects nonpartisanship has on the patron (and by extension, the democratic process and society in general), because the policy of nonpartisanship extends all the way to my core identity of sexuality and gender, there are inevitable chilling effects on me as a person. Spending five days a week in the closet makes it harder to express my true self when I'm with friends or in the comfort of my own home, because a semi-closeted life begins to feel has become normal, and therefore somewhat comfortable. Enacting my professional ethics by taking the homosexual highroad requires extra energy, and sometimes I end the day feeling drained. On those days, I struggle with my decision to stay closeted to my patrons. What would my hero, the late librarian Barbara Gittings, think? Would Gittings, who in the '60s and '70s protested against the federal government ban on gay employees, helped change the classification of homosexuality as a mental disorder, and co-founded the Gay and Lesbian Task Force of the American Library Association, commend my adherence to the principles of library service?

For me, it comes down to this: by doing my part to ensure that people have free access to all information, I am maintaining the democratic foundation of this nation. And that foundation must remain intact if we ever expect it to support the human and civil rights of all people. So to those who accuse me of having a homosexual agenda, yes, I do have one: to provide the best and most unbiased information services possible, whatever the cost.

Patricia's Child, Patrick's Penis & the Sex of Reference: A Lesbian Librarian's Log of Perverse Patronage

Shawn(ta) D. Smith

I am a 27-year-old, Afro-Caribbean, lesbian, reference librarian. These traits matter when I'm behind the desk. A positive face-to-face reference interview is often contingent upon my ability to engage in sexual play or harassment. As a new librarian, practicing for only two years after my May 2008 library school graduation, I am still learning the social etiquette of reference. One thing not discussed in library school was gender, sexuality, and sex presentation at the Desk. When applying the standards for appropriate reference outlined by the Reference and User Services Administration (RUSA), I have learned through various encounters of sexual play and harassment, that librarianship is ill-equipped for addressing the needs relating to sexuality in general, but of lesbian librarians, specifically. As I write this essay, I am interim Public Services Coordinator at the Pratt Institute Library (Brooklyn Campus), as well as part-time Young Adult (YA) Reference Librarian at the Central Branch of Brooklyn Public Library. This essay will outline my experiences at the reference desk and charge the reference desk as a sexual space, one that has the obligation of navigating through the realms of flirtation and harassment, depending on the sex (male/female) and intention of the patron, but always outside of the control of the librarian.

For myself, responding to a patron's information needs must include consideration of the library user's social-behavioral understandings of a lesbian, of black people, and of sexually "attractive" women. Had I received this understated perspective during library school, I would have been better equipped as an entering librarian, and less hesitant during my continued practice.

What they don't (can't) teach us in library school

The Director of the GSL Learning Resources Center at Bronx Community College taught my Introduction to Library Science course. Among other intricacies in the profession, Professor Lawton discussed the role of gender in the library field. His non-traditional teaching style was apparent by the way he suspiciously closed the door at the beginning of the first session. Each student sat upright, closed our blank notebooks, and Professor Lawton lectured. We discussed prevalent disparities of this gendered profession, like the imbalance of men in management positions. In varying ways, he instilled in me the memory of one prevailing statement: "What they don't (can't) teach you in library school is that 'identity' matters." In my introduction to libraries, I understood that who you are in the world will be who you are at the reference desk. The reference desk does not erase your gender or your race or your sexual orientation.

Having been granted a glimpse of what they won't teach us in Library School in my introductory course, my fire was indeed fueled for the documentation of negative experiences to follow. I never bothered to crosscheck this comparison of gender disparity, but instead, grew intrigued by the application of an analysis of gender in the library science field. Suddenly, I wondered if I chose the profession because it was indeed a woman's space. In that class, I decided that this distortion was yet another attribute to the profession – I had become a librarian in order to have majority women colleagues. Entry into management was something I would consider later. As a very rare breed of black-male-librarian, Professor Lawton played a large role in the construction of my ability to include my many identities as a part of my work, my style, and my understanding of what it means to be a librarian. It is "I and I" who sits alone at the desk; and so I claim 27 years, Jamaican, Rasta, Guatemalan, Garifuna, Lesbian, Black, Brooklynite, writer, reference librarian.

On a day that I was absent, upon my return, a student sitting to my left whispered into my ear an update for what I missed from the previous class. Due to poorly written papers, Professor Lawton expressed deep disappointment and alarm, ripping the cushion of comfort and laxity that we had fallen into due to his informal teaching style. Nervously, I inched towards his desk after class and he gifted me with a singular reproach. I shed tears with him that day, revealing my fear of entering another space in life where I would have to forcefully penetrate in order to succeed. I didn't want to be an imposition. I didn't want to be a lesbian in a straight world, or black in a white profession. I assumed he felt solace in my fears, and grounded in my tears, also not wanting to be the only black man at every table. On some very universal level, I surmise we are all struggling with the inability to compromise who and what we are into confining spaces. To "come out" or "be in" a closet": I assumed he had his own dilemma. Professor Lawton is also instrumental in the advocacy for the appointment of black male librarians as faculty in the City University of New York. What I learned from Professor Lawton: that in any field, but especially in librarianship, our jobs are to never compromise but instead, to redefine our spaces. That night, 1/2 hour after class ended, we walked to the F train together, sharing our stories. It was then that Professor Lawton offered me an interview for my first library position as an intern at Bronx Community College. That is where my journey began.

A Lesson In (the Sex of) Reference

Graduate assistants from Pratt and Queens College alike have relayed similar anxieties of being thrown onto the reference desk, with a librarian on-call in a nearby room. Aside from copy-cataloguing old books from the basement storage, my primary responsibility was Reference. Nevertheless, the challenge was refreshing. I enjoyed being the primary source for needy students on the eve of their due dates. Quickly, I learned the ropes of the ready reference sources, the online databases, and the university-wide OPAC. Providing information was not my primary concern. Attentive in my technical services, and information sources courses, I was ready to plunge into the sporadic accessibility issues of a community college population. Most days, I'd troubleshoot paper jams in the printers, instruct second-language learners on the classification system, or practice the mouse-clicking function with returning students still unfamiliar with computer hardware. Whether the reference desk had a line, or a two-hour lull, I felt confident in my knowledge base as a new librarian.

Trouble began with a returning patron. In his mid-forties, Patrick (not his real name) came to the desk with his laptop, often requesting help uploading his newest software. His cues for inappropriate behavior were grounded in my realization that he knew the answers to most of his reference questions. Over the span of days, it was upon his third approach to the reference desk that he began to ask personal questions about my day, post-work engagements, and my love life. Overall, one could limit his interactions to "small talk." As a Brooklynite, I was privy to the virtues of men when in enclosed spaces with attractive women; my daily hour-and-a-half commute to the Bronx was filled with making new friends. And this is how I treated Patrick, as a virtuous man, simply interested in meeting a seemingly available woman. However, the etiquette of the reference desk was not the same as the subway. When a man crossed a boundary on the street, I was free to walk away, curse him out, or most often, ignore the interaction completely. Yet at the desk, always aiming to apply the skills recently adapted in library school, I found myself at an unfamiliar crossroads.

When I realized that Patrick's persistence in obtaining my attention, and my number, was strong-willed, I told him that I was not interested. He couldn't believe that he was unable to win me over. Aside from bringing me gifts, he did his best to woo me toward his gaze. One very slow day at the reference desk, annoyed and frustrated, a day where Patrick would likely hang around for a good portion of his stay there, in no need of reference help, but still adamant on hoarding for my attention, I felt I could resolve the issue of our interactions, my discomfort and his persistence, by coming out. I told Patrick that I am a lesbian. This revelation was prefaced with my reiteration to him that it was not his fault that I was not interested. My naïveté assumed that this was the end of our circular conversation. Instead, he translated this fact as an invitation for sex, and began to relay obscene sexual innuendos. My eyes swelled and I called in sick the following day.

Shortly afterward, I attended a mandatory sexual harassment workshop provided by the Department of Human Resources. Led by a previously accused professor and head of the sexual harassment committee, I and three other participants transformed the small workshop into a nurturing support group. During this group, I revealed my current issue without mention of my sexuality, only specific to the behavior of the patron. A consensus was made that prior to filing a sexual harassment claim, one ought to exercise two very vital actions: clarity and consistency.

Lesson #1: Remain Clear & Consistent with Returning Patrons

Had I led Patrick to believe that his behavior was acceptable? Was I clear about my distaste for his presence? Unlike my usual ways for interacting with men in common situations such as the subway or the street corner, I had been uncharacteristically complacent towards his advances. The workshop gave me a new outlook on my behavior. I was prepared to face Patrick during our next encounter.

As the semester began to shift away from midterms, the library traffic waned. My next shifts were in the New Media Center with Professor Lawton, followed by back room cataloguing with the Head Cataloguer. As something of a vacation from the reference desk bustle, I didn't mention my sexual harassment issues, but simply enjoyed the pacing of instructing students on the use of projectors or VHS machines, and the monotonous solitude of title entries and MARC encoding. Professor Lawton must have sensed my change of temperament and recommended I make a written log of my internship experience. "You never know when you'll need to refer back," he said. His recommendation was helpful to this article and my own development as a librarian.

Lesson #2: Keep a Log

As with most weekdays, my reference shift closed the library. Patrick came in that following week during the late hour. I was renewed and confident until he rubbed his body close to where my hand was resting. On the opposite side of the desk he peered forward. His movements were exaggerated. I was cautious because this was our first encounter following my coming out. In a low voice that I have still been unable to retract from my memory, he said, "My dick is so hard, would you like to rub it?"

Had I not logged his words, I would not be able to properly relay them. My log is my tangibility. When I see his pepper-haired skin surrounding his thick beige lips sound these words, I hear my keyboard elongate each syllable, extending this sexual interlude, this tongue raping. With my log, I own these words. Without a log, in time I would likely manipulate their syntax, their simplicity, their passive aggressive urgency. My log is my evidence. My log is the manifestation of my coming out, a transcription of his words. "My dick is so hard" then he licks his lips, "would you like to rub it?"

In the sexual harassment workshop, we practiced saying "NO!" The instructors believed that this word was underused. "No," was commonly seen as an insult, or an invitation towards conflict. We were instructed that "NO!" was the first step towards clarity.

Lesson #3: Saying "NO!" exercises your clarity muscles

Methodically, I stood up. I looked Patrick in the eye, and I said, without hesitation, "NO!" This was followed by clear instructions, as I had rehearsed days before.

"No. I do not. You make me uncomfortable. You make me feel as if I cannot come to work. Because of you, I feel as if I am in an unsafe work environment. Do not approach this desk with that mess. If I have to say it again, I will call security, and have you expelled from this library. Do you understand?"

Patrick's eyes began to water. He removed his hat. And walked away. The following day, Patrick came in and apologized. Exclaiming that he had no idea of my discomfort, he assured me that I would not have to worry about him any longer. I smiled, thanked him for his honesty, and returned to my work.

How "Good" Lesbian Librarians get Fucked

I'd like to say that Patrick was my last encounter of sexual harassment while being out at the desk. But instead, I've had plenty more; Patrick was the first of many. Since this encounter, however, I have given considerable thought to my own behaviors and more broadly, the social architecture of the reference desk. Why is it that so often patrons engage in various forms of sexual communication at the desk? Furthermore, not all of our sexual communication at the desk is harassing. I often wonder how things would have been different if "Patrick" was "Patricia." If an attractive woman came to the desk to talk about life and relationships, would I have treated her differently? If I were a straight woman, how would I have received Patrick upon his initial approach, so to prevent it from becoming perverted?

Before I continue, I'd like to bring forward a point for discussion: Patrick's reaction. Without a single urge to defend his actions, Patrick was completely apathetic to my clearly voiced discomfort. Perhaps as someone without the genetic capability of promoting male sexual advances (as I like to consider "lesbian" to be in its most essentialist definition), I immediately felt discomfort in his informal communicative approach. Yet, as I relive this experience, I wonder if Patrick was actually innocent of harassing, and guilty only of his own heterosexuality. As I cannot speak for his personal experience or intentions, I can simply say that the role of the librarian is to "service" the patron. Patrick not only saw me as an attractive woman (with a seemingly feminine gender presentation), but he also saw me as a librarian. Librarians do not say *NO!* An apt description of the Reference Librarian position is one that says *Yes!* We find answers; we probe; we engage; we leave the patron with the most resources available for their continued research. Librarians go the extra mile.

As with most beginning reference courses, I had an assignment that required us to approach three different reference desks with an obscure reference question in order to analyze the librarian's behaviors. This was how we learned the traits of good and bad reference desk behavior. Classmates reported back their findings. Often two out of three trips were encounters of "bad behavior," including short answers, no eye contact, or wrong answers due to lack of probing. Conversely, "good behavior" was found when librarians smiled, said hello and engaged in brief informal conversation, stood up and roved the stacks, handed the patron the book, or provided in-depth bibliographic instruction. Although the class surmised that the "good librarians" likely sensed that we were library students, thereby providing top service, generally, it was agreed that good service requires a single formula: service and attention.

Patrick was likely reacting to my role as a very new, excited, and "by the book" librarian. As with all of my patrons, I gave Patrick a terrible amount of attention. Coming from an attractive woman, he likely misconstrued that attention as flirting. Perhaps Patrick was not familiar with this type of attention from anyone, an attractive woman, or a librarian. For Patrick, I do not see it unlikely that my initial stand-up, bright smile, attentive ear, and care-filled posturing could be anything but sexual if coupled with a nice smell, soft skin, and youthful glow.

As someone who can relate to female attraction, the sex-positive part of me wants to cut him some slack, and say, "hey bro, I get it, and I'd want *me* to rub my dick too." But the reference desk isn't a play party. Unlike two players at a play party, the patron and the librarian do not have a chance to negotiate their desires. Instead, at the reference desk, the patron puts his needs on the table; the good librarian obliges, asks for more, until the patron is spent.

As someone who is a trained professional librarian, however, the sex-positive part of me is shelved during a reference interview. There is no sex involved when I'm considering final papers as the final marker for a student's final semester. Every day at the library, I am aware that the reference interview can mean the difference between a failing or a passing grade, between paying tuition for another semester or acquiring full-time employment. In short, a reference interview can feed a family; there is no room for play at the reference desk. Whether at a community college, private art school, or public library, the reference desk is a pivotal entryway for patrons utilizing the library's resources.

Yet, prior to penetrating the desk, a patron need not be aware of the dynamic functions of the reference desk. To the patron, the reference desk can be anything they like. The library profession has constructed the reference desk as a vehicle for accessibility. Therefore, a patron is not wrong if she/he views the reference desk as a source of recreation, without boundaries or negotiated principles. Specifically, the reference desk can very well be nothing more than a place where a pretty librarian sits on Saturdays between 1:00 p.m. and 6:00 p.m. Generally, the reference desk has the potential to become a breeding ground for sexual interaction. As a result, the reference interview requires a formula that properly incorporates sex, gender, and physical presentation as factors that may affect its success.

How then, do we construct this formula?

Lesbian-Librarian Specific Reference Rules?

Part of Central Library's mission – as with most public libraries – is "to provide the people of Brooklyn with free and open access to information for education, recreation and reference." This is the library of my childhood and the model for my impression of libraries. It has always been my dream to work at BPL (which had during my employment, its first black woman executive director), but more specifically, the Central Branch, which overlooks Prospect Park and shares Eastern Parkway with the Brooklyn Botanic Gardens and the Brooklyn Museum A most beautiful place to visit and work, Central Library has wings and tiers. Its architecture is inclusive with its mission; a satellite view will reveal that the building is shaped like a symmetrical open book, with the youth wing on its left side, perhaps as the front matter. This is where I reside, at the reference desk, receiving the patrons who choose to enter the building and turn left to the initial smiling face.

Yet, its multitudes of splendor aside, I challenge a literal analysis to the inherent mission of BPL, and libraries as a whole, in the rendering of the phrase "free and open access." Consider the implications of such a service to a limitless amount of patronage. At the public library reference desk, there is no closed constituency. Although my title is young adult librarian, I receive inquiries from various types of patrons, including teens, but also their parents, job seekers, college students, young adults over 20 who have aged out, but find familiarity in the YA section of the library, as well as the homeless, the lonely, and those who often memorize my schedule in order to drop by when they need someone to whom they can relay their internal monologues. If in writing, the rules are to service the information needs of our patrons, some moments arise when the duty to provide "free and open access" requires a reconsideration of exactly how "open" that access may be.

But what are the rules for reference service?

The June 2004 *Guidelines of Behavioral Performance for Reference and Information Service Providers* was edited to reflect the changing face of reference service since its original 1996 publication. However, this shift in language is responsive to changing technologies in the field of

Patricia's Child, Patrick's Penis & the Sex of Reference 249

librarianship, and to my surprise, not reflective of this majority female profession with concerns around gender, sexuality, and safety. The RUSA guidelines begin with the unit of measure for a successful reference transaction:

> *In all forms of reference services, the success of the transaction is measured not only by the information conveyed, but also by the positive or negative impact of the patron/staff interaction. The positive or negative behavior of the reference staff member (as observed by the patron) becomes a significant factor in perceived success or failure. (MOUSS)*

The tools for ensuring positive interactions are based on five main areas of behavior: 1) Approachability, 2) Interest, 3) Listening/Inquiring, 4) Searching, and 5) Follow up (MOUSS).

Although the areas seem general enough, the sub-areas slowly begin to mirror the attributes of a finishing school. The ways in which a lesbian librarian interacts with a heterosexual man may require different behavioral roles for positive communication. Eye contact, smile, stand up, move closer, probe for conversation, then encourage the patron to return, seem a breeding ground for sexual harassment. I urge lesbian librarians to consider the same methods of interaction with a lesbian patron of mutual attraction. Would your movements and gestures be the same? Would you spend additional time on her question? How would she react to you?

Due to my experience with Patrick, I'd like to offer a counter experience with a returning patron who comes to the public library during my weekend shifts, often twice a month. Patricia (also not her real name), a mid-forties woman of my height and posture came to the young adult room harboring a reader's advisory question. As many patrons frequent the public library recreationally, most of the day is spent recommending books, creating book lists, learning the material, and tidying displays for patron consumption. Patricia wanted to know about a "good book." Applying the RUSA rules, I approached her as I saw her aimlessly sifting through the aisles. We made eye contact and smiled at each other. After her initial request, I asked, "What have you read before? Give me an example of your definition of a 'good book!'" We went on perusing the aisles while conversing about female protagonists and popular fiction. I assured her that she would love Edwidge Danticat's *Krik Krak*, but that she must read *Breath, Eyes, Memory* to get a true sense of her writing style. Also, I told her how to access additional copies, how to place books on hold, and how to renew online. Our reference interview was quite formal. Yet,

I wasn't surprised to see Patricia the following week, reporting back on her favorite story in the collection. This time, Patricia came with her long locks firmly braided to each side, and a crisp collared shirt. We were clearly flirting behind the guise of the reference interview.

The Patricia anecdote doesn't end that we fall in love and move to a state where marriage is legal. She did, however, offer to "hang out" after work. It was then that I realized how a straight woman might have felt uncomfortable in this situation, in contrast to how I felt: supremely flattered and excited. Additionally, I also realized that because we never once strayed outside of the standard reference interview (likely out of nervous necessity), there was a chance that I could have been heterosexual, and thereby feel uncomfortable or even harassed. I never came out to Patricia. And Patricia never officially came out to me.

One Saturday, she approached the reference desk without a reader's advisory question, but instead her ten-year-old son. He was held at the shoulders beneath her pressuring hands.

"Be nice, say hello," she sang to him as she squeezed him harder.

Nervously, she exclaimed that she thought the two of us should meet. He reluctantly said hello, and I, shocked and a bit confused, shook his little hand.

Patricia instills a new question for me: when male patrons enter the realms of sex with a lesbian librarian, it is likely that they are experiencing what Patricia was feeling: a sexual connection, or simply put, flirting? Furthermore, should we then equate Patricia's child with Patrick's penis?

Flirtation vs. Harassment

Using the main areas for a successful reference interview, I argue that for a lesbian librarian, the following scenario is flirting when the patron is female, and harassment when the patron is male:

> *The patron approaches the reference desk. The librarian averts her attention from the computer screen to the patron. She smiles and greets the patron then asks an open-ended question. The patron states his or her claim. The librarian maintains or re-establishes eye contact with the patron throughout the transaction. The librarian is sitting with her eyes intently on the computer screen searching through the catalog. When answering a question, as the probing continues, the patron stares at the librarian's neck or at her blouse instead of the computer screen. The librarian reaches for the patron's book to see what*

she or he is already reading. The patron intentionally brushes her hand in the exchange. The librarian retracts gently, and to diverge the encounter, decides to get up and walk the patron to the stacks. The patron walks behind the librarian and the librarian notices the patron stare deeply at her body as she moves towards the stacks.

I will stop here, if the patron is male, then although the lesbian librarian is following standard protocol, she should have a revised standard way to continue the interaction without denying service, and without making the patron feel ill at ease for his own heterosexuality. If that patron is female, then the lesbian librarian will have her own code of behavior for how to interact with other women in a sexual manner.

Unfortunately, in a predominantly heterosexual world, the patron who performs the above behaviors is most often male. In addition, as the above scenario is autobiographical, it occurs with men across race and class lines. Perhaps because of my age and race, I appear single and accessible. Black women are historically hypersexualized. If I were similar in age and race to my colleagues: 15-20 years older, white, or heterosexual, perhaps my issues would be different. Characteristically based, moments such as these occur for me every day that I am on the reference desk. Men continuously ask me to give them hugs or my number, reach to touch me, buy me treats from the café, inquire about my home life, or propose to walk me out after the library's closing.

I have also manipulated my appearance. I have worn suits to the reference desk as well as jeans. Form-fitting clothes seem to make no difference from loose fitting clothing. My knotty-dred-rasta-locs have been pulled back as well as left to hang against my shoulders. After Patrick, I shaved the right side and back of my hair, so to appear "more gay." Although fellow queer people sense the camaraderie, straight people simply think my appearance "cool." In my experience, many men request service from me at the reference desk, as they would a waitress at Hooters. We young, female, reference librarians are vulnerable at the reference desk; we are bound to our placement for the duration of our shifts, as if our hands were tied to the headboards and the patrons held the whip in their hands.

A heterosexual woman may know how to navigate through interactions of service-seeking men. As lesbian librarians however, our observed disinterested behavior in sexual attention from men, may significantly limit our ability to provide positive service.

Which is why, alternately, when a black lesbian enters the room, I test my theory. I have a handful of service-seeking Patricia's (black lesbian patrons) who come to the desk on a given month. Whether we're flirting or simply enjoying the mutual company of one another, I am unsure. However, I do not discourage their multiple questions, and in fact, provide a formal reference interview, likely how it was intended, while enjoying the play and the information.

My world is lesbian. I have volunteered at the Lesbian Herstory Archives for over three years. I have only lesbian friends, and am a collective member of the oldest feminist theater space in NYC, WOW Café Theater, where I co-produce Queer and Trans People of Color Theater. Due to holding three positions (one of which is at an LGBT organization), there is little time for recreation outside of work, and no time to learn the mores of heterosexuality. Male librarians are the only men with whom I communicate, and these interactions are typically limited to work. Instead of a course on heterosexuality, however, without compromise, I urge for librarianship to disclose the unspoken: sex (as romance, as love, as flirting, as play, as touching, as being touched, as being groped, as servicing, as being fucked, as violence, as humiliation, as rape, as harassment) at the reference desk. In these sometimes-empty-cold-grand architectural buildings, human contact affects people in sometimes-sexual ways. Yet, in this predominantly women-led profession, lesbian librarians are likely to be the ones at greatest risk. Unlike straight women, at no point will we think it endearing to be propositioned by a man at work. It may be up to us lesbians, out at the desk, to start the conversation. As a 27-year-old, Jamaican, Rasta, Guatemalan, Garifuna, Lesbian, Black, Brooklynite, writer, reference librarian, in this log, I am ready to stop compromising, to clearly and consistently say *NO!*, and to continue on the journey towards redefining our spaces, our reference desks, and our libraries.

Who's with me?

Endnotes

1. A play party is a consensual sex party where the players negotiate agreements for how each would like to play. I've had the great fortune of attending Ignacio Rivera's, *The Play Party Named Desire*. It is a closed party for queer women and trans folks of Color and their queer and trans white allies. During my second time attending, a first timer sat beside me. Habitually, I faced her and asked, "Are you finding everything that you need?" She said she was nervous, but ultimately, she wanted to have an orgasm. My default, cheerful librarian response led me to smile, "I can assist you with that." We began to negotiate. She said she wanted to be touched, but not penetrated. I said that I didn't want to be touched or undressed. We

went on like this for some time, until an agreement was made for how we would play. Amidst a room of onlookers, I secured my latex barrier and dutifully serviced my player-patron until her body cringed and wrapped itself around mine.

2. Shortly after my employment, I moved to Eastern Parkway, only two blocks away from the Library so that I could walk to work and enjoy the scenic splendor. This act of locating myself so close to the library further complicates the issue of being a lesbian librarian. Working in the community means that I constantly bump into patrons on the way to the laundry or Sunday Brunch. As I happen to be hand-in-hand with a lover, crossing paths with patrons and their family makes being out at the desk my only option.

3. I am aware that the fault in this analysis is when comparing a child to a penis, lesbians, thereby do not have vaginas (or rather the need for sex), but instead have children (or rather the need for companionship/coupling/the u-haul/love/relationships/processing/trust/commitment). As someone who attends play parties, I counter this gap in analysis by furthering the point that heterosexual men likely do also want the need for the aforementioned. However, it is the fault of the heterosexism at play in the structured mores of the reference desk that gave Patrick no cues for anything other than a handjob. With Patricia, I did not engage in sex-play, but due to my learned ability to adequately communicate with women, offered real, conscious and consensual flirtation.

4. ... or not. I don't want to connote here that older or white librarians do not get sexually harassed at the reference desk. Instead, I would like to consider that women of the same age and race demographic have different rates of harassment at the desk if their sexual orientations are the variable.

Work Cited

MOUSS Management of Reference Committee. *Guidelines for Behavioral Performance of Reference and Information Service Providers*. Reference and User Services Association. Rev. ed. American Library Association, June 2004. Web. 31 Dec. 2009.

On Being *As If*, Imagination and Gay Librarianship

William Thompson

I begin with a quandary. I am not and never have been a gay librarian. On the other hand: I am gay, am a librarian, do gay-oriented library scholarship (per this contribution), produce gay-themed programming, and advocate for gay materials in the collection. If anyone is a gay librarian, I must be. Then why say I have never been a gay librarian? Because, though I am comfortable doing what might be called "gay librarianship," I don't feel as if I am free to give "gay librarian" as a self-description for the simple reason that I am not a gay librarian by profession. That is my quandary. What does it mean to be a gay librarian when there is almost no professional space for gay librarians as such? As a rule, my library, like most libraries, does not formally organize professional positions by sexuality. Rather, library positions are formally recognized by function: "reference librarian," "metadata librarian," "systems librarian," and so on.

These functions are related to the library's overall mission, that of making information available to its patrons. Jobs are built around these functions. New functions and new jobs come into being. We recently created a position for a "marketing librarian," e.g. someone who will market the library to our patrons. Sexuality is not, generally speaking, formally recognized as being useful in this regard. We do not imagine libraries or librarians in this way. We tend to imagine library positions in other ways. This institutional act of the imagination is of the sort that Slavoj Zizek would characterize as ideological, that is to say, a fantasy that structures and gives consistency to "social reality" (30, 92). The social reality in this case is librarianship. As Zizek would put it, we act "as if" there are no gay librarians, though we know there are gay librarians (34). Why do libraries act in this way? Possibly because as educational institutions, they are an example of what Louis Althusser called "ideological state apparatuses," institutions whose mission is to support the ideology of the ruling class (98). This ideology historically does not include overt support for gay persons or other oppositional identities, as, for example, feminists or libertarians. Therefore, we don't build jobs around these kinds of identities – though we do build professional identities around our jobs. Though I have met a number of self-described libertarians I have yet to meet someone who would describe him or herself as a libertarian librarian by profession, yet I have no doubt there are libertarian librarians out there doing what might be called libertarian librarianship in practice, if not in name. The same, I suspect, is true of most gay librarians. We are gay librarians by an oppositional act of the imagination. We act *as if* we were gay librarians and *as if* there were a gay public for our gay librarianship, which we believe there to be. We know this because we are part of that gay public, that mass collection of strangers who have glimpsed one another in crowds, in bars, in gay pride parades, in dance clubs, in newspapers, in magazines, on television, and in films.

This experience is what literary and queer theorist Michael Warner calls "stranger relationality," the knowledge that there are many others whom I don't know, but with whom I know I share common interests – a fact that tends to empower me (74). Put simply, stranger relationality is the knowledge that one is not alone, that one belongs to an indefinite, but related, collective. A public created via stranger relationality is not unlike Benedict Anderson's concept of the "imagined community," a collective of people who don't know one another personally, but "where in the minds of each lives the image of their communion" (6). This kind of collective communing is a modern phenomenon in that it requires a sense of scale that was difficult for people to achieve before print and related media. We are aware of distant others, others who are like us, but whom we will never meet. Anderson gives the example of bourgeois factory owners in Lille and Lyon who did not know one another personally – and never would – but who could enter into a relationship via the newspapers that reported on the market, on labor conditions, on government regulation, etc. (77). One can enter into a virtual relationship with distant others in this way and learn from them or vote like them. As Anderson notes, it is impossible to imagine an illiterate bourgeois because they are in no small part an effect of literacy (77). The bourgeoisie learn to be bourgeois through schools, media of various sorts, and apprenticeship in professional life and professional organizations, all of which imply a literate public. Through this communion, these strangers create community, a sense of mutual belonging that allows someone to use the phrase, "my fellow Americans," without our *feeling* as if they are speaking nonsense. If we pause a moment and reflect, we may think, "What is it, really, that all Americans have in common?" and the feeling of rationality and community may collapse. Typically, we don't pause. We listen. We may not agree, but we recognize or imagine ourselves as the addressee of this discourse. We believe in the nation and in our belonging to the nation (Anderson 26). Participating in a public means being the acknowledged recipient of, and possibly, the creator of, the discourses addressed to that public, not all of which we might find agreeable (Warner 67). It is in the experience of being addressed that we recognize ourselves as the intended recipient of a particular gay message, whatever it might be: a book, a personal ad, even a slur.

If someone says "that's so gay" in my hearing, as has happened, I react in the way that I do because I am gay. Even if I was not the target of the quasi-slur, that message is intended in part for me. I am part of its public. It tells me something about the current state of affairs as regards the imagined dignity of gay people. And if I let it stand, then that shapes the discourse about being gay among both heterosexuals and gay persons. Likewise, if walking through the library where I work, I see a rainbow flag sticker on the top of a laptop and I react with an affirming smile, it's because that rainbow flag was addressed in part to me, as an act of solidarity, of reassurance, of consolation.

Because publics are the recipients of messages, publics are intimately bound up with the media that convey those messages. The reverse is also true. All forms of media have publics, that is to say persons they imagine they are addressing and who are recognizing themselves as being addressed by that media. It is for this reason that Warner, Anderson, and other theorists of publics and imagined communities focus on media and the use of media. Media of various sorts are largely the means of the "communion" that allows publics and imagined communities to come into existence. Warner and Anderson have examined the historical importance of print as a means of creating publics and shaping imagined communities. The importance of media has to do with what Anderson calls the "modularity" of imagined communities (4). By modularity, he means that imagined communities are not rigidly tied to any one geography or ethnicity. Rather, as mediated acts of the imagination they can be copied and transmitted by media. Consider the importance of the Internet to the creation of contemporary imagined communities, e.g. Facebook or jihadist web sites. Imagined communities function as models. The feminist movement learned from the civil rights movement and the gay rights movement can learn from both of those because these powerfully-imagined communities are not rigidly tied to any person or place. Warner likewise notes that for publics to come into existence, the ability for messages to circulate among them must also exist: "Anything that is addressed to a public is meant to undergo circulation" (91). What is modular has the ability to circulate, to move literally from place to place, person to person, but also across time. Materials in a library are a perfect example of the ability for messages to circulate among a public. The public responds by creating messages of its own, either quite literally in the form of new materials (new music, new films, new books) or by asking for messages of a similar kind. Circulation is what allows for a public or imagined community to co-imagine and co-create themselves. News must circulate among us if we are to discuss and debate it – and be changed by that debate and, thus, change the debate itself.

I would argue that libraries are a form of broadcast media and our collections and services are messages we send to our publics. Library collections are an example of imagining a community or public. Warner describes this process in terms of writing, when he states, "writing to a public helps to make a world insofar as the object of address is brought into being partly by postulating and characterizing it. This performative ability depends, however, on that object's not being entirely fictitious – not postulated merely, but recognized as a real path for the circulation of discourse" (91-92). In the case, for instance, of a gay fiction collection in a library, the "postulated object of address" would be that class of persons (not all of whom might self-identify as gay) who have an interest in the lives of GLBT persons. Without data of some sort, we must imagine and believe in this class of persons' existence. However, belief is not enough. The ability for a discourse to work effectively depends on the reality of such a class of persons among whom it can circulate. We might postulate the existence of extraterrestrials and create a collection for them, but if they don't exist, then the materials may not circulate. I say "may not," because it is always possible that there is another public, one we have not imagined, that will receive this collection. This is one of the productive risks of librarianship. We may do more (and less) than we intend. Think, for example, of the camp use that gay persons make of films such as *The Women* or *Whatever Happened to Baby Jane?* So while the circulation of, say, gay and lesbian materials is not absolute ironclad proof that a defined public exists for them it is highly suggestive that such a public exists. Moreover, the messages that libraries send are complex in that they are not simply the information included in, say, Alison Bechdel's *Fun Home*, but also the idea that a library values the same kind of discourse and its potential addressees that Bechdel is imagining. In short, a library holding *Fun Home* on its shelves co-imagines with Bechdel a public among which this item will circulate. This is an assumption of value. I am not alone in what I value. And, then, as Benedict Anderson points out, the book or film itself will likely present itself as typical, not necessarily in terms of its plot (which might be quite fantastic), but as presenting characters that viewers and readers can identify with and, so, read themselves into a text. A novel is something that could happen to us if ... As a result, the pleasure of novels (and movies) is that they seem to happen to us. They seem "as if" (Anderson 29-36). This "as if-ness" allows us to reflect on our own lives and experiences; Edmund White suggests that even formally conservative realist fiction has had a powerful liberating effect for women, blacks, and gays in that it allows people to imagine themselves into new lives (6-8). Dan Chiasson, in a recent review of James Schuyler's posthumous collection *Other Flowers: Uncollected Poems* in the *New York Review of Books*, remarks of Schuyler, "... like many a loner he mollified his solitude with reading, where he found models for how to live – as an artist, as a gay man – that his real life denied him" (44). The philosopher Martha Nussbaum, while writing in defense of the humanities, notes D. W. Winnicott's definition of play as "potential space" that opens up between people. Nussbaum believes that engagement with the humanities allows for a sophisticated form of play to occur where adults can "experiment with the idea of otherness in ways that are less threatening than the direct encounter with another may be" (14).

In other words, my work as a gay librarian is to help create publics or imagined communities through the collections I build and the programming I create in partnership with my colleagues and funding agencies, and I hope through the medium of these collections and programming to empower the people among whom these collections circulate or who attend or "attend to" the programming. For example, by providing a wide variety of gay and lesbian films, containing diverse views of gay and lesbian experience, I was hoping to provide solidarity among gay people. I was hoping, and still do hope, that the mere existence of the collection would send a message that gay life and gay love matter in the same way that heterosexual life and love matter, that when gay people wanted to find materials that reflected their experience, those materials would exist. It is for this reason that materials from Western Illinois University's gay and lesbian film collection can be borrowed via interlibrary loan by anyone in the country. This is an example of the deliberate processes I mentioned earlier – and of the self-conscious gay library activism I just mentioned. Previous to the creation of this collection, WIU had a restrictive interlibrary loan (ILL) policy regarding VHS and DVD formats. With few exceptions, we did not loan out our films. However, it was part of the conditions of the grant that funded this collection that its materials would be available to other Illinois libraries. In fact, this was one of the attractive features of the grant because I understood how difficult it can be to get access to gay and lesbian films in small towns and rural areas. Even larger metropolitan areas are not likely to provide easy access to a diversity of gay and lesbian films. I remember when I was first coming out how hungry I was for gay and lesbian narratives, for stories that would help me understand what it meant to be gay, which would put me in touch with a gay and lesbian world larger than that of my own experience. I remember the thrill I experienced when I saw *Lianna, Desert Hearts, Victor/Victoria,* and *Parting Glances.* These films emboldened me. The lives they depicted, each in their very different ways, showed me what a public gay life might be like. I wanted gay people in small towns to have the opportunity to see the same diversity of films that people did in larger cities, to have the same diverse consolations. For that reason, I advocated for our ILL policy to be liberalized beyond the requirements of the grant, which stated that the collection should at minimum circulate among our Illinois consortia. I wanted the collection to be available to anyone in the country who wanted to use it. That came to pass. Our films travel the state and nation. But they also stay close to home. It has gratified me greatly when members of the local gay community thank me for providing the films they watch with their loved ones or use in classes.

Messages inherently assume value because a sender asks them to be heard. Materials are placed in collections so that they may be used. Libraries and librarians recognize this value because we have taken the time to develop intentional and elaborate protocols (collection development plans, circulation policies, ILL policies, cataloging policies, and building hours) for crafting and sending or, for that matter, preventing these kinds of messages. Messages that are not heard – materials that do not circulate – are regarded as less valuable and may be removed from the collection. It is striking to think of collections in libraries as speaking to "lost publics," but that certainly happens. Imagine out-of-date science materials or the collected works of novelists whose publics have passed on or are waiting to be re-imagined. The threatened loss of a public has preoccupied libraries and librarians. I mean here the concern that libraries are perhaps too closely associated with a form of stranger relationality and communal imagining (print) that seems to be threatened with abandonment by its public. Indeed, it is partly for this reason that I proposed a grant for a GLBT film collection, feeling that it would be more likely to be used than a gay literature collection. I also felt that the granting agency would be more open to a film collection – and for the same reason. In a sense, the GLBT film collection has a shadow collection, the collection or collections

I could have created instead and which, given the current funding crisis in higher education, may never be created at my library.

Imagined communities or publics can work in surprising ways, for there are many such communities and publics and they are not always in harmony. Consider the numerous instances in which *Heather Has Two Mommies*, to name the most famous example, has been challenged. The point I am making here is not so much about an impulsive or over-cautious bureaucratic response to a controversial work, but about the power an imagined public can have over libraries or any other institution that addresses a public or publics. When the public looks at an institution like a library, they often imagine it to be a reflection of themselves, their values and their beliefs, in no small part because those values and beliefs were shaped by institutions like libraries, schools, churches, etc. Creating this kind of identification between the public and the institution is an example of the specularity that Althusser posits as a chief mechanism for identity formation (122). If the public sees an image in the mirror that surprises it or that disturbs it, it may get riled, ideologically speaking. If the reflection in the ideological mirror has changed, then maybe the public has changed, too. For the mirror reflects me. This mutual reflection between publics and institutions is powerful. For that reason libraries take a very deliberate interest in creating collections or in refusing to create them. This deliberateness is not a bad thing. One can point to policies (as, for example, regarding challenges to materials) that deliberately protect controversial materials. It is this very deliberateness that allows us to create usable gay and lesbian collections. Without strong rules about access and privacy, for instance, a GLBT collection might not get used. Our awareness of the importance of privacy to the publics that use our collections has caused us to establish protocols that protect privacy (though in the aftermath of 9/11 no privacy protocols are unassailable) and, by protecting privacy, allow the stranger relationality effect to occur. I am allowed to receive a message privately (by checking out a book or a film), all the while knowing by the date stamps on the checkout slip that unknown other recipients of this discourse have been there before me. It is the job of the "as if" gay librarian to imagine collections and policies that will allow for GLBT stranger relationality to occur.

I want to return to my status of "as if" a gay librarian. The state of "as if" is by nature not a formal, but an imaginary one. Formally, I am a reference and instruction librarian. Informally, I have been responsible for creating a rather large, and still growing, gay and lesbian film collection for my institution. Creating this collection involved a number of formal processes typical of library work: grant writing, acquisition, cataloging, promotion and changes to policies, in particular the ILL policy. On the other hand, creating this collection was not something I was formally expected to do as part of my job. Rather, it was something I imagined and pursued on my own, informally, outside the boundaries of my position. The same is true of the gay and lesbian programming I do in and for the library. For example, I organized a successful speakers series on the topic of "Libraries, Museums, Archives and Sexuality," bringing speakers from around the region to discuss how their collections represented, or failed to represent, sexual experience. None of this gay librarianship is expected of me. What is expected of me is to work at the reference desk, provide bibliographic instruction and interact with a couple of academic departments for collection development purposes. My library would have functioned quite "normally" if I did not do the gay and lesbian work I did – and do – for the simple reason that it is quite normal to assume the absence of a gay public to whom the collection ought to respond. It is the way things traditionally have been and usually are. On the other hand, I find the informal nature of my gay librarianship, its "as if-ness," to be an advantage. Recognition, as Patchen Markell notes in his excellent *Bound by Recognition*, comes with a price of its own. As he writes:

> *If a radical identity crisis can be paralyzing, an excessively firm grip on identity – an excessive investment in having your acts reflect and express who you take yourself to be – can be paralyzing, too. . . . [I]t can lead you to simplify your own sense of who you are for the sake of having a maximally coherent and stable evaluative orientation; it can lead you to neglect those human goods that cannot be pursued as part of a plan. (60-61)*

Because being a gay librarian is not formally recognized, unlike my role as a reference librarian, I am free to do gay librarianship when and in whatever way I choose, whereas when I work at the desk as a reference librarian or as in the classroom as a teacher I am bound by the stated and unstated rules that govern those particular activities as, for example, the times I am supposed to be there, the materials to be covered that day, the methods of evaluation to be used, the professional demeanor expected to be on display, and so forth. None of that exists for me when I work as a gay librarian. I have no job description, no enforceable plan for that activity. It's open territory and I like it that way. Still, not being recognized, not being part of a plan has its drawbacks. Next year the library is going to have a formal gay pride event for the first time, but only because I am pushing this. I have every confidence that if tomorrow I were to decide not to organize a gay film for National Coming Out Day, my library would take no particular notice of this absence. It is likely that no one else would be ordered to do this. This is not because the university is homophobic (in fact we have a very gay positive anti-discrimination statement) but because the normal running of the library does not yet imagine the need for this kind of event. Likewise, I have to fight every year to get minimal funding to develop the GLBT film collection. If I didn't do it, likely no one would. But that's what you sign up for when you become, by imagining it, a gay librarian – the responsibility of imagining a gay public who will want gay materials, and then, having imagined that public, being responsive to them by addressing them with collections and programming. I like to think that things are different now after nine years of my "as if" gay librarianship. And, no doubt, they are. The film collection exists. The gay-themed programming happened. I believe these responses to the gay public to be moral acts of the imagination. Because they are moral acts, they are liable to be opposed by others whose imaginations picture a different public in our towns and our institutions, a public that is imagined not to include gay people, or to include them only as objects of clinical study or moral opprobrium. If normality is defined by that absence, then the world, including the library, will *feel* full and complete without gay materials or with materials that imagine only a certain kind of gay person. That is the trick of normality, its seeming plenitude and completeness. The counter-trick of activism, in this case of gay librarianship, is to deny this plenitude, to locate a gap in normality, and then proceed to fill it by imagining and instantiating a new norm, one that includes gay, lesbian, bisexual and transgendered persons. The difficulty is that people are comfortable with the plenitude that normality provides. Nothing *feels* like it is missing. The inertia that this imagined completeness creates is a powerful political and ideological weapon for stifling change. As Warner says, "When any public is taken to be *the* public, those limitations invisibly order the political world" (107). But again, some absences are more deeply felt than others. The absence of new information in the sciences would be quickly felt. If we cut our subscriptions to scientific journals there would be an outcry. The absence of a gay film collection might not be felt as deeply, nor would the absence of an openly gay librarian. In order for these absences to be felt, a public for the materials and for the librarian needs to be imagined. And that is the job of the gay librarian or the feminist librarian or the evangelical librarian. We have to imagine our publics. We have to believe in them. That is our moral responsibility. We must act as if our publics exist even when our institutions passively tell us they do not. Because we know they do exist. We are that public. We have to hope that they will believe in us, that they will act as if gay librarians exist.

Being gay has influenced my practice of librarianship. From the earliest moment that I knew I was gay, being queer taught me that the world was bigger than it seemed, that there were possibilities, realities other than those proposed by family, school, church, the law, etc. This led me to the insight that "everything is both exactly the way it seems and yet not what it seems." This was my halting, teenage way of expressing the idea that there are multiple "worlds" and we inhabit them disjunctively or simultaneously. To my mind, simultaneity is the preferred way, to be both gay and a librarian; gay and Catholic; gay and whatever else it is I am. It is not always comfortable or even logical being "gay and ..." but the complexities and compromises make for a richer life. It wasn't always this way for me. My experience of being gay when I first discovered a romantic interest in other males (I was twelve) was that these feelings must remain a terrifying secret. As I grew older, terror was replaced by fascination. I can recall as a teenager sitting in a 24-hour doughnut shop, right across the street from the gay bar in my city. I remember the bar as housed in a nondescript, windowless concrete block structure on a seedy stretch of road that also included the town's pornographic movie theater. Every now and then, the door to the bar would open and a multicolored light, hot and bright as a flashbulb, pulsed into the darkness, brilliantly illuminating the doorway as people went in and out. The light, I suppose, came from the dance floor. I never found out because I never went to that bar. I simply observed it. But for a long time the memory of an unexceptional, banal concrete block facade containing a brilliant, jewel-like light symbolized to me what gay life must be – hidden, glamorous, theatrical, more concentrated and brilliant than the world around it. I inevitably grew up (a little anyway), and came to understand that life led in that bar, or those like it, could be as dreary as any other. Nonetheless, that initial image of a concrete box bursting with a brilliant interior light remained the image of a hidden world, sparkling within the ordinary one.

Years later I came across a line from the French poet Paul Eluard which expressed this plurality in a way that resonates powerfully with me: "There is another world but it is inside this one." That was it, the interiority of the gay world to the larger world. The knowledge, and the experience, of another world hidden alongside the visible informs, for example, my attraction to Catholicism, academic life,[1] and unionism, all of which operate,

---

1. See, for instance, the cliché of universities not being part of the "real world."

each in their own way, in an interior relation to the larger world. By this I mean that they are removed from the world and yet, because interior to it, are contained within it, and like a seed at the core of a peach or apple, are pregnant with possibility for change. Libraries also occupy an interior relation to the regular world. They are places within other places. A school library, a university library, a city library is often "inside" another, larger structure. The structure could be institutional and bureaucratic – a library belongs to a city or county. Libraries are often literally internal to other structures, e.g. school libraries are within the confines of the school. The town library where I grew up was set off from the surrounding area by a park with a lake. University libraries often think of themselves this way, i.e. the metaphor of the library as the "heart of the university." Yet libraries are not only in an interior relation to the larger world, but also encapsulate the world, remediating it through print or some other format, all of it arranged by the world-doubling taxonomies of Dewey or Library of Congress. So as a young person, I looked for the traces in the library of the gay (though I didn't yet know that word) world I intuitively knew must be hidden inside it, the "library inside the library," if you will. I was looking for a message from the collection. In due course, I found it in the works of Oscar Wilde, for whom I developed an adolescent crush, one which I have never completely abandoned. Wilde drew me to theater (another world within the world) as a young person – I was quite active in theater through high school and college – and after. Theater, like librarianship, is an interior and reduplicative discourse, splitting the world between the "real" one outside of the theater and the "as if" one that lives inside, and further splitting that world into that which occurs on stage and that which occurs backstage. In theater, as in libraries, everything could always be different – and will be. There will be other shows, other directors, other actors – all on the same stage. Likewise, there is nothing inevitable about what goes on in a library. In a mass, the floor upon floor of shelf upon shelf of materials can *seem* massive, implacable, unchanging. Being gay has always meant a strong invitation to ask questions: "Is this the way things must be?" "Can't we imagine something else?" In the case of libraries the answer is, "Yes, of course." I try to bring this queer knowledge to my practice of librarianship, a queer knowledge that also accords with the library's role in addressing its many and varying publics. It is our job as gay librarians to commune with these publics, to imagine a space, or better, to create an imaginative space, the library, where individuals and publics can connect and so move from "as if" to "as is" and back again. Because imagining never stops.

Works Cited

Althusser, Louis. "Ideology and the Ideological State Apparatus." *Lenin and Philosophy and Other Essays*. New York: Monthly Review, 2001. 85–126. Print.

Anderson, Benedict. *Imagined Communities*. London: Verso, 1991. Print.

Chiasson, Dan. "'A Hat off a Yacht...'." *New York Review of Books* 27 May 2010: 43-45. Print.

Nussbaum, Martha. "Skills for Life: Why Cuts in the Humanities Teaching Pose a Threat to Democracy Itself." *Times Literary Supplement* 30 April 2010: 13-15. Print.

Markell, Patchen. *Bound by Recognition*. Princeton: Princeton UP, 2003. Print.

Warner, Michael. *Publics and Counterpublics*. New York: Zone Books, 2005. Print.

White, Edmund. "Today the Artist is the Saint Who Writes His Own Life." *London Review of Books*. 17.5 (9 Mar. 1995): N. pag. *London Review of Books*. Web. 25 May 2010.

Zizek, Slavoj. *The Sublime Object of Ideology*. London: Verso, 1989. Print.

Contributors

Maria T. Accardi is co-editor of *Critical Library Instruction: Theories and Methods.* She is Assistant Librarian and Coordinator of Instruction at Indiana University Southeast in New Albany, Indiana, just across the river from Louisville, Kentucky, where she lives, reads, writes, and plays Scrabble with her partner, the poet Constance Merritt.

Paul Blobaum is the Health and Human Services liaison librarian at Governors State University, University Park, Illinois. He holds the rank of Associate Professor. Professor Blobaum serves as co-editor of the "Specialty of the House" column, *Journal of Hospital Librarianship,* and has recently published in that journal as well as the *Journal of the Medical Library Association.*

John Bradford is Head of Automation & Technical Services at the Villa Park Public Library and co-author of *Gay, Lesbian, Bisexual, and Transgendered Literature: A Genre Guide.* He volunteers at the Leather Archives & Museum and is active in the Chicago Hellfire Club and the Windy City Bondage Club.

Donna Braquet is the Life Sciences Librarian at the University of Tennessee, Knoxville. She has been instrumental in establishing an LGBT & Ally Resource Center on her campus and has recently received tenure and been promoted to Associate Professor.

Jim Van Buskirk worked as Program Manager of the James C. Hormel Gay & Lesbian Center at the San Francisco Public Library from 1992 to 2007. His writing has appeared in various books, newspapers, magazines, radio broadcasts, and websites. For more information, please visit: www.jimvanbuskirk.com.

Matthew P. Ciszek is Head Librarian at Penn State Shenango and has worked in management positions in academic and law libraries and as a systems librarian and trainer for library automation vendors. He holds a Master of Library Science from SUNY-University at Buffalo.

Kellian Clink is a reference and instruction librarian. She feels incredibly privileged to be a part of students' college community. Her philosophy of life is to be a conduit of joy unless she is honoring her inner curmudgeon that day.

Ryan Donovan is a senior librarian with the New York Public Library. He has served as a committee member on the ALA Stonewall Book Awards and written reviews for *School Library Journal*. He is an active blogger for www.nypl.org, and keeps a library-themed blog at: ryanthelibrarian. blogspot.com

Andy Foskey is a reference librarian who once made a dress out of trash bags for a queer prom. He is a Sagittarius and enjoys contemplating social justice issues in librarianship. Someday he would like to meet Lynda Barry.

Lia Friedman is a gardener, ocean lover & librarian based in southern California. As Head of Public Services & Instruction and Outreach Librarian at the UCSD Arts Library, Staff Librarian for *Make/Shift* magazine, and a member of Radical Reference, Lia was recognized as a 2009 "Mover and Shaker" by *Library Journal*.

Martin Garnar is the Reference Services Librarian at Regis University in Denver, CO, and also teaches professional ethics for the University of Denver's Library and Information Science program. He and his partner Mark live in Denver's Berkeley neighborhood with their much-loved miniature dachshunds Franklin & Francesca.

Johnnie Gray is the Interlibrary Loan Librarian for Christopher Newport University in Newport News, VA. He graduated in 2008 with his MLIS from the University of Pittsburgh.

Ellen Greenblatt currently works at Auraria Library, University of Colorado Denver. Previously she worked at the State University of New York at Buffalo Libraries, Princeton Theological Seminary Library, and Princeton

University Library. Active in LGBTIQ librarianship for over a quarter century, she edited *Serving LGBTIQ Library and Archives Users: Essays on Outreach, Service, Collections and Access,* co-edited *Gay and Lesbian Library Service,* served on the EBSCO LGBT Life Database Advisory Board, co-chaired the ALA Gay and Lesbian Task Force and chaired its book award committee. She has presented on this topic at international, national, regional, and state conferences. Additionally, she teaches an on-line graduate course on "LGBTIQ Resources and Issues" at the San Jose State University School of Library and Information Science.

Chris Hartman is Systems Librarian at Fort Lewis College in Durango, Colorado, and faculty advisor for the school's LGBTT student organization. When she isn't busy coming out, she likes to hike, bike, sew and (of course) read.

Richard Hulser is chief librarian, Los Angeles County Natural History Museum. Besides trying to enjoy life and not take himself too seriously, he discusses future information access and visualization on his blog at http://cybrarianviews.com. He was the first openly gay candidate for SLA president when he ran in 2000.

BWS Johnson is armed and considered dangerous. Please do not encourage radical Librarianship by reading this tripe. Definitely do not send offers of employment or inquires about consulting to Bwsjohnson@yahoo.com, nor should you swim for two (2) hours after reading this tripe despite aforementioned advisory.

Marcel LaFlamme served as director of library services at Independence Community College from 2008–2010. He is currently pursuing a Ph.D. in cultural anthropology at Rice University.

Brenda Linares is the Finance Manager and Administrative Librarian at the Louis Calder Memorial Library of the University of Miami Miller School of Medicine. She is an ALA Spectrum Scholar and a former NLM Associate Fellow. She thanks her parents, sister, friends, and mentors for all their love and support.

Kimberli A. Morris is currently a law librarian at the Penn State University Dickinson School of Law. Over her career she has worked primarily at US law school libraries, but has also had the chance to work internationally in Uganda and Iraq, and in a jail law library.

Tracy Nectoux is the Quality Control and Metadata Specialist for the Illinois Newspaper Project. She enjoys an amazing life in an amazing city with amazing people. She hopes to leave the world a better place than she found it.

Ann O'Neill is a happily out professor teaching the next generation of librarians.

Jason D. Phillips is a Government Information Reference Librarian at Georgetown University. His next projects are two invited co-authored articles for *The Serials Librarian* concerning GLBT lifestyle and scholarly periodicals. He thanks his family, friends, and colleagues for their constant support, and a special thanks to Harrison for simply being amazing.

Nicola Price is the pseudonym of a librarian at a U.S. state legislative library.

Robert Ridinger is a full professor in the Northern Illinois University Library, and has been active in advocating for gay and lesbian subjects for over 25 years through publications and research presentations to both local and national audiences. He is a board member of the Leather Archives and Museum.

K.R. Roberto is the serials/electronic resources librarian at the University of Denver. He recently co-edited *She Was a Booklegger: Remembering Celeste West* with Toni Samek and Moyra Lang, and also edited 2008's *Radical Cataloging: Essays at the Front;* his current research involves queerness and cataloging.

Shawn(ta) Smith, your Lesbian Librarian, wants to bring separatism back. She is a YA Librarian at Brooklyn Public Library, Archivette of the Lesbian Herstory Archives, and producer of Rivers of Honey, Cabaret Theater for Women and Trans Artists of Color. Her art, writing, and sex focus primarily on Black Lesbians.

Emily Vardell is Director for Reference, Education, and Community Engagement at the Louis Calder Memorial Library of the University of Miami Miller School of Medicine. She is proud to be a Fulbright Scholar and former NLM Associate Fellow. Many thanks to family and friends for their love, encouragement, and guidance.

Roger Weaver is the Institutional Repository & Digital Collections Librarian at the Missouri University of Science and Technology in Rolla Missouri. Life in a small town means driving an hour to the nearest shopping mall. What's a gay boy to do?

David White is a recently retired cataloger from the Library of Congress and lives in San Antonio, Texas. He has previously worked in public libraries in San Antonio, Louisville, Kentucky, and New York City.
William Thompson is an Associate Professor at Western Illinois University.

Rachel Wexelbaum is a librarian, teacher, and writer. Currently she is the "Confessions of a Librarian" columnist for www.lambdaliterary.org.

Index

AIDS,
  see *To the Friend Who Did Not Save My Life*
American Library Association (ALA), 147*n*2
  non-discrimination policy and, 212-214
  see also Gay, Lesbian, Bisexual, and Transgendered Round Table of the American Library Association (GLBTRT of ALA)
Anderson, Benedict,
  see imagined community, critical views of
Anti-Defamation League, 170
Art Libraries Society of North America (ARLIS/NA), 148*n*4
Art Libraries Society of North America Special Interest Group, 148*n*4

Bringing Out Roland Barthes, 155-156 [quoted], 162 [quoted]

Commission,
  University of Tennessee, 69-71
  see also domestic partnership benefits
  see also gender equality policy
  see also non-discrimination policy
community,
  see imagined community, critical views of
curator,
  defined, 155

discrimination,
  acts of, 55-56, 92-94, 189, 194, 207,
discrimination policy,
  see non-discrimination policy
diversity,
  LIS curricula and, 209
  recruitment initiatives and, 210-212
  visibility and, 210-214
  vs. affirmative action, 207-210
domestic partnership benefits, 45, 102, 176-178, 193-194
  see also Commission, University of Tennessee
  see also gender equality policy
  see also non-discrimination policy

EAGEL at IBM, 152

Family Friendly Libraries, 233*n*1
Four Corners Gay and Lesbian Alliance for Diversity (4CGLAD), 172
  see also Four Corners Lesbian Network
Four Corners Lesbian Network, 171-172
  see also Four Corners Gay and Lesbian Alliance for Diversity (4CGLAD)
Fred Martinez,
  see Two Spirit
The Full Spectrum, 36-37

Galaxy.com, 101
gay community,
  see imagined community, critical views of

gay marriage,
  see same-sex marriage
Gay, Lesbian, Bisexual, and Transgendered Round Table of the American Library Association (GLBTRT of ALA), 38*n*6, 212-214, 225-226
gender equality policy, 40-41
  see also Commission, University of Tennessee
  see also domestic partnership benefits
  see also non-discrimination policy
GLBTRT of ALA,
  see Gay, Lesbian, Bisexual, and Transgendered Round Table of the American Library Association (GLBTRT of ALA)
Guibert, Herve,
  see *To the Friend Who Did Not Save My Life*

Hauptman, Robert,
  see reference services, ethical considerations
homosexual agenda, 237

identity politics, 222-224
  defined, 222
ideological state apparatuses,
  defined, 255-256
imagined community,
  critical views of, 256-265
Inge, William Motter,
  brief history of, 156-157
  collection availability of, 161
  collection celebrating, 158-159
  plays of, 157
  posthumously published work, 160
  suicide of, 157-158
  Tennessee Williams and, 157
  see also William Inge Theater
Institutional Review Board (IRB), 73

James C. Hormel Gay & Lesbian Center, 108
Jesuit,
  defined, 188

Koster, Gregory,
  see reference services, ethical considerations

Leather Archives & Museum (LA&M), 102, 135-136
LGBTQ,
  Iraq law and, 183-185
  Uganda law and, 181-183
  see also Gay, Lesbian, Bisexual, and Transgendered Round Table of the American Library Association (GLBTRT of ALA)
librarianship,
  gender and, 242
  flirtation and, 249-250
  flirtation vs. harassment and, 250-252
  non-partisan, 237-240
  sexual harassment and, 243-248

Milk [motion picture], 221-222 [quoted]
Miller, D.A.,
  see *Bringing Out Roland Barthes*
MOUSS,
  see reference interview, *Guidelines of Behavioral Performance for Reference and Information Service Providers*

non-discrimination policy, 37-38, 45, 55, 64-65, 102, 132-133, 192-193
  see also American Library Association (ALA), non-discrimination policy and
  see also Commission, University of Tennessee
  see also domestic partnership benefits
  see also gender equality policy
non-partisan librarianship,
  see librarianship, non-partisan

Our Sister's Keeper, 172

Index

play party,
   defined, 252-253

Reference and User Services Association (RUSA),
   see reference interview, *Guidelines of Behavioral Performance for Reference and Information Service Providers*
reference interview,
   Guidelines of Behavioral Performance for Reference and Information Service Providers, 248-249, 253
   trust, 228-229
reference services,
   ethical considerations, 226-227
same-sex marriage, 111, 183-185
sexuality,
   social networking and, 20-21, 39-40, 141-144
   workplace and, 18-21, 27, 37
social networking,
   see sexuality, social networking and
Special Libraries Association (SLA), 147*n*1
   Diversity Leadership Development Program, 152-153
   GLBT presence within,
     process of, 148-153
Stonewall Book Awards, 40*n*8, 135
stranger relationality,
   defined, 256
   see also imagined community, critical views of
Swan, John,
   see reference services, ethical considerations

To the Friend Who Did Not Save My Life, 161
transgender,
   guide to transitioning, 126-127
Trident International, 135
Two Spirit, 168, 171-172

Uganda,
   see LGBTQ, Uganda law and

Voices of Diversity,
   brief history of, 71-76
   challenges of, 76-78
   conclusion to, 81
   opportunities of, 76
   personal perspectives,
     Donna, 80-81
     Roger, 78-80

Warren, Michael,
   see imagined community, critical views of
William Inge Theater, 158
   see also Inge, William Motter

CPSIA information can be obtained at www.ICGtesting.com
262317BV00002B/1/P